SAT Math Prep

A Workbook with 480 Questions & Explanations

SAT Math Prep: A Workbook with 480 Questions & Explanations

This publication was written and edited by the team at Ivy Global.

Editor-in-Chief: Corwin Henville

Producers: Lloyd Min and Junho Suh

Editors: Alex Emond, Grace Bueler, Mark Mendola, Sacha Azor

Contributors: Thea Bélanger-Polak, Stephanie Bucklin, Nathan Létourneau, Bessie Fan, Ian Greig, Elizabeth Hilts, Lei Huang, Geoffrey Morrison, Ward Pettibone, Arden Rogow-Bales, Kristin Rose, Nathan Tebokkel, and Isabel Villeneuve

About the Publisher

Ivy Global is a pioneering education company that delivers a wide range of test prep and consulting services.

E-mail: publishing@ivyglobal.com
Website: http://www.ivyglobal.com

Contents

Chapter 4: Passport to Advanced Math

Chapter 5: Additional Topics

Introduction
Chapter 1

Section 1
About This Book

Welcome, students, parents, and teachers! This book is designed to prepare students for the SAT exam, a standardized exam created and administered by the College Board, which is required by many colleges and universities in the United States as part of the admissions process.

The goal of this book is to provide practice drills to help students improve their SAT score by targeting specific skills. There are 119 unique question types on the SAT and this book includes a set of drills for every single type of Math question. Detailed answer explanations are also included for those drills. This book does not, however, include instructional content outside of the answer explanations, nor does it include a practice test. For practice tests, we recommend purchasing the Ivy Global SAT 6 Practice Tests book (ivy.gl/6PT) for the best available practice tests. For further instruction, we recommend Ivy Global's comprehensive SAT Guide which can be found at ivy.gl/satguide or contacting us for experienced tutoring help at ivyglobal.com/sat/tutoring.

How to Begin

We recommend using this book after taking a practice test and scoring it with our free Cloud scoring tool. Free practice tests can be found online at prep.ivyglobal.com and detailed scoring analysis for those exams at cloud.ivyglobal.com. In addition to receiving a score, scoring a practice test on Cloud will provide you with detailed analysis of your test performance broken down by question type like the following example:

Math Questions Breakdown					
Category/Topic		Correct	Incorrect	Omitted	Total
Heart of Algebra		12	10	0	22
Measures of Centre and Spread (H16)		3	0	0	3
Solve Systems of Equations (H12)		2	1	0	3
Graphs and Tables of Linear Functions (H8)		0	3	0	3
Create Linear Equations (H1)		1	2	0	3
Solve Linear Equations (H2)		4	0	0	4
Input/Output Pairs for Linear Functions (H7)		1	1	0	2

This information will allow you to identify the types of questions that could use improvement. You can then look up those question types with the table of contents in this book and practice!

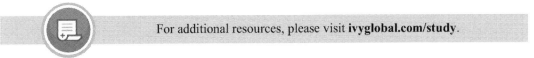
For additional resources, please visit **ivyglobal.com/study**.

Heart of Algebra
Chapter 2

Chapter 2
Heart of Algebra

Questions in the Heart of Algebra domain test your fundamental Algebra skills. You'll need to create, interpret, manipulate, and solve algebraic equations. Not every question that requires you to use algebra falls within the Heart of Algebra domain: some advanced algebra tasks fall into the Passport to Advanced Math domain, algebra problems that include imaginary numbers fall into Additional Topics, and you may need to use some algebra to solve problems in any domain.

There are 18 specific question types in this domain:

	Heart of Algebra		
H1	Create Linear Equations	H10	Create Systems of Equations in Context
H2	Solve Linear Equations	H11	Graphs and Tables of Systems of Equations
H3	Interpret Linear Equations	H12	Solve Systems of Equations
H4	Number of Solutions for a Linear Equation	H13	Interpret Parts of Systems of Equations
H5	Model with and Create Linear Functions	H14	Number of Solutions for a System of Equations
H6	Interpret Linear Functions	H15	Create Linear Inequalities
H7	Input/Output Pairs for Linear Functions	H16	Interpret Linear Inequalities
H8	Graphs and Tables of Linear Functions	H17	Graphs and Tables of Linear Inequalities
H9	Create Linear Functions Given Slope or Points	H18	Solution Sets of Linear Inequalities

Create Linear Equations
Part 1

These problems ask you to create and use linear equations. You will need to create and use linear equations to solve for variables, rewrite another equation in terms of a variable, solve words problem by creating and using linear equations, or interpret a variable using the context of a scenario described in a word problem.

DIRECTIONS

Select the best answer among four choices and circle the corresponding letter or record it on a separate sheet of paper.

NOTES

1. You may use a calculator, but not all problems require the use of a calculator.
2. Variables and expressions represent real numbers unless stated otherwise.
3. Figures are drawn to scale unless stated otherwise.
4. Figures lie in a plane unless stated otherwise.
5. The domain of a function f is defined as the set of all real numbers x for which $f(x)$ is also a real number, unless stated otherwise.

1

If $a = -2b + c$, $a = 6$, and $c = -4$, what is b?

A) −5

B) −2

C) 1

D) 2

2

If $p = -3$, $q = 7$, and $r = -2$, what is the value of $(p + r)(qr - r)$?

A) −16

B) 12

C) 30

D) 60

3

If $\dfrac{a}{b} = 6$ and $\dfrac{b}{c} = -10$, what is the value of $\dfrac{a}{c}$?

A) −60

B) $-\dfrac{3}{5}$

C) $\dfrac{3}{5}$

D) 60

4

If $x + y = -12$ and $y = 7$, what is the value of x?

A) −19

B) −5

C) 5

D) 19

5

If $5x + 9$ is 7 less than $3x$, what is the value of $2x$?

A) -24

B) -16

C) -8

D) -2

6

If Alice has 7 pets in total, consisting of birds, turtles, and hamsters, which expression is equivalent to the number of pets she has?

A) birds + turtles – hamsters

B) birds × hamsters × turtles

C) birds + (hamsters + turtles)

D) 7 – (birds + turtles + hamsters)

7

A town has a single wind turbine which produces 16,000 kWh of energy per day. If the town uses 11,000 kWh a day, how much energy, in kWh, goes unused over the course of 3 days?

A) 5,000

B) 15,000

C) 33,000

D) 48,000

8

Jerry works as a secretary at an office for 15 dollars an hour, 8 hours a day. If he wants to save up enough money for a $9,000 car, what is the minimum number of days he must work to be able to afford the car?

A) 1,125

B) 600

C) 90

D) 75

9

Will makes 20 dollars an hour, and Saima makes 0.75 times Will's wage. Over the course of 10 hours, how many more dollars does Will make than Saima?

A) 200

B) 100

C) 50

D) 15

10

If $q = 11a + 3$ and $a = \frac{1}{2}j - 1$, what is the value of q in terms of j?

A) $5j - 8$

B) $\frac{11}{2}j - 14$

C) $\frac{11}{2}j - 8$

D) $\frac{11}{2}j + 2$

11

Tamara is practicing her basketball free-throws. If she hits 10 shots in a row on Monday and always hits 2 more shots in a row than the day before, how many free throws does she hit, in a row, on Friday?

A) 14

B) 16

C) 18

D) 20

12

Kristen opens a bank account where she earns a bonus of $3 at the end of each week. She deposits $20 at the beginning of her first week, $13 the second week, $18 the third week, and $22 the fourth week, without withdrawing any money. How many dollars are in her bank account after the end of four weeks?

A) 78

B) 82

C) 85

D) 88

Answers & Explanations

1. The correct answer is (A). If you substitute the given values for a and c into the equation, you get $6 = -2b - 4$. If you solve for b, you get $b = -5$.

2. The correct answer is (D). If you substitute the given values for p, q, and r into the expression, you will get $(-3 - 2)(7 \times (-2) - (-2))$, which you can simplify to $-5 \times -12 = 60$.

3. The correct answer is (A). You can express $\frac{a}{c}$ in terms of the given ratios as $\frac{a}{b} \times \frac{b}{c}$ to eliminate b. This product is $6 \times -10 = -60$.

4. The correct answer is (A). You can substitute the given value for y into the equation $x + 7 = -12$ and solve for x to get $x = -19$.

5. The correct answer is (B). First, set up the equation $5x + 9 = 3x - 7$, then solve for $2x$: $5x - 3x = -7 - 9$, so $2x = -16$.

6. The correct answer is (C). The question is asking you to write out an expression equal to the total number of pets that Alice owns. It doesn't matter that she has 7 pets in total, because the expression will be some equivalent form of birds + hamsters + turtles. (C) is equivalent to this expression since the brackets do not change the result of the addition.

7. The correct answer is (B). The amount of energy that goes unused is equal to the amount of energy they use subtracted from the amount of energy produced. If you use d as a placeholder for the number of days, you can write this out as an equation:
Energy Sold = Energy Made – Energy Used Energy Sold = $16000d - 11000d$
Energy Sold = $5000d$

8. The correct answer is (D). If Jerry works 8 hours a day at a wage of 15 dollars per hour, he makes $8 \times 15 = 120$ dollars a day. He wants to save up 9,000 dollars, so he should work for $\frac{9000}{120} = 75$ days.
If you got (B), you found out how many hours he should work, not how many days.

9. The correct answer is (C). You want to find the difference in total wages earned, so first find out how much each person made individually. Will makes 20 dollars an hour, or $\$20 \times 10 = \$200$ in ten hours; Saima makes 0.75 times the amount Will does, so $0.75 \times \$200 = \$150$ in ten hours. Therefore, Will makes $\$200 - \$150 = 50$ dollars more than Saima.
If you chose (A) or (B), you probably found the amount Will or Saima makes in ten hours and stopped there. If you chose (D), you probably found the amount of money Saima makes per hour and stopped there.

10. The correct answer is (C). The second equation is already arranged such that a is in terms of j, so all you need to do is substitute the value of a into the first equation and solve for q:

$$q = 11\left(\frac{1}{2}j - 1\right) + 3$$

$$q = \frac{11}{2}j - 11 + 3$$

$$q = \frac{11}{2}j - 8$$

11. The correct answer is (C). The number of free throws Tamara hits increases by 2 each day. She hits 12 on Tuesday, 14 on Wednesday, 16 on Thursday, and 18 on Friday.

12. The answer is (C). It is important to notice that for this question, Kristen deposits money at the beginning of the week and earns interest at the end of the week. In addition, you should know from the question that the interest Kristen earns does not depend on how much money she has in her bank account – she earns $3 at the end of each week regardless of how much she deposited or how much money is in her account. As a result, you can represent her transactions in a table such as the one below to calculate the total amount of money she has.

Week	Deposit	Interest	Total
1	20	3	$20 + 3 = 23$
2	13	3	$23 + 13 + 3 = 39$
3	18	3	$39 + 18 + 3 = 60$
4	22	3	$60 + 22 + 3 = 85$

If you chose (A), you may have thought that she earns 3% interest on the total amount of money in her bank account. If you chose (B), you may have thought that she didn't earn a bonus in her fourth week.

Solve Linear Equations
Part 2

These problems ask you to solve linear equations in one variable. You may need to solve for a variable in a given equation, or you may need to use an equation to solve a word problem. You may also need to solve equations in terms of variables.

DIRECTIONS

Select the best answer among four choices and circle the corresponding letter or record it on a separate sheet of paper.

NOTES

1. You may use a calculator, but not all problems require the use of a calculator.
2. Variables and expressions represent real numbers unless stated otherwise.
3. Figures are drawn to scale unless stated otherwise.
4. Figures lie in a plane unless stated otherwise.
5. The domain of a function f is defined as the set of all real numbers x for which $f(x)$ is also a real number, unless stated otherwise.

1

If $x + 1.4 = -5.5$, what is the value of x?

A) −6.9

B) −4.1

C) 4.1

D) 6.9

2

If $5x - 12 = 44$, what is the value of x?

A) 6.4

B) 8.0

C) 11.2

D) 12.4

3

If $n - 8.1 = -2.9$, what is the value of n?

A) −11.0

B) −5.2

C) 5.2

D) 11.0

4

If $k + 6 = 12 - k$, what is the value of k?

A) 3

B) 4

C) 6

D) 9

5

If Zoë can read 2 critically acclaimed novels each month, how many such novels can Zoë finish in a year?

A) 2

B) 12

C) 24

D) 48

6

Coincidentally, the percent humidity in an office is always equal to 10 times the total number of centimeters of rainfall from the previous day. If 0.2 centimeters of rain fell every hour for 24 hours on Friday, what is the percent humidity in the office on Saturday?

A) 2.4 %

B) 4.8 %

C) 24 %

D) 48 %

7

$$-x = 8x + 3$$

Given the equation above, what is the value of x?

A) 3

B) $\dfrac{1}{3}$

C) $-\dfrac{1}{3}$

D) -3

8

A coyote runs at top speed from Sebastopol to San Andreas, a distance of 141 miles. If the coyote's top speed is 37 miles per hour, how many hours will its trip take?

A) 0.26

B) 2.62

C) 3.81

D) 5.22

9

The value $a = \dfrac{1}{2}b$ is substituted into the linear equation $y = 2a + 3b - \dfrac{1}{2}a$. What is the simplified equation in terms of b?

A) $y = 3b$

B) $y = \dfrac{13}{4}b$

C) $y = \dfrac{15}{4}b$

D) $y = \dfrac{19}{4}b$

10

If $-5y = 2q - 10t$ and $3y = 8q + 5t$, what is the value of q?

A) $-\dfrac{2y}{9}$

B) $\dfrac{y}{18}$

C) $\dfrac{18}{y}$

D) $2y$

Answers & Explanations

1. The correct answer is (A). To solve for x, subtract 1.4 from each side of the equation to get $x = -5.5 - 1.4 = -6.9$.

2. The correct answer is (C). You can solve for x by adding 12 to each side to get $5x = 44 + 12$. Then, you can divide both sides by 5 to get $x = \dfrac{56}{5} = 11.2$.

3. The correct answer is (C). To solve for n, you can add 8.1 to each side of the equation to get $n = -2.9 + 8.1$, which simplifies to $n = 5.2$.

4. The correct answer is (A). You can isolate k on the left side of the equation to get $k + k = 12 - 6$, then solve for $k = 3$.

5. The correct answer is (C). If Zoë can read 2 books in a month, and there are 12 months in a year, that means that Zoë can read $2 \times 12 = 24$ books per year.

6. The correct answer is (D). If you call the percent humidity p and the number of centimeters of rainfall r, you can see that $p = 10r$ from the first sentence of the question. If 0.2 centimeters of rain fell each hour for 24 hours, that means that $0.2 \times 24 = 4.8$ centimeters of rain fell in total. This is equal to r, so you can plug in the value 4.8 to the original expression to solve for p: $p = 10(4.8) = 48$.

7. The correct answer is (C). First, you can combine like terms on each side of the equation. Adding x to both sides and subtracting 3 from both sides gives you $-3 = 9x$. Dividing both sides by 9 gives $-\dfrac{3}{9} = x$, or $-\dfrac{1}{3} = x$.

8. The correct answer is (C). If the coyote runs at 37 miles each hour, then you can multiply 37 by the number of hours the coyote runs to find the total distance travelled. So, we can set up the equation $37 * h = 141$ where h is the number of hours the coyote runs. Dividing both sides by 37 shows that $h = 3.81$.

9. The correct answer is (C). Since the first equation is already in terms of b, all you have to do is substitute the value of a into the equation and simplify.

$$y = 2\left(\frac{1}{2}b\right) + 3b - \frac{1}{2}\left(\frac{1}{2}b\right)$$
$$= 2\left(\frac{1}{2}b\right) + 3b - \frac{1}{4}b$$
$$= b + 3b - \frac{1}{4}b$$
$$= 4b + \frac{1}{4}b$$
$$= \frac{15}{4}b$$

10. The correct answer is (B). To solve this question, you could recognize that by multiplying the second equation through by 2 and adding it to the first equation, you can eliminate the variable t.

$$-5y = 2q - 10t$$
$$6y = 16q + 10t$$
$$y = 18q$$

Now, all you have to do is solve for q.

$$q = \frac{y}{18}$$

Interpret Linear Equations
Part 3

These problems ask you to interpret a constant, variable, factor, or term in context for a given linear equation in one variable. These problems will usually take the form of a word problem that describes the situation that is modeled by the equation, and you will need to make logical inferences based on that description.

DIRECTIONS

Select the best answer among four choices and circle the corresponding letter or record it on a separate sheet of paper.

NOTES

1. You may use a calculator, but not all problems require the use of a calculator.
2. Variables and expressions represent real numbers unless stated otherwise.
3. Figures are drawn to scale unless stated otherwise.
4. Figures lie in a plane unless stated otherwise.
5. The domain of a function f is defined as the set of all real numbers x for which $f(x)$ is also a real number, unless stated otherwise.

1

If $a = bx$, where b is a constant, and $a = 72$ when $x = 18$, for what value of x does $a = 8$?

A) 2

B) 4

C) 16

D) 32

2

Robert randomly picks five candies from a bag. Any time he picks a red candy, he picks an additional candy to replace it. If he picks a total of $x + 5$ candies, which of the following does x represent?

A) The number of total candies he picks

B) The number of red candies he picks

C) The number of non-red candies he picks

D) The total number of candies in the bag

3

A saleswoman is paid $0.1c + 90$ dollars each day, where c is the total cost of the items she has sold. What does the number 90 represent in this expression?

A) Her total daily salary, in dollars

B) The commission she makes on her sales throughout the day, in dollars

C) The amount of money she makes per hour, in dollars

D) The flat rate, in dollars, that she makes no matter what she sells

4

Greig can eat 3 pieces of sushi per minute, but as the number of sushi pieces he eats increases, his eating speed decreases. If s is equal to the number of rolls he has eaten, which of the following could model his sushi eating speed, in pieces per second?

A) $3s$

B) $3 - 0.1s$

C) $\dfrac{1}{20} - \dfrac{1}{600}$

D) $\dfrac{1}{20} + \dfrac{1}{600}$

5

As a server, Vlad earns tips in addition to his hourly wage. Vlad estimates his dollar earnings in a single shift, y, using the equation $y = x(12 + t)$, where t is the average amount of tips he earns in an hour. What does the variable x represent in this equation?

A) Vlad's hourly wage

B) Vlad's total average hourly earnings

C) The number of hours in Vlad's shift

D) Vlad's average earnings in a shift

6

Aria gives her houseplant a new fertilizer that increases its growth rate by 3 inches per month. If the height of Aria's plant y over some number of months x is represented by the expression $y = x(b+3)$, what could the constant b represent?

A) The amount of fertilizer given.

B) The number of weeks that have passed.

C) The growth rate of her plant with fertilizer.

D) The growth rate of her plant without fertilizer.

Answers & Explanations

1. The correct answer is (A). You can find the value of b by plugging in the given values for a and x to get $72 = b \times 18$, which simplifies to $b = 4$. Now you can solve the equation $a = 4x$ by plugging in $a = 8$ to get $x = 2$. The correct answer is (B).

2. The correct answer is (B). You know that Robert picks at least 5 candies out of the bag. You also know that Robert pulls out an extra candy any time he picks a red candy. If Robert picks out an extra candy every time he picks a red candy, then each time he picks a candy he will keep picking extra candies until he gets one that isn't red. That means he will always end up with 5 candies that aren't red. He will also end up with an unknown number of red candies, represented by the variable x.

3. The correct answer is (D). Since 90 is always added to the expression regardless of how many items the saleswoman sells, it is the rate that she makes no matter what she sells. Even if she sells nothing all day, she'll still make $0.1(0) + 90 = 90$ dollars, which is her "flat rate."

4. The correct answer is (C). Since Greig's speed goes down as the number of pieces he's eaten goes up, that means that the entire expression (his speed) will go down as s (the number of pieces) increases. The only two expressions where this is true are (B) and (C). Furthermore, you know that the expression represents his sushi eating speed in pieces per second. When he's eaten 0 pieces, option (B) shows his speed as 3 pieces per second, which is much faster than what the question states his speed is, three pieces per minute. So, the correct option is (C), which correctly shows his beginning speed as $\frac{1}{20}$ of a piece per second, or three pieces per minute.

5. The correct answer is (C). We know that Vlad earns both wages and tips. We can also distribute x across the terms in parentheses to get just two terms on the right side of the equation: $y = 12x + tx$. If t represents the average amount that Vlad makes in tips in an hour, and y represents Vlad's total earnings in a shift, then we can make sense of those two terms by inferring that Vlad has an hourly wage of $12. If Vlad works x hours in a shift, he will earn $12x$ in wages and tx in tips, or a total of $x(12 + t)$.

6. The correct answer is (D). The number of months x is being multiplied by the constant (b+3) to find the plant's total height. This means that every month, the plant grows by (b+3) inches. Since you've been told that the fertilizer increases the growth rate by 3 inches per month, you know that the +3 represents the extra growth from the added fertilizer. Therefore, since it's being added to b, that must be the original growth rate of the plant before fertilizer was added.

Number of Solutions of Linear Equations

Part 4

These problems ask you to determine the conditions under which a linear equation in one variable has no solutions, one solution, or infinitely many solutions.

DIRECTIONS

Select the best answer among four choices and circle the corresponding letter or record it on a separate sheet of paper.

NOTES

1. You may use a calculator, but not all problems require the use of a calculator.
2. Variables and expressions represent real numbers unless stated otherwise.
3. Figures are drawn to scale unless stated otherwise.
4. Figures lie in a plane unless stated otherwise.
5. The domain of a function f is defined as the set of all real numbers x for which $f(x)$ is also a real number, unless stated otherwise.

1

$$6x = ax + 3$$

For what value of a will the above equation have no solutions?

A) 6

B) 3

C) The equation will never have any solutions

D) The equation will have a solution no matter what a is

2

Joelle writes the equation $\frac{1}{2}(m) + 4$ to express his present age, where m is equal to Mary's present age. If Joelle and Mary were born at the same time, at how many different times in Joelle and Mary's lives will the equation above be true?

A) 0

B) 1

C) 2

D) It will always be true

3

Which of the following equations intersects the y-axis an infinite number of times?

A) $y = 0$

B) $y = x$

C) $x = 0$

D) $y = \dfrac{1}{x}$

4

Which of the following equations does not intersect the x-axis?

A) $2(y + x) = 2x$

B) $3y + 3 = x$

C) $y - 5 = x + y$

D) $4(y + x) = 2(2x - 3)$

5

What value of x satisfies the following equation?

$$12 + 8x - 7 = 5x + 5 - 2x$$

A) Infinitely many solutions

B) 0

C) 1

D) No solution exists

Answers & Explanations

1. The correct answer is (A). It can never be true that $6x = 6x + 3$, since $6x$ cannot ever be equal to itself plus three. To check this algebraically, you can subtract $6x$ from both sides to get the incorrect statement $0 = 3$, which confirms that there is no possible solution.

2. The correct answer is (B). If was born at the same time as Mary, and Mary's age is equal to m, then Joelle's age is also equal to m. Thus, you can write the expression $m = \frac{1}{2}(m) + 4$ to compare their ages.

   There are two values for m that satisfy this equation: 8 and -8. However, a person's age is never negative during their lifetime, so the equation can only be true once: when Joelle and Mary are 8 years old.

3. The correct answer is (C). One way to answer this is to draw out each line:

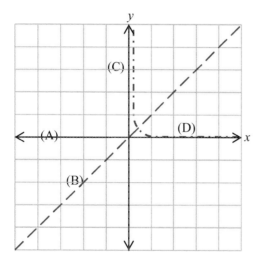

   Based on this sketch, (A), (B) and (D) intersect the y-axis once or not at all, which leaves (C). This also makes sense: for a line to intersect the y-axis an infinite number of times, that means the line must *be* the y-axis.

4. The correct answer is (D). In order for two lines (or one line and a linear axis) to never intersect, they must have the same slope. The x-axis has a slope of 0; in other words, it is a horizontal line. You can rewrite each of the options to determine which has a slope of 0 and is a horizontal line: the only answer option for which this is true is (D), which simplifies to the equation $y = \frac{3}{2}$.

5. The correct answer is (B). To solve this, simplify the equation and isolate x:
$$12 + 8x - 7 = 5x + 5 - 2x$$
$$5 + 3x = 5 - 2x$$
$$5x = 0$$
$$x = 0$$

Create Linear Functions

Part 5

These problems ask you to create and use linear functions to solve problems in a variety of contexts or model a relationship between quantities.

1

If $a = 4$ and $b = -15$, what is the value of $2a - b$?

A) -11

B) -7

C) 19

D) 23

2

The function $t(x) = 12.5x + 30$ represents Tom's pay based on the number of hours he has worked, x, plus a base salary. Daisy works at the same store. If her hourly pay is $6.25 more than Tom's and she receives $3 more in base salary than Tom, which of the following functions represents Daisy's pay?

A) $d(x) = 6.25x + 30$

B) $d(x) = 12.5x + 33$

C) $d(x) = 18.75x + 30$

D) $d(x) = 18.75x + 33$

3

In order to recover a beached sailboat, the tide on a beach needs to be greater than 1.3 m high. The height of the tide between 6:00AM to 8:00AM is given by the linear equation $y = 0.25x + 0.4$, where x is the number of 30-minute intervals that pass after 6:00AM and y is the height of the tide. If the point where $x = 0$ represents the height of the tide at 6:00AM, will the sailboat be recovered by 8:00AM?

A) Yes, the tide at 8:00AM is higher than 1.5m.

B) Yes, the tide at 8:00AM is between 1.3m and 1.5m.

C) Yes, the tide at 8:00AM is exactly 1.3m.

D) No, the tide at 8:00AM is less than 1.3m.

4

Christine is a card collector. If she has 2 cards when she starts her collection and each week the number of cards in her collection is 3 less than 3 times the amount she had last week, which of the following represents the number of cards she has, a, in terms of how many she had last week, b?

A) $a = 2b + 3$

B) $a = 3b - 1$

C) $a = 3b - 3$

D) $a = 3b + 2$

5

A cell phone provider charges its customers a flat fee of $25 per month, plus $1 for every 10 minutes the customers spend talking. Which of the following equations represents the monthly charge in dollars, y, in terms of the number of minutes that the customers spend talking, x?

A) $y = 10x + 25$

B) $y = 25x + 10$

C) $y = \dfrac{x}{10} + 25$

D) $y = \dfrac{x}{25} + 10$

Answers & Explanations

1. The correct answer is (D). You can substitute the given values for a and b into the expression to get $2(4) - (-15)$ $= 8 + 15 = 23$. If you got (B), you may not have realized that subtracting -15 is equivalent to adding 15, and subtracted 15 from 8 instead. If you got (C), you may have found the value of $a - b$ instead of $2a - b$.

2. The correct answer is (D). To solve this question, first identify the pieces of the function that represents Tom's pay. $12.50 is his hourly wage, and x is the number of hours he works. $30 is his base salary. Daisy's hourly pay is 6.75 more: $12.50 + $6.75 = $18.75. Daisy's base salary is $3 more than Tom's base salary: $30 + $3 = $33. Therefore, the equation for Daisy's pay must be $d(x) = 18.75x + 33$.

3. The correct answer is (B). To solve this question, first determine how many 30-minute intervals have passed from 6:00 AM to 8:00 AM. Two hours have passed, or 120 minutes, which is $\frac{120}{30} = 4 \times 30$-minute intervals. Substitute $x = 4$ into the function to get $y = 0.25(4) + 0.4 = 1.4$. Since the output is 1.4 which is greater than 1.3, the boat can be recovered.

4. The answer is (C). The question tells you that the number of cards she has this week, a, is equal to 3 less than the number she had last week, b, which means that $a = 3b - 3$. If you chose (B), you may have included the initial 2 cards she had when finding the general formula.

5. The correct answer is (C). Because the company charges $1 for every 10 minutes that the customers talk, the charge per minute is $\frac{1}{10}$ dollars, meaning the slope of the linear equation should be $\frac{1}{10}$. The flat fee is $25 per month, meaning customers pay $25 even when they do no talking, so the y-intercept of the line should be 25. (C) is the option that satisfies both requirements. If you picked (A) you might have thought that customers were charged $10 for every minute they talk.

Interpret Linear Functions

Part 6

These problems ask you to interpret the meaning of an input/output pair, constant, variable, factor, or term in a linear function that represents a context.

DIRECTIONS

Select the best answer among four choices and circle the corresponding letter or record it on a   .
separate sheet of paper.

NOTES

1. You may use a calculator, but not all problems require the use of a calculator.
2. Variables and expressions represent real numbers unless stated otherwise.
3. Figures are drawn to scale unless stated otherwise.
4. Figures lie in a plane unless stated otherwise.
5. The domain of a function f is defined as the set of all real numbers x for which $f(x)$ is also a real number, unless stated otherwise.

1

A line with a slope of 2 passes through the points $(2, 0)$ and $(a, -6)$. What is the value of a?

A) -2

B) -1

C) 0

D) 1

$$2 = \frac{-6-0}{a-2}$$

$$2 = \frac{-6}{a-2}$$

$$2(a-2) = -6$$
$$2a-4 = -6$$
$$2a = -2$$
$$a = -1$$

2

The population of a colony of seals can be modelled by the function $p(t) = -100t + 20{,}000$, where $p(t)$ is the number of seals and t is the number of years since 1993. What does the term $-100t$ mean in this context?

A) In 1993, there were 100 seals in the colony

B) Each year, the number of seals decreases by 100

C) In 100 years from 1993, there will be no more seals

D) One seal leaves the colony every 100 years

3

The point (2, 6) lies on the graph of the speed of an object after a specified starting time. If the object's speed in <u>meters per second</u> can be modelled by the equation $v(t) = 3t$, what could the point (2, 6) indicate?

A) The object is accelerating at 3 m/s²

B) The object started from a position of rest

C) Six seconds after starting, the object is travelling at 2 m/s

D) Two seconds after starting, the object is traveling at 6 m/s

4

A guitarist uses the function $f(p) = 2 + 1.7p$ to calculate how much power, in watts, her effects pedals will use. If p represents the number of pedals, what does the coefficient 1.7 represent?

A) The number of watts used by her guitar on its own

B) The total number of watts available

C) The number of watts that each pedal uses

D) A correction factor to convert between units

5

Jared and Vinny make up a two-person rowing team. Vinny's rowing speed depends on Jared's speed. Vinny's speed in meters per second is determined by the function $v(x) = j(x) - 7$, and Jared's speed in meters per second is determined by the function $j(x) = \dfrac{8x}{3}$, where x is the speed of the water's current in the direction that Jared and Vinny are rowing. If $x = 7$, what is Vinny's speed, in meters per second, to the nearest whole number?

A) 12

B) 19

C) 28

D) 56

Answers & Explanations

1. The correct answer is (B). You know the slope of the line and almost the coordinates of two points: use the equation for slope to determine the missing value:

    a. $m = \left(\dfrac{y_1 - y_2}{x_1 - x_2}\right)$

    b. $2 = \left(\dfrac{0 - (-6)}{2 - a}\right)$

    c. $2(2 - a) = 6$

    d. $2 - a = 3a$

    e. $a = -1$

2. The correct answer is (B). As t increases, -100 will be multiplied by greater and greater numbers, resulting in a more and more negative number. This means that more and more seals are being subtracted each year. After one year, when $t = 1$, 100 seals are subtracted. After two years, when $t = 2$, 200 seals are subtracted. This continues on, subtracting another 100 seals each year.

3. The correct answer is (D). Since you know that the graph is of an object's speed over time, you know that speed is plotted on the y-axis and time is plotted on the x-axis (as time almost always is). The point (2, 6) shows an x-value (or in this case, t-value) of 2. This means that time that has passed is equal to 2. Similarly, the y-value (or $v(t)$ value) is equal to 6, which means that the speed is 6. So, after 2 seconds, the speed of the object is 6 m/s.

4. The correct answer is (C). Since 1.7 is being multiplied by p, the number of pedals, then for every pedal added, the total wattage will increase by 1.7. This means that each pedal uses 1.7 watts.

5. The correct answer is (A). Since Vinny's speed depends on Jared, you first have to find Jared's speed at $x = 7$. To do this, substitute $x = 7$ into $j(x)$: $j(7) = \dfrac{(8)(7)}{3} = \dfrac{56}{3}$. Next, substitute this value into Vinny's speed function: $v\left(\dfrac{56}{3}\right) = \dfrac{56}{3} - 7 = 11.\underline{6} \approx 12$.

Input/Output Pairs of Linear Functions

Part 7

These problems ask you to find one quantity in a linear function when given the other quantity.

DIRECTIONS

Select the best answer among four choices and circle the corresponding letter or record it on a separate sheet of paper.

NOTES

1. You may use a calculator, but not all problems require the use of a calculator.
2. Variables and expressions represent real numbers unless stated otherwise.
3. Figures are drawn to scale unless stated otherwise.
4. Figures lie in a plane unless stated otherwise.
5. The domain of a function f is defined as the set of all real numbers x for which $f(x)$ is also a real number, unless stated otherwise.

1

The function $f(x)$ is defined as $\frac{4}{3}x + k$, where k is a constant. If $f(3) = -1$, what is the value of $f(9)$?

A) −5

B) 3

C) 7

D) 10

$-1 = \frac{4}{3}(3) + k$

$4 + k = -1$

$k = -5$

$12 + (-5) = 7$

2

Excluding one end, a rope has knots every 6 inches along its length. If the rope is 30 feet long, how many knots does it have?

A) 5

B) 15

C) 30

D) 60

3

What is the value of $g(x) = 9x - 32$ when $x = 9$?

A) 59

B) 49

C) 39

D) −14

4

The number of people living in Mena's neighborhood is described by the function $f(x) = 14x + 812$, where x is the number of months that have passed since he moved in. If there are now 1092 people living in his neighborhood, how many months ago did Mena move in?

A) 18

B) 20

C) 58

D) 78

5

The equation $3p + 15 = 0.6s - 3$ models the relationship between the expected number of sea lion pups p in a colony based on the number of adult sea lions s. If there are 100 adults in a given colony, how many pups would be expected?

A) 12

B) 14

C) 18

D) 36

6

Given the function $f(x) = 3(x+2) - 5$, what is the value of x where $f(x) = 10$?

A) 0

B) 3

C) 5

D) 9

Answers & Explanations

1. The correct answer is (C). Since $f(3) = 1$, you know that $\frac{4}{3}(3) + k = -1$. You can solve this equation to get $k = -5$. To find $f(9)$, plug in $x = 9$ to get $\frac{4}{3}(9) - 5 = 7$. If you chose (A), you may have stopped when you found the value of k.

2. The correct answer is (D). If the rope has one knot every 6 inches, it has $\frac{1 \text{ knot}}{6 \text{ in.}} \times \frac{12 \text{ in.}}{1 \text{ foot}} = 2$ knots per foot of length. You can model the number of knots k in a rope of length l feet by writing out $2l = k$. Since the rope is 30 feet long, it will have $2 \times 30 = 60$ knots.

3. The correct answer is (B). To solve this question, simply substitute $x = 9$ into the function and solve:
$$g(9) = 9(9) - 32$$
$$= 81 - 32$$
$$= 49$$

4. The correct answer is (B). To solve this question, first consider how the function models the situation. In this problem, $f(x)$ models the number of people in a neighborhood given x, the number of months since Mena moved in. The model suggests that 812 people were there when Mena arrived, and an additional 14 arrived each month.

To determine how many months Mena has been there given the current number of people, set up an equation with the model on one side, and the current number of people $f(x)$ on the other, and then solve for x:
$$14x + 812 = 1092$$
$$14x = 280$$
$$x = 20$$

5. The correct answer is (B). To solve this problem, plug the given number of adult sea lions into the equation that models the relationship and then solve for p.
$$3p + 15 = 0.6s - 3$$
$$3p + 15 = 0.6(100) - 3$$
$$3p + 15 = 60 - 3$$
$$3p + 15 = 57$$
$$3p = 42$$
$$p = 14$$

6. The correct answer is (B). If $f(x) = 10$, then you can set 10 equal to the given function and solve for x:
$$10 = 3(x + 2) - 5$$
$$10 = 3x + 6 - 5$$
$$10 = 3x + 1$$
$$9 = 3x$$
$$3 = x$$

Graphs and Tables of Linear Functions
Part 8

These problems ask you to make connections between verbal, tabular, algebraic, and graphical representations of a linear function.

DIRECTIONS

Select the best answer among four choices and circle the corresponding letter or record it on a separate sheet of paper.

NOTES

1. You may use a calculator, but not all problems require the use of a calculator.
2. Variables and expressions represent real numbers unless stated otherwise.
3. Figures are drawn to scale unless stated otherwise.
4. Figures lie in a plane unless stated otherwise.
5. The domain of a function f is defined as the set of all real numbers x for which $f(x)$ is also a real number, unless stated otherwise.

1

What is the slope of a line that passes through the points $(3, 21)$ and $(12, -6)$?

A) -3

B) $-\dfrac{5}{3}$

C) $\dfrac{5}{3}$

D) 3

$$\frac{-6-21}{12-3} = \frac{-27}{9} = -3$$

2

The following chart shows the increase in Ellie's height in cm over the past 5 years. If this information was modeled as a linear relationship in the form $y = mx + b$, where x represents the number of years since 2010, which of the following equations gives the correct relationship?

Year	2010	2011	2012	2013	2014
Ellie's height (cm)	155.3	156.5	157.7	158.9	160.1

$+ 1.2$

A) $y = 0.2x + 155.3$

B) $y = 0.9x + 155.3$

C) $y = 1.1x + 155.3$

D) $y = 1.2x + 155.3$

3

Paper Cranes	Minutes
1	2
2	4
3	6

Grace is timing her friend Thea's ability to fold paper cranes, keeping track of her results in the table above. Which of the following equations correctly models the number of cranes, c, in terms of the number of minutes that pass, m?

A) $c = 2m$

B) $c = \dfrac{1}{2}m$

C) $c = m + 1$

D) $c = m + 2$

4

Which of the following is an equation of the line $0 = 3y - 9x + 21$ in point-slope form?

A) $-9x + 3y = -21$

B) $(y - 4) = 3(x - 1)$

C) $(y + 4) = 3(x - 1)$

D) $(y + 4) = -3(x - 1)$

① plugin (x−1)

then x = 0

5

Which of the following statements is true if $y = 5x$ and $g = x + 4$ are lines in the plane?

A) y and g are parallel lines.

B) y and g are perpendicular lines.

C) g is increasing faster than y.

D) y and g intersect at $(1, 5)$.

6

Biologists have been tracking the population of wolves in a National Park for the past five years. How has the population of wolves been changing over time, as shown in the graph below?

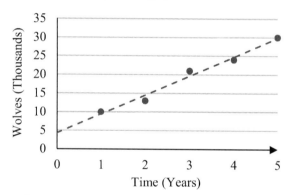

A) Increasing

B) Decreasing

C) Changing with no clear pattern

D) Staying constant

7

The population of rabbits in a particular region over 5 years is shown in the graph below. If the current trend continues, how many rabbits will there be in 6 years, to the nearest thousand?

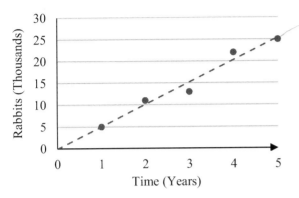

A) 25,000

B) 27,000

C) 29,000

D) 30,000

8

In which sections of the graph shown below is the slope of the function negative?

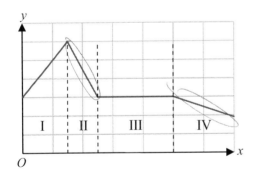

A) I only

B) I and III only

C) II and IV only

D) II, III, and IV only

9

Two sailboats sail directly away from the shore. If sailboat *R* starts closer to shore and travels faster than sailboat *Q*. Which of the following graphs could represent each boat's distance from the shore over time?

A)

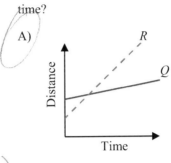

B)

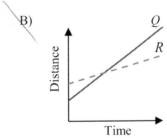

C)

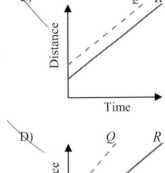

D)

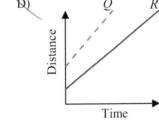

Line c has an equation of $y = 5x + 9$. What is the slope of line k, given that it is perpendicular to line c?

A) $-\dfrac{1}{5}$

B) $\dfrac{1}{5}$

C) 5

D) 9

Which of the following pairs of equations represents two lines that are perpendicular to each other?

A) $y = 7x + 12$ and $y = \dfrac{1}{7}x - 3$

B) $y = \dfrac{1}{2}x + 1$ and $y = 2x - 9$

C) $y = 3x + 10$ and $y = -3x$

D) $y = -\dfrac{1}{5}x - 4$ and $y = 5x - 6$

The average processing speed of a piece of hardware has increased over the past 7 models. The engineers creating this hardware have found the increase in average speed to be a linear function dependent on the model number (the first model is Model #1, the second is Model #2, etc.) The following graph shows the data that the engineers have collected. If the equation of the graph is written in the form $y = mx + b$ where y is the speed of the hardware in megahertz and x is the model number, what is the value of m?

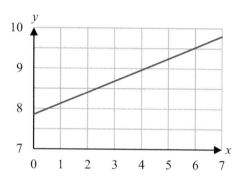

A) 0.15

B) 0.3

C) 1.2

D) 7.8

13

A bean sprout is placed in a dish with 50mL of water. Every day, the remaining quantity of water is measured. It is found that the bean sprout absorbs 2mL of water every day. Which of the following graphs represents the relationship between the number of days elapsed and the quantity of water remaining?

A)

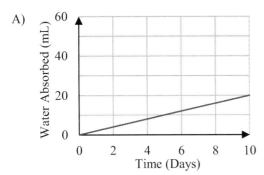

B)

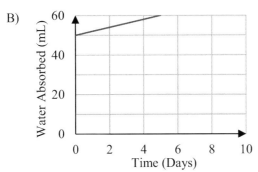

C)

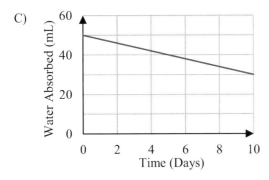

D)

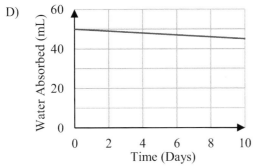

14

Which of the following graphs represents a line with a slope of $-\dfrac{3}{2}$?

A)

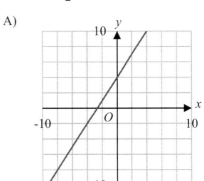

B)

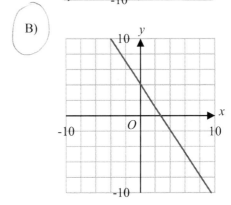

C)

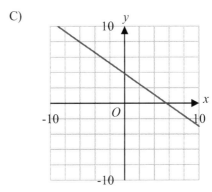

D)

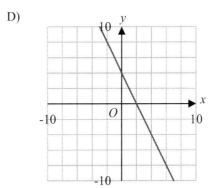

15

Which of the following equations represents a line that is parallel to the line graphed below?

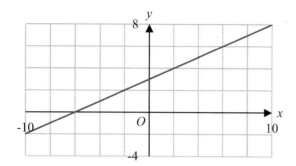

A) $-2x + 5$

B) $-\dfrac{1}{2}x + 5$

C) $\dfrac{1}{2}x + 5$

D) $2x + 5$

16

Two cars drove away from a common point. The graph below shows how far away they were from that common point, in kilometers, over a ten-hour period. After how many hours were the two cars the same distance away from the common point?

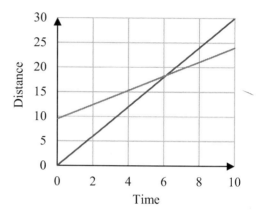

A) 6

B) 9

C) 15

D) 18

17

In the (x, y) coordinate plane shown below, two lines are parallel to each other. What is the value of g?

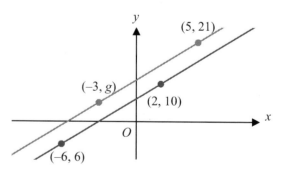

A) −5

B) −3

C) 5

D) 21

Which of the following figures shows a line with a slope of $-\dfrac{1}{2}$?

A)

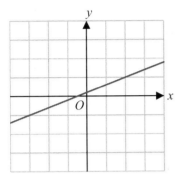

B)

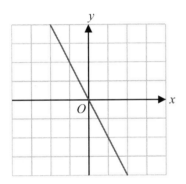

C)

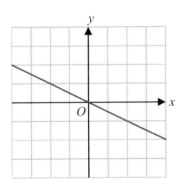

D)

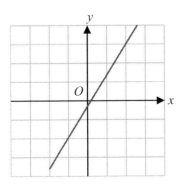

Which of the following equations represents a line in the (x, y) coordinate plane parallel to the one shown in the figure below?

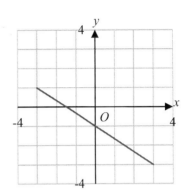

A) $y = -\dfrac{3}{2}x - 1$

B) $y = -\dfrac{2}{3}x - 35$

C) $y = \dfrac{3}{2}x$

D) $y = -x + 27$

Answers and Explanations

1. The correct answer is (A). To calculate the slope of the line using those two points, remember that slope is the change in y over the change in x: $\frac{y_1 - y_2}{x_1 - x_2} = \frac{21 - (-6)}{3 - 12} = \frac{27}{-9} = -3$.

2. The correct answer is (D). Since all of the y-intercepts of the answer choices are the same, all you need to determine is the slope. The slope is the change in the y-value for every unit increase in the x-value. In this context, the y-variable is Ellie's height, since it is dependent on the x-value, which is the number of years since 2010. Every year, Ellie's height increases by 1.2 cm. So, the slope of the line, m, must be 1.2.

3. The correct answer is (B). You can see from the chart that for every 1 minute that passes, the number of cranes increases by 2. That means the slope is equal to 2, which you can verify using the point slope formula: $m = \frac{4-2}{2-1} = \frac{2}{1} = 2$. The only equation which has a slope of 2 is (A), the correct answer. You can also plug in points to test that your answer is correct.

4. The correct answer is (C). If you remember that point-slope form is $(y - y_1) = m(x - x_1)$, where m is the slope of the line and (x_1, y_1) is a point on the line, then you can instantly eliminate (A). Since all of the remaining answers end include $(x - 1)$, you can use the value $x = 1$ to test further. Plug $x = 1$ into the equation of the line to solve for the y coordinate:

$$0 = 3y - (9 \times 1) + 21$$
$$-3y = -9 + 21$$
$$y = -4$$

    This eliminates answer choice (B). If the point has the coordinates $(1, -4)$, then the equation of the line should include $(y + 4)$. Now, you can plug another random value into the original equation to find another point on the line; $x = 0$ is a good value to use. Plugging in $x = 0$ gives you the point $(0, -7)$. Finally, use the two points $(0, -7)$ and $(1, -4)$ to solve for m, the slope: This eliminates answer choice (D), since that point does not work when plugged in.

$$m = \frac{-7 + 4}{0 - 1}$$
$$m(0 - 1) = (-3)$$
$$-m = -3$$
$$m = 3$$

5. The correct answer is (D). You can eliminate (A) and (B) because the slope of y is 5, and the slope of g is 1. These slopes are neither equal nor negative reciprocals of each other, so they are not parallel or perpendicular lines. You can eliminate (C) because "increasing" refers to the rate of change, or the slope; the line with the larger slope is increasing at a faster rate, and y has a larger slope than g. You are left with (D), which you can prove by setting y = g and solving for both the x and y coordinate:

$$5x = x + 4$$
$$4x = 4$$
$$x = 1$$

Substituting x into either of the line equations will give you the y coordinate of their intersection:
$$y = (1) + 4 = 5$$

6. The correct answer is (A). Each year, the number of wolves is larger than the number of wolves the previous year; to show this, the trend line has a positive slope. Therefore, you can say that over time, the population of wolves is increasing.

7. The correct answer is (D). To solve this question, the only thing you need to find is the slope. Notice that for each unit increase in the x direction, there is a 5 unit increase in the y direction; each year there are 5 thousand more rabbits. Therefore, one year after 25 thousand rabbits at the five-year mark, there will be 30 thousand rabbits.

8. The correct answer is (C). The slope is negative when the line on the graph is decreasing from left to right. I shows the graph increasing, so you can eliminate (A) and (B). III shows no change at all, and a slope of zero is not a negative slope, so you can eliminate (D).

9. The correct answer is (A). Sailboat R starts closer to shore, so line R's y-intercept must be smaller than line Q's y-intercept. This eliminates (B). Sailboat R also travels faster than sailboat Q, which means that its line has a greater slope. (A) is the only graph that contains both of these elements.

10. The correct answer is (A). First, recognize that the equation for line c is in slope-intercept form, $y = mx + b$, where m is the slope of the line. The slopes of two perpendicular lines are negative reciprocals of each other, so if the slope of line c is 5, then the slope of k is $-\frac{1}{5}$.

11. The correct answer is (D). Slopes of perpendicular lines are negative reciprocals of each other. The only pair of lines whose slopes follow this rule is (D).

12. The correct answer is (B). The value of m in this question is equivalent to the slope of the line in the graph. Using the equation slope $= \frac{\text{rise}}{\text{run}}$, you will find that $m = \frac{\text{rise}}{\text{run}} = \frac{0.3}{1}$.

13. The correct answer is (C). The question tells you that the graph should represent the quantity of water remaining. Since the plant absorbs 2 mL of water every day, the quantity of water remaining should decrease over time. This eliminates (A) and (B). To distinguish between (C) and (D), look at the slopes of the graphs: you can see that in (D), the plant absorbs $\frac{1}{2}$ mL every day, whereas in (C) the plant absorbs 2 mL every day.

14. The correct answer is (B). The question asks you to identify the graph with a slope of $-\frac{3}{2}$. Since the slope is negative, you know that the line must point down to the right. This eliminates choice (A). Of the remaining choices, you can use the gridlines to identify which graph has a slope of $-\frac{3}{2}$ by remembering that slope = $\frac{\text{rise}}{\text{run}}$. (B) is the only line that has a decrease of 3 units in y-value for every 2 unit increase in x-value.

15. The correct answer is (C). Lines that are parallel to one another have the same slope. You can find the slope of the line in the graph by remembering that slope = $\frac{\text{rise}}{\text{run}}$. For every 2 unit increase in the x-coordinate, the y-coordinate increases by 1. This means that the slope of the line is $\frac{1}{2}$. The only line that has this slope is (C).

16. The correct answer is (A). To answer this question, you should find the point of intersection between the two lines. From the graph, you can see that the two lines intersect at $t = 6$.

   If you chose (D), you probably found the distance, d, at the intersection point instead of the time, t.

17. The correct answer is (C). Since parallel lines have the same slope, you can compare the two slopes to find the missing coordinate. The lower line has a slope of $\frac{10-}{2--} = \frac{16}{8} = 2$, so the slope of the other line is also 2. Solve the slope equation for g:

$$2 = \frac{(21-g)}{(5-(-3))}$$
$$2 = \frac{(21-g)}{8}$$
$$16 = 21 - g$$
$$g = 5$$

18. The correct answer is (C). The question asks you to identify a line with a slope of $-\frac{1}{2}$. Since the given slope is negative, you know that the line must go down as you move right on the x-axis. This allows you to eliminate options (A) and (D). A slope of $-\frac{1}{2}$ means that the line moves down by $\frac{1}{2}$ units for every unit you move to the right on the x-axis, as seen for the line in (C). (B) is incorrect as the line moves down by 2 units for each unit on the x-axis.

19. The correct answer is (B). To identify the equation of a line parallel to the given line, you must determine the slope of the line in the figure. To do so, you can pick two points where the coordinates of the line are obvious, for example, (0, –1) and (3, –3). Given these points, you can divide the difference in y-coordinates by the difference in x-coordinates to get $\frac{-3-(-1)}{3-0} = -\frac{2}{3}$. The only one of the answer options with the given slope is (B). You don't need to worry about the constant added at the end of the equation– when looking for a parallel line, the only thing that matters is the slope.

Create Linear Functions Given Slope
Part 9

These problems ask you to create a linear function given two input/output pairs, one input/output pair and the rate of change, or the rate of change of a perpendicular line.

DIRECTIONS

Select the best answer among four choices and circle the corresponding letter or record it on a separate sheet of paper.

NOTES

1. You may use a calculator, but not all problems require the use of a calculator.
2. Variables and expressions represent real numbers unless stated otherwise.
3. Figures are drawn to scale unless stated otherwise.
4. Figures lie in a plane unless stated otherwise.
5. The domain of a function f is defined as the set of all real numbers x for which $f(x)$ is also a real number, unless stated otherwise.

1

What is the slope of the line perpendicular to $g = mx + 5$ that intersects line g at the point (3, 14)?

A) 3

B) $\dfrac{1}{3}$

C) $-\dfrac{1}{3}$

D) -3

2

A city planner is mapping out a city's streets on an (x, y) coordinate plane. If the equation of Maple Street is given by $y = -\dfrac{1}{2}x + 8$, which of the following is the equation of a street that will intersect Maple Street at a right angle?

A) $-2x + \dfrac{4}{3}$

B) $-\dfrac{1}{2}x + 5$

C) $\dfrac{1}{2}x + 11$

D) $2x + 7$

In the (x, y) coordinate plane shown below, lines m and k intersect at a 90° angle. If line m passes through the points $(0, 0)$ and $(4, 3)$, which of the following can be the equation of the line k?

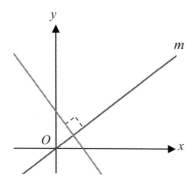

A) $y = -\dfrac{3}{4}x + 3$

B) $y = -\dfrac{4}{3}x + 3$

C) $y = \dfrac{3}{4}x + 3$

D) $y = \dfrac{4}{3}x + 3$

The line $g(x)$ is perpendicular to the line $f(x)$. If $f(x) = 5x - 3$, which of the following is a possible equation for $g(x)$?

A) $5x - 3$

B) $\dfrac{1}{5}x - 2$

C) $-\dfrac{1}{5}x + 7$

D) $-5x + 3$

Aurelia is running a fireworks display. If she presses the trigger five times, 55 fireworks are launched. If she presses the trigger nine times, 103 fireworks are launched. Which function might represent this relationship, if x is the number of times she presses the trigger?

A) $f(x) = 11x$

B) $f(x) = 11x + 4$

C) $f(x) = 12x - 5$

D) $f(x) = 13x - 2$

Which of the following equations represents a line that is perpendicular to $y = -3x - 2$ and intersects the point $(-2, 4)$?

A) $y = -\dfrac{1}{3}x + \dfrac{14}{3}$

B) $y = \dfrac{1}{3}x + \dfrac{14}{3}$

C) $y = \dfrac{1}{3}x + \dfrac{10}{3}$

D) $y = \dfrac{1}{3}x + \dfrac{2}{3}$

The line m, shown on the xy-plane below, is perpendicular to k. If m has as slope of 1, which of the following pairs of points may lie on k?

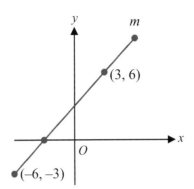

A) $(1,0)$ and $(7,0)$

B) $(0,0)$ and $(2, 4)$

C) $(0,0)$ and $(-4, -2)$

D) $(0,3)$ and $(6, -3)$

Answers and Explanations

1. The correct answer is (C). To find m, simply plug in the point (3, 14) into the equation for g:

$$14 = (m \times 3) + 5$$
$$9 = 3m$$
$$m = 3$$

   Since you know the line is perpendicular to $g = mx + 5 = 3x + 5$, its slope will be equal to $-\frac{1}{m}$, or $-\frac{1}{3}$.

   If you got (A), you probably just found the slope of line g and stopped there.

2. The correct answer is (D). Because the lines must intersect at right angles, the two lines must be perpendicular to one another. Since slopes of perpendicular lines are negative reciprocals of each other and the slope of the given line is $-\frac{1}{2}$, the slope of any line perpendicular to it must be 2. (D) is the only answer choice that has a line with a slope of 2.

3. The correct answer is (A). Since you are given two points on m, you can find its slope using the slope equation to get $\frac{4 - 0}{3 - 0} = \frac{4}{3}$. Since k is perpendicular to m, its slope will be the negative reciprocal of the slope of m, to get $-\frac{3}{4}$. Out of the answer options, only (A) represents a line with a slope of $-\frac{3}{4}$.

4. The correct answer is (C). Perpendicular lines have negative reciprocal slopes, so if $f(x)$ has a slope of 5, $g(x)$ must have a slope of $-\frac{1}{5}$. Since (C) is the only option with this slope, it is correct.

5. The correct answer is (C). You can see that based on the number of times Aurelia presses the trigger, a different number of fireworks are launched. These two pairs of numbers can be written as two points: (5, 55) and (9, 103). Since all the answer options are linear functions in standard form, you can start by finding the slope between the two points: $m = \frac{103 - 55}{9 - 5} = \frac{48}{4} = 12$. Since (C) is the only function with a slope of 12, it must be the correct answer.

6. The correct answer is (B). The slopes of perpendicular lines are negative reciprocals of each other. Since you are looking for a line that is perpendicular to $y=-3x-2$, the slope of any perpendicular line must be $\frac{1}{3}$. This rules out answer choice (A). To find the y-intercept, substitute the given point $(-2,4)$ into the slope intercept form of the line and solve:

$$y = \frac{1}{3}x + b$$

$$4 = \frac{1}{3}(-2) + b$$

$$4 + \frac{2}{3} = b$$

$$b = \frac{14}{3}$$

Only (B) has the correct slope and y-intercept.

7. The correct answer is (D). To find which points can lie on k, you must first find the slope of k, which is the negative reciprocal of the slope of m. The slope of m is 1, which means that the slope of k must be -1. Using the slope equation, you can find that the two points in (A) have a slope of 0, (B) has a slope of 2, and (C) has a slope of -0.5, so they can all be eliminated. As a result, (D) is correct – the slope of (D) is $\frac{3-(-3)}{0-6} = -1$.

Create Systems of Equations
Part 10

These problems ask you to create and use a system of linear equations in two variables to solve problems in a variety of contexts or interpret solutions in terms of the context.

1

If $p - r = 11$ and $q - r = -5$, what is the value of $p - q$?

A) -16

B) -6

C) 6

D) 16

2

Sylvia buys a snack-pack of nuts as an after lunch treat. She notices that there are twice as many cashews as almonds, so she eats ten cashews and sees there are still five more cashews than almonds. How many almonds were in the snack-pack?

A) 45

B) 30

C) 15

D) 5

3

Ali and Hubert are splitting a jar of p candied pecans. If the amount Ali takes, a, is three times half the amount that Hubert takes, h, how many pecans did Hubert eat, assuming that all the pecans got eaten?

A) $\dfrac{5}{2}p$

B) $\dfrac{2}{5}p$

C) $\dfrac{3}{2}a$

D) $a - p$

Raymond is 175 cm tall. He stacks 9 soda cans and 8 jars of jam on top of each other, and measures that the entire stack is 11 cm shorter than him. He then makes a stack of 12 soda cans and 7 jars of jam and notices that that stack is 18 cm taller than him. How tall is one soda can?

A) 7 cm

B) 8 cm

C) 9 cm

D) 12 cm

Sara realizes that if she had x quarters and y dimes then she would have $2.60, but if she had y quarters and x dimes she would only have $1.25. What is $x + y$?

A) 9

B) 10

C) 11

D) 12

Alizah is comparing the prices of two apple orchards. At the first orchard, it costs $30 to rent a basket for collecting apples, and every pound of apples collected costs $5. At the second orchard, baskets are free, but the apples cost $20 per pound. How many pounds of apples would Alizah need to collect at each orchard for their costs to be the same?

A) 2

B) 3

C) 4

D) 5

Answers and Explanations

1. The correct answer is (D). To determine the value of $p - q$, you can subtract the second equation from the first to eliminate r: $p - q = (p - r) - (q - r)$. You can then substitute the value of these expressions to get $11 - (-5) = 16$.

2. The correct answer is (C). Before Sylvia eats the snack, there are twice as many cashews as almonds, so you can write the relationship $c = 2a$ where c is the original number of cashews and a is the original number of almonds. After she eats 10 cashews ($c - 10$), there are still five more cashews than almonds ($a + 5$). So, $c - 10 = a + 5$. You can solve the system for a, the number of almonds, but substituting $2a$ in for c in the second equation:

    $$(2a) - 10 = a + 5$$
    $$a = 15$$

3. The correct answer is (B). If Ali and Hubert split the jar of pecans, then you know that $a + h = p$. The question also tells you how much Ali takes in terms of the amount Hubert takes: $a = \frac{3}{2}h$. You can substitute the a in the first equation with $\frac{3}{2}h$ to get the new equation $\frac{3}{2}h + h = p$, or $\frac{5}{2}h = p$. Therefore, $h = \frac{2}{5}p$. If you got (A), you may have written the amount of pecans total and stopped there. If you got (C), you may have written the amount of pecans Ali takes and stopped there. If you got (D), you may have mistaken $a - p$ with $p - a$, which is also equal to the amount Hubert takes.

4. The correct answer is (D). You can set up a system of equations using the given information. If the height of a soda can is s and the height of a jam jar is j, you know that $9s + 8j = 175 - 11$, and $12s + 7j = 175 + 18$. You can simplify these to get $9s + 8j = 164$ and $12s + 7j = 193$. You can now multiply the first equation by 4 and the second equation by 3 and subtract the second from the first to get $36s - 36s + 32j - 21j = 77$. You can simplify this to get $11j = 77$, which means that $j = 7$. You can now substitute $j = 7$ into either of your original equations to get $s = 12$. If you picked (A), you might have found the height of a jam jar instead of a soda can.

5. The correct answer is (C). You can set up a system of equations using the given information: $0.25x + 0.10y = 2.60$ and $0.10x + 0.25y = 1.25$. You can multiply the first equation by 2 and the second equation by 5, and subtract the first from the second, to get $1.25y - 0.20y = 6.25 - 5.20$. You can simplify this to get $1.05y = 1.05$, which means that $y = 1$. You can substitute $y = 1$ into either of your original equations to find that $x = 10$. Finally, $10 + 1 = 11$.

6. The correct answer is (A). The first orchard has a base cost of $30, plus a variable number of $5 pounds of apples. So, the cost y of x pounds of apples is represented by y = 5x + 30. In the second orchard, there is no base fee but each pound costs $20, so the cost y of x pounds of apples is represented by y = 20x. Since you're trying to find when the two orchards have equal cost, simply set each expression equal to the other:

    $$5x + 30 = 20x$$
    $$30 = 15x$$
    $$2 = x$$

    Alizah would need to buy 2 pounds of apples for the two costs to be equal.

Graphs and Tables of Systems of Equations
Part 11

These problems ask you to make connections between tabular, algebraic, and graphical representations of a system of linear equations in two variables.

1

The table of values of two linear functions is given below. If they intersect at the point (a, b), what is the value of $a + b$?

x	$f(x)$	$g(x)$
1	3	5
4	9	20

A) −2

B) −1

C) 1

D) 2

2

$$y - 2 = ax$$
$$y = -ax$$

In what quadrant of the xy-plane does the solution to the above system of equations lie, given that a is a negative whole number?

A) I

B) II

C) III

D) IV

Which of the following systems of equations would create the pair of lines shown below?

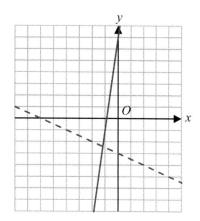

A) $y = 3(3x + 2) \ \backslash\backslash \ y = -\dfrac{1}{2}x - 3$

B) $y = 3x + 2 \ \backslash\backslash \ y = -\dfrac{1}{2}x - 3$

C) $y = 3x + 2 \ \backslash\backslash \ y = -(x + 3)$

D) $y = 3(3x + 2) \ \backslash\backslash \ y = -(x + 3)$

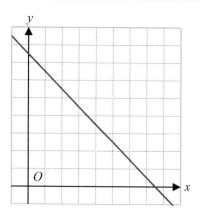

y	x
14	7
8	4
2	1

The table of values above shows some values that lie on line g, while the graph shows line h. At what point do g and h intersect?

A) $(8, 4)$

B) $(5, 10)$

C) $(10, 5)$

D) $(8, 2)$

What is the slope of a line perpendicular to the line shown below?

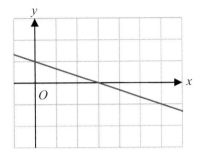

A) −3

B) $-\dfrac{1}{3}$

C) $\dfrac{1}{3}$

D) 3

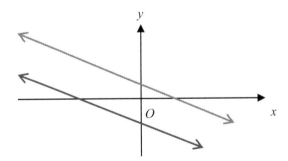

6

If a and b are both positive integers, which of the following could represent the system of equations above?

A) $y = ax + b \mid y = ax - b$

B) $y = -ax + b \mid y = ax + b$

C) $y = ax - b \mid y = -ax - b$

D) $y = -ax + b \mid y = -ax - b$

x	y_1	y_2
−1	−1	−9
0	0	−6
2	2	0
4	4	9

Given the table above representing two linear equations, which of the following could represent the system of equations above?

A) $y = 3x - 3 \mid y = -x$

B) $y = 3x - 6 \mid y = x$ ←

C) $y = \dfrac{1}{3}x - 3 \mid y = -x$

D) $y = \dfrac{1}{3}x - 6 \mid y = x$

Answers and Explanations

1. The correct answer is (D). To solve this, first you must write the equations for $f(x)$ and $g(x)$. The table gives two points for each line: $(1, 3)$ and $(4, 9)$ for $f(x)$, and $(1, 5)$ and $(4, 20)$ for $g(x)$. Using the slope formula, the slope of $f(x)$ is $\frac{9-3}{4-1} = \frac{6}{3} = 2$. The slope of $g(x)$ is $\frac{20-5}{4-1} = \frac{15}{3} = 5$. You can plug both slopes and two points into the point-slope form of linear equations: $f(x) - 3 = 2(x - 1)$ and $g(x) - 5 = 5(x - 1)$. Putting them both into standard form gives $f(x) = 2x + 1$ and $g(x) = 5x$. Set each function equal to the other and solve for x:

2. The correct answer is (A). To begin, it's helpful to put the first equation into standard form: $y = ax + 2$. If a is a negative whole number, then the first equation will have a negative slope, while the second equation $y = -ax$ will have a positive slope. The y-intercept of the first equation is 2, and the y-intercept of the second equation is 0. You can sketch out a potential graph, perhaps with $a = -1$, to show yourself what that might look like:

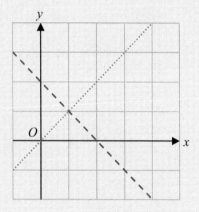

   From this sketch, it's clear that both lines intersect in quadrant I. To confirm, you can test other values of a to find that the lines always intersect in quadrant I.

3. The correct answer is (A). To solve this problem, use the graph to estimate the slope and intercepts of each line, and then select the equation that matches. Remember that you can draw on your test booklet, which can be helpful:

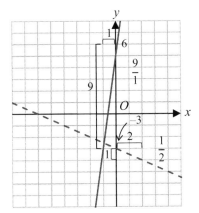

The solid line crosses 1 vertical gridline for each 2 horizontal gridlines, and it slopes downward, so it has a slope of $-\frac{1}{2}$, and it intercepts the y-axis at -3, so its formula is $-\frac{1}{2}x - 3$. That appears in answer choices A and B, so we can eliminate C and D.

The dotted line crosses 9 vertical gridlines for each 1 horizontal gridline, and it slopes upward, so it has a slope of $\frac{9}{1}$ or 9, and it intercepts the y axis at 6, so its formula is $9x + 6$. None of the answer choices has that formula exactly, but 3 is a factor of both 9 and 6, and if we factor that equation we get $3(3x + 2)$. That appears in answer choice A and D, and we've already eliminated C and D, so A must be correct!

4. The correct answer is (B). The easiest way to solve this is to use your pencil to sketch out the line of h by plotting the points given and then connecting them with a line.

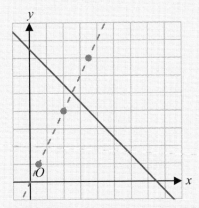

Based on this sketch, you can see that the two lines intersect at about (5, 10). The other answer choices are nowhere near that point, so the correct answer is (B). If you wanted to double check, you could write both equations and solve them. Line g has a y-intercept of 15, and a slope of -1, so its equation is $y = -x + 15$. Using the slope formula, you can find that line h has a slope of $\frac{8-2}{4-1} = 2$. You can then use point-slope form to write out the equation of the line, or notice that with a slope of 2 the line will have a y-intercept of 0. Either way, you'll end up with an equation equivalent to $y = 2x$. Setting the two equations equal to each other as $-x + 15 = 2x$ gives you $x = 5$, and plugging that x-value back into either equation gives you $y = 10$.

5. The correct answer is (D). To find the slope of a perpendicular line, you must take the negative reciprocal of the slope of the first line. You can see the rise over run of the line above is $-\frac{1}{3}$, so the perpendicular slope must be 3. You can also sketch out each potential slope to determine which is perpendicular to the first line.

6. The correct answer is (D). You can see that both lines have a negative slope, since they slope downward to the right. That means that both lines must have negative slopes. The only pair of equations for which this is true is (D). To double check, you can notice that one line has a y-intercept above the x-axis, and one line has a y-intercept below the x-axis, both of which match the lines in option (D).

7. The correct answer is (B). To begin with, you can see that y_1 is always the same value as x, which means that its equation is $y = x$. That eliminates (A) and (C). To find the equation for the second set of values, you can use the slope formula to determine whether the slope is $\frac{1}{3}$ or 3:

$$m = \frac{0 - (-6)}{2 - 0} = \frac{6}{2} = 3$$

Since (B) is the option that contains a line with a slope of 3, it is correct.

Solve Systems of Equations
Part 12

These problems ask you to solve a system of linear equations in two variables.

DIRECTIONS

Select the best answer among four choices and circle the corresponding letter or record it on a separate sheet of paper.

NOTES

1. You may use a calculator, but not all problems require the use of a calculator.
2. Variables and expressions represent real numbers unless stated otherwise.
3. Figures are drawn to scale unless stated otherwise.
4. Figures lie in a plane unless stated otherwise.
5. The domain of a function f is defined as the set of all real numbers x for which $f(x)$ is also a real number, unless stated otherwise.

1

What ordered pair (x, y) satisfies the following system of equations?

$$2x - 2y = 6$$
$$x - 3y = 5$$

A) $(-2, 1)$

B) $(-1, 2)$

C) $(1, -2)$

D) $(2, -1)$

2

If (a, b) is the solution of the following system of equations, what is the value of $b - a$?

$$y = -x + 8$$
$$y = 5x - 4$$

A) 2

B) 4

C) 6

D) 8

If the solution to the following system of equations is $x = a$ and $y = b$, what is $a + b$?

$$3y - x = 6$$
$$5y + 2x = -1$$

A) −4

B) −2

C) 2

D) 4

$$8x - 4y = 24$$
$$2y - 3x = 2$$

The two lines above intersect at which of the following values of y?

A) 4

B) 14

C) 20

D) 22

The lines $y = 3x + 6$ and $y = 4x + 13$ intersect at the point (a, b). What is $a + b$?

A) −22

B) −12

C) −8

D) −2

~~Philosophy Amazing Grace Ballet Rose EDT~~

Marc Jacobs Perfect EDP

Jimmy Choo by Jimmy Choo EDP

Zara x Jo Malone stunningly venille EDC

✓ Juliette Has a Gun superdose EDP

✓ Givenchy Irresistible EDP

Ariana Grande Moonlight EDP

✓ Jo Malone waterlily EDC

Prada Candy EDP

✓ Givenchy L'interdit EDP

✓ Dolce & Gabbana L'imperatrice EDT

✓ Glossier You EDP

✓ Juliette Has a Gun Magnolia bliss EDP   break

✓ Valentino Donna Born in Roma Coral Fantasy EDP

✓ Jo de Janeiro Cheirosa EDP

✓ Chanel Chance Eau Tendre EDT

✓ Zara wonder Rose EDT

cocoa seeds
Glow Drops

(as a hobby)

cinculure general

0.5

0.3 4 1 oz
    2

1.7oz — 50mL

3.3oz — 100mL
for samples

0.28

Answers and Explanations

1. The correct answer is (D). First, you can use the second equation to solve for x in terms of y to get $x = 3y + 5$. Then, you can substitute this expression for x into the first equation to get $2(3y + 5) - 2y = 6$, which you can solve to get $y = -1$. You can confirm that choice (D) is correct by solving for x using this value of y: $x - 3(-1) = 5$, so $x = 2$.

2. The correct answer is (B). First, you have to solve the system of equations. Since both equations are written as an expression equal to y, the two equations are equal and you can combine them as $-x + 8 = 5x - 4$, which you can solve to get $x = 2$. Then, you can solve $y = -2 + 8$ to get $y = 6$.

    Finally, since $(2, 6)$ is the solution of the system of equations, you can plug in the values of a and b to evaluate the expression $b - a = 6 - 2 = 4$.

3. The correct answer is (B). Although you could use substitution to solve this system of equations, the easiest method is elimination. If you multiply the first equation by 2 and add it to the second equation, you get $6y + 5y - 2x + 2x = 12 - 1$, which, after simplifying, becomes $11y = 11$, which tells you that $y = 1$. You can substitute $y = 1$ into either of the two equations and solve for x to find that $x = -3$. Finally, $1 + (-3) = -2$.

4. The correct answer is (A). Finding the intersection point of two lines is equivalent to solving the system given by their equations. Since these equations are already arranged so that y is isolated, you can set both right-hand sides equal to each other to get $3x + 6 = 4x + 13$. Rearranging this and isolating for x gives you $x = -7$. You can substitute this value into either equation to get $y = -15$. Finally, $-7 + (-15) = -22$.

5. The correct answer is (D). The simplest way to solve this system is using the combination method. First, multiply the entire second equation by 2 so that the y-terms will cancel out: $4y - 6x = 4$. Then, combine both equations vertically.

$$-6x + 4y = 4$$
$$+ \ 8x - 4y = 24$$
$$2x = 28$$
$$x = 14$$

Now, you can plug the x-value into either equation to find the y-value:

$$2y - 3(14) = 2$$
$$2y - 42 = 2$$
$$2y = 44$$
$$y = 22$$

Solving Systems of Equations
Part 13

These problems ask you to interpret a solution, constant, variable, factor, or term based on the context of a system of linear equations in two variables.

1

$$y = x - 1$$
$$y = \frac{1}{2}x + a$$

What must be true of a for the two lines above to intersect where $x > 0$?

A) $a < 1$

B) $a < -1$

C) $a > 1$

D) $a > -1$

2

The growth of Mateo's two bamboo plants can be modeled by $y_1 = 2.3x + 3$ and $y_2 = 3.2x + 1$ respectively, where y is the height of each plant and x is the number of days that have passed since Mateo started measuring their growth. If $y_1 = y_2$ for a given value of x, which of the following must be true at that point in time?

   I. The plants have been growing for an equal amount of time.

   II. The plants have reached equal heights.

   III. The plants are growing at equal rates.

A) II

B) III

C) I and II

D) I, II and III

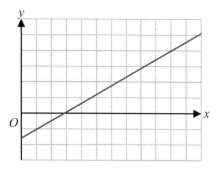

The distance-time graph of Car A driving along a highway is shown above. Car B departs a few minutes later from a different location, but travelling along the same highway in the same direction as Car A. If Car B eventually overtakes Car A, what is a possible equation for Car B?

A) $y = \dfrac{1}{2}x$

B) $2y = x + 1$

C) $y = \dfrac{1}{3}x + 5$

D) $y = x - 2$

As a storm approaches, the wind speed from the East can be modelled by $s = 1.6t + 2.34$ and the wind speed from the North can be modeled by $s = 1.12t + 4.6$. If s is the speed of the wind in each direction and t is the time that has passed since the storm began, which of the following is true?

A) The initial speed of the Northern wind was greater than the initial speed of the Eastern wind.

B) The initial speed of the Eastern wind was greater than the initial speed of the Northern wind.

C) The initial speed of the Northern wind was equal to the initial speed of the Eastern wind.

D) The initial speed of the Northern wind and the initial speed of the Eastern wind cannot be determined.

In the number of weeks w since the beginning of 2019, the number of books b in one library is modeled by the equation $b = 3w + 2012$, while the number of books b in a second library is modeled by the equation $b = 2w + 1900$. If the rate at which the libraries acquired new books before 2019 is the same as the rate at which they acquired new books during 2019, which of the following statements is true?

A) The two libraries had the same number of books at the beginning of 2019.

B) The two libraries had the same number of books at some point before the beginning of 2019.

C) The two libraries will have the same number of books at some point after the beginning of 2019.

D) The two libraries have never had and will never have the same number of books.

Answers and Explanations

1. The correct answer is (D). The easiest way to approach this is to sketch out a diagram. Draw out the first line, and then draw out some potentials for the second line, perhaps with the value of a at 1 and -1:

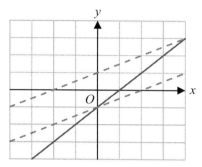

From this diagram, you can see that if $a = 1$, the two lines will intersect at $(4, 3)$. At that point, x is greater than zero. If $a = -1$, the lines will intersect at $(0, -1)$. At that point, x is equal to 0, but not greater. You can see that if a continued to decrease, the intersection would move further and further to the left, into negative values of x. However, if you increase the value of a even a tiny fraction from -1, the intersection of the lines will shift slightly to the right, where x is greater than 0. This means that as long as the value of a is greater than -1, the lines will intersect where x is greater than 0.

2. The correct answer is D. You can see from the graph that the slope of Car A's line is approximately $\frac{3}{5}$. If Car B is to overtake Car A,

    it must be traveling at a higher speed, and therefore have a greater slope. (A) and (C) have slopes less than $\frac{3}{5}$, and rewriting (B) in standard

    form shows that it does as well. That leaves (D). To double check, if you plot $y = x - 2$, you can also see that this option will eventually intersect the Car A's line and then rise above it.

3. The correct answer is (C). Since y is the height of each plant and $y_1 = y_2$, you know that both heights are the same, so II must be true. The question also states that the heights are equal for a given value of x, which means you must plug in the same value of x into both equations. This means that the same number of days have passed for each plant, so I is true. Since the "rate" of growth in a linear equation is the slope of the line, and each line has a different slope, III is not true.

4. The correct answer is (A). At the beginning of the storm, no time has passed, so $t = 0$. When $t = 0$, the two wind speeds are 2.34 from the North and 4.6 from the East. The initial speed of both winds is represented by the constant added to each expression. Since $4.6 > 2.34$, then it's true that the initial speed of the Northern wind was greater than the initial speed of the Eastern wind.

5. The correct answer is (B). One way to solve this problem is by considering the rate of change of each line and the initial value of each line. First, since the first equation has a slope of 3 and the second equation has a slope of 2, the first library must be acquiring books at a faster rate than the second library. Secondly, when $w = 0$ at the beginning of 2019, the first library had 2012 books and the second library had 1900 books.

Using this information, you can first eliminate (A), since the two libraries had different numbers of books at the beginning of 2019. Since the first library had more books at the beginning of the year and is also acquiring books more quickly, the second library will never catch up in the future, which eliminates (C). Since these lines have different slopes, you know that they must intersect at some point, and at that point the two libraries will have the same number of books, so (D) cannot be true. That leaves the correct answer, (B). If you were to sketch out the graphs, you'd see that the two lines intersect at about $w = -112$, or 112 weeks before the beginning of 2019.

Number of Solutions of Systems of Equations
Part 14

These problems ask you to determine the conditions under which a system of linear equations in two variables has no solution, one solution, or infinitely many solutions.

DIRECTIONS

Select the best answer among four choices and circle the corresponding letter or record it on a separate sheet of paper.

NOTES

1. You may use a calculator, but not all problems require the use of a calculator.
2. Variables and expressions represent real numbers unless stated otherwise.
3. Figures are drawn to scale unless stated otherwise.
4. Figures lie in a plane unless stated otherwise.
5. The domain of a function f is defined as the set of all real numbers x for which $f(x)$ is also a real number, unless stated otherwise.

1

$$y = mx + 3$$
$$y = x + 1$$
$$y + 5 = -x$$

If the system of equations above has exactly one solution, what is the value of m?

A) 5

B) 3

C) $\dfrac{5}{3}$

D) $\dfrac{3}{5}$

2

How many solutions are there for the following system of equations?

$$6y = 12x + 1$$
$$\frac{3}{2}y - 3x = \frac{1}{4}$$

A) 0

B) 1

C) 2

D) Infinitely many

3

What is the minimum possible number of intersections for the following lines, given that $a \neq b$?

$$y + ax - 4 = 0$$
$$y + bx - 4 = 0$$

A) 0

B) 1

C) 2

D) Infinitely many

4

How many solutions are there to the following system of equations?

$$3x + 2y = -5$$
$$-4y = 10 + 6x$$

A) 0

B) 1

C) 2

D) Infinitely many

5

For the system of equations below, which of the following statements is true about the value of b?

$$3x + 4y = -2$$
$$9x = -12y + b$$

A) If $b = -6$ the system has infinitely many solutions

B) If $b = -6$ the system has exactly two solutions

C) If $b = -6$ the system has exactly one solution

D) If $b = -6$ the system has no solutions

6

For what value of n does the following system of equations have an infinite number of solutions?

$$-2x + 7y = -6$$
$$6x + ny = 18$$

A) -21

B) -3

C) 11

D) 21

$-3, n$ot 3

Ant

Answers and Explanations

1. The correct answer is (C). If the system has one solution, then all three lines intersect at the same point. First you can solve the system of the two equations that are given, and then determine what value of m makes the third line also intersect that same point.

    First, rewrite the equations so they're all in the same form, and then solve for y through combination:

    $y + 5 = -x \rightarrow y = -x - 5$

    $$y = -x - 5$$
    $$+ y = + x + 1$$
    $$2y = -4$$
    $$y = -2$$

    Once you have the y-value, plug it back in to either equation to determine that $x = -3$. So, all three lines intersect at the point $(-3, -2)$. From there, you can simply plug that pair of values into the third equation and then solve for m.

    $$(-2) = m(-3) + 3$$
    $$-5 = -3m$$
    $$5/3 = m$$

2. The correct answer is (D). First, you should rewrite both equations so that they are in standard form.

    $$6y = 12x + 1 \rightarrow y = 2x + \frac{1}{6}$$
    $$\frac{3}{2}y - 3x = \frac{1}{4} \rightarrow y = 2x + \frac{1}{6}$$

    You can see that they are both the same equation, which means that they are the same line. Two lines directly on top of each other intersect at every single point along both lines, so the system has infinitely many solutions.

3. The correct answer is (B). First, rewrite both equations in standard form: $y = -ax + 4$ and $y = -bx + 4$. If a did equal b, the two lines would be identical, in which case there would be infinitely many intersections. However, since $a \neq b$, the lines must have different slopes. Two lines with different slopes always have exactly one intersection.

4. The correct answer is (D). You can rearrange the second equation to $-6x - 4y = 10$, which is simply the first equation multiplied by -2. Therefore, any pair (x,y) that satisfies the first equation will also satisfy the second equation. Since the first equation represents a line, there are infinitely many pairs (x,y) that satisfy it. Therefore, the system has infinitely many solutions. Another way to say that there are "infinitely many solutions" to these equations is to say that these equations are identical.

5. The correct answer is (A). You can rearrange the first equation and multiply it by 3 to get $9x = -12y - 6$. You can see that if $b = -6$ in the second equation, then the two equations are the same, meaning that the system has infinitely many solutions. However, if $b \neq -6$, there will be no solution, since it is impossible for $9x + 12y$ to both equal -6 and not equal -6 at the same time. An easy way to understand this geometrically is that the lines represented by these equations have the same slope, so they are parallel. If they also have the same y-intercept, which is b, then they will be the same line and there will be infinitely many solutions.

6. The correct answer is (A). The system of equations will have an infinite number of solutions only if the equations are the same. If you compare the two pairs of known terms, $-2x$ with $6x$ and -6 with 18, you can see that each term in the second equation is -3 times the corresponding term in the first equation. Therefore, to make the two equations equivalent, n must be -3 times the middle term of the first equation, $-3 \times 7 = -21$. If you got (D), check that you multiplied 7 by -3, not 3.

Create Linear Inequalities
Part 15

These problems ask you to create and use linear inequalities in one or two variables to solve problems in a variety of contexts or interpret solutions in terms of the context.

1

What is the solution to the inequality $|x + 5| < -2$?

A) $x < -7$

B) $x > -7$

C) The solution set includes all real numbers.

D) The inequality has no real solutions.

2

A manufacturing plant produces steel rods. The rods can only be sold if they are within 2 cm of the expected length of 3 meters. If l is the length of the rod in meters, which of the following inequalities describes the lengths of rods that can be sold?

A) $|1 + 2| \leq 3$

B) $|1 - 0.02| \leq 3$

C) $|1 + 3| \leq 2$

D) $|1 - 3| \leq 0.02$

3

If x is between 30 and 70, which of the following inequalities describes all the possible values x can represent?

A) $|x + 30| < 70$

B) $|x - 30| < 70$

C) $|x + 50| < 20$

D) $|x - 50| < 20$

4

If $|2x - 3| > 9$, what is the value of x?

A) $x < 6$ or $x > 3$

B) $x > 6$ or $x < -3$

C) $-3 < x < 6$

D) $-6 < x < 3$

5

Given that $3|2x + 6| - 9 < 27$, what are the possible solutions of x?

A) $x < -3, x > 9$

B) $9 > x > -3$

C) $-9 < x < 3$

D) $x < -9, x > 3$

6

A racehorse is only qualified for the Shaughnessy Classic race if it weighs between 900 and 1100 lbs. Which of the following absolute value expressions represents the possible weight, in x lbs, of a racehorse that is qualified for the Shaughnessy Classic?

A) $|900 - x| > 100$

B) $|900 - x| < 100$

C) $|1000 - x| > 100$

D) $|1000 - x| < 100$

$900 \le x \le 1100$

7

If $2x + 11 < 23$, what is the solution set for x?

A) $x < 6$

B) $x < 12$

C) $x < 17$

D) $x < 34$

VSC

8

If $3x - 7 < x + 8$, which of the following is a possible value of x?

A) 3.5

B) 7.5

C) 12.5

D) 33.5

Which of the following is the solution of the inequality $3n - 4 > 7n + 12$?

A) $n < -4$

B) $n > -4$

C) $n < 4$

D) $n > 4$

In order for her car to be able to travel the 50 miles to her cottage, Zoë needs at least 4 gallons of gas. Her car can hold up to 16 gallons of gas. If Zoë puts gas in her car and then drives to her cottage and back, which of the following inequalities must be true, if x represents the amount of gas left in her car?

A) $x \leq 8$

B) $8 \leq x \leq 16$

C) $4 \leq x \leq 12$

D) $x \geq 16$

4 gallons

Answers and Explanations

1. The correct answer is (D). Since the absolute value of a number will always be positive, $|x + 5|$ cannot be less than –2 for any value of x, since that would imply that $|x + 5|$ is negative.

2. The correct answer is (D). To set up this inequality, you want to compare the length of a rod, l, to its ideal length of 3 meters. For the rod to be fit for sale, the difference between those two values, $|l - 3|$, must be no greater than 2 cm or 0.02 m, which is represented by the inequality in (D).

3. The correct answer is (D). The unknown number x can be represented by the inequality $30 < x < 70$. To describe that in absolute value terms, take the midpoint of 30 and 70, which is 50, then observe that x cannot be more than 20 units more or less than 50. As a result, you know that the magnitude, or absolute value, of the difference between x and 50 must be less than 20.

4. The correct answer is (B). To solve $|2x - 3| > 9$, first solve $(2x - 3) > 9$, which is equal to $x > 6$. Then, you can solve for $-(2x - 3) > 9$, which is $x < -3$. Thus, you can conclude that x can only be less than –3 or greater than 6.

5. The correct answer is (C). To solve for $3|2x + 6| - 9 < 27$, first isolate $|2x + 6|$ to get $|2x + 6| < 12$. You can then treat $|2x + 6|$ as $(2x + 6)$ for one solution and $-(2x + 6)$ for the other to get $x < 3$ and $x > -9$.

6. The correct answer is (D). Since the weight of the racehorse must be between 900 and 1100 lbs. to be qualified, its weight must be less than 100 lbs. away from the mean, 1000 lbs., of these two numbers. Therefore, for any value of x between 900 and 1100, x will not deviate more than 100lbs. away from the mean of 1000 lbs., as shown by (D).

7. The correct answer is (A). You can isolate x in the inequality by subtracting 11 from both sides to get $2x < 12$, then dividing both sides by 2 to get $x < 6$.

8. The correct answer is (A). First, you can simplify the inequality by isolating x to get $x < 7.5$. Only (A) satisfies this inequality. (B) is incorrect since the symbol $<$ means x must be less than but not equal to the endpoint of 7.5.

9. The correct answer is (A). Simplify the inequality by adding 4 to and subtracting $7n$ from each side of the inequality to get $-4n > 16$. Then, divide each side by –4 to get $n < -4$. Don't forget to reverse the direction of the inequality because you are dividing by a negative number.

10. The correct answer is (A). If she is making a round trip, then you know she needs twice as much gas, or 8 gallons of gas. Since she just used 8 gallons of gas to drive to her cottage and back, and she could have had at most 16 gallons in her car to begin with, she now has at most 8 gallons in her car, so $x \leq 8$.
    If you picked (B), you may have thought x represented the amount of empty space in her gas tank.

Interpret Linear Inequalities

Part 16

These problems ask you to interpret a constant, variable, factor, or term of a linear inequality in one or two variables in a context.

$20 > 2.5b + 5$

$\{20\ b$

1

If $|4 - a| < b + 2$, for which of the following values of b will the inequality have no real solutions?

A) −3

B) −1

C) 4

D) 10

2

Barry goes to the fair with $20 in his pocket. The number of bags of berries b that Barry can afford to buy is represented by the expression $20 > 2.5b + 5$. The constant 5 would most likely represent which of the following?

A) The price of one bag of berries.

B) The price of admission to the fair. flat rate

C) The number of bags of berries that Barry starts with.

D) The amount of time that Barry spends buying berries.

3

Alia is redesigning her yard, and she wants to install p number of planters filled with t number of trees using the expression $p \geq \frac{1}{3} t$. What is the most likely reason that Alia uses the coefficient 1/3 in this expression?

A) The trees cost $0.33 each.

B) The planters cost $0.33 each.

C) No more than 3 trees can fit in a planter.

D) There should be at least 3 times as many planters as trees.

4

The number of photos p that Gal can fit on her poster is represented by expression $30 > p$. Gal gets a new poster board, and the expression changes to $30 > \frac{1}{2}p$. What does the second expression most likely indicate about the new poster board?

A) The new poster board is $\frac{1}{2}$ the size of the old one.

B) The new poster board is 2 times the size of the old one. ←

C) The new poster board costs $\frac{1}{2}$ as much as the old one.

D) The new poster board costs 2 times as much as the old one.

5

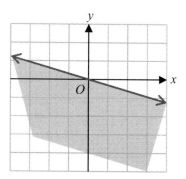

If a is a positive integer and $y \leq ax$, which transformation of a will result in the graph seen above?

A) $-a$

 B) $\frac{1}{a}$

C) $-\frac{1}{a}$

D) $|a|$

Aady 3/14
camp 01/31
Jules 11/15
Nick B/1
Amam 3/10

(handwritten notes at top of page)

$$\frac{b+2}{-2} \frac{< 0}{-2}$$
$$b < -2$$

Answers and Explanations

1. The correct answer is (A). Since the left side of the inequality is an absolute value, the inequality will have no solutions if this absolute value is less than or equal to zero since an absolute value must always be positive. This is the case when $b + 2 < 0$, or $b < -2$. Only (A) satisfies this condition.

2. The correct answer is (B). The left side of the inequality represents the $20 Barry has in his pocket, since it must be greater than the amount of money Barry spends at the fair. Each bag of berries costs $2.50, since his cost increases by that much for every bag of berries he buys. However, he pays $5 regardless of how many berries he buys. This must be some constant cost, which in this case could be the price of admission to the fair.

3. The correct answer is (C). With simple expressions, it can be helpful to translate the expression into words. $p \geq \frac{1}{3}t$ translates to "the number of planters must be greater than $\frac{1}{3}$ the number of trees." In other words, there are more trees than planters, but the number of planters must be at least $\frac{1}{3}$ the number of trees. For example, if Alia gets 6 trees, she would need 2 planters so that both could hold the maximum of 3 trees. If she gets more planters, then there are fewer trees in each planter, which works fine. However, if she gets fewer planters, the trees will not all fit.

   (A) and (B) are incorrect because pricing is not part of her consideration, and because it wouldn't make sense that she must spend more money specifically on planters or on trees. (D) is incorrect because it gets the ratio backwards.

4. The correct answer is (B). The first expression shows that she can put less than 30 photos on her poster board, which is presumably as many as can fit on the size. The second expression may have a coefficient of $\frac{1}{2}$, but by simplifying the expression you can see that it is equal to $60 > p$. Now, Gal can fit 60 posters on the board, which means that it is twice as large.

5. The correct answer is (B). Linear inequalities follow many of the same rules as linear equations, and in this case, the slope of the inequality can be look at similarly to the slope of a linear equation. If a is a positive integer at first, you know that the line will have a positive slope. The graph shows a line with a negative slope, so the answer cannot be (B) or (D), both of which will end up with positive values of a. You can also see that the line is more horizontal than vertical, so the slope must be between 0 and -1. The only option that gives a value within that range is (C).

Graphs and Tables of Linear Inequalities

Part 17

These problems ask you to make connections between tabular, algebraic, and graphical representations of linear inequalities in one or two variables in a context.

DIRECTIONS

Select the best answer among four choices and circle the corresponding letter or record it on a separate sheet of paper.

NOTES

1. You may use a calculator, but not all problems require the use of a calculator.
2. Variables and expressions represent real numbers unless stated otherwise.
3. Figures are drawn to scale unless stated otherwise.
4. Figures lie in a plane unless stated otherwise.
5. The domain of a function f is defined as the set of all real numbers x for which $f(x)$ is also a real number, unless stated otherwise.

1

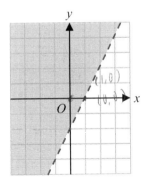

Which of the following inequalities is represented by the graph above?

A) $y < 2x - 2$
B) $y > 2x - 2$
C) $y \le 2x - 2$
D) $y \ge 2x - 2$

2

Which of the following number line graphs represents the solution set to the inequality $3x + 5 \le -2x$?

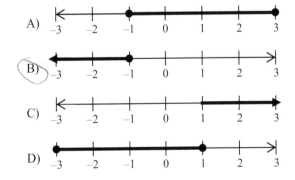

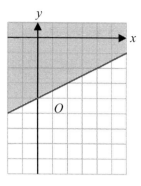

Which of the following inequalities is represented by the graph above?

A) $y < \dfrac{1}{2}x - 4$

B) $y > \dfrac{1}{2}x - 4$

C) $y \le \dfrac{1}{2}x - 4$

D) $y \ge \dfrac{1}{2}x - 4$

x	y
2	3
3	1
4	20
5	−5
6	19

Given the table of (x, y) pairs above, which of the following inequalities could describe the relationship between x and y?

A) $y < 4x - 3$

B) $y < 3x$

C) $y > -x$

D) $y > 2x - 12$

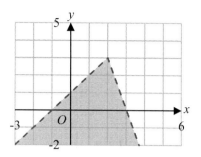

Which of the following systems of inequalities could be represented by the graph above?

A) $y < x + 1$ and $y < -3x + 9$

B) $y < x + 1$ and $y > 3x - 9$

C) $y > x + 1$ and $y > -3x + 9$

D) $y > x + 1$ and $y < 3x - 9$

$$y \geq x - 2 \qquad 0 \geq -2 \checkmark$$
$$y < -2x \qquad 0 < 0 \; \times$$

Which of the following graphs represents the above system of inequalities?

A)
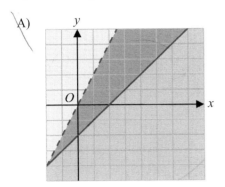

B)
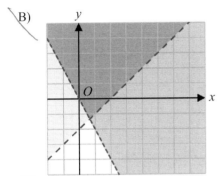

C)
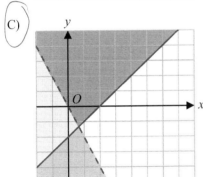

D)
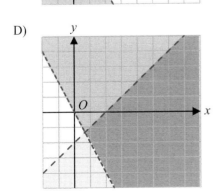

Which of the following inequalities represents the number line shown below?

A) $-3 < x < 2$

B) $-3 \leq x \leq 2$

C) $-\dfrac{3}{4} \leq x \leq \dfrac{1}{2}$

D) $-\dfrac{4}{3} < x < \dfrac{1}{2}$

Which of the following inequalities represents the number line shown below?

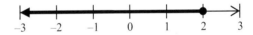

A) $4 + 6x \leq 10$

B) $4 + 6x < 10$

C) $\dfrac{1}{4} + \dfrac{3}{16}x \leq \dfrac{5}{8}$

D) $\dfrac{1}{4} + \dfrac{3}{16}x < \dfrac{5}{8}$

Answers and Explanations

1. The correct answer is (B). You can see that the line on the graph is dotted, meaning that it is representing either > or <, as opposed to a solid line which would represent ≤ or ≥. This eliminates (C) and (D). Since the shaded region is above the line, that means that the values of y that satisfy the inequality are greater than the line itself, which matches (B). You can test this by picking a point in the shaded region and plugging it into the inequality to ensure the expression remains true.

2. The correct answer is (B). Identifying the correct number line is easier if we begin by simplifying the given inequality:

$$3x + 5 \leq -2x$$
$$5x + 5 \leq 0$$
$$5x \leq -5$$
$$x \leq -1$$

   The number line for $x \leq -1$ should extend to the left to show a "less than" relationship, have a solid dot on -1 to show the "or equal to" relationship, and should have an arrow to show that the domain of solutions extends beyond the area of the printed number line. Only (B) has all of those features.

3. The correct answer is (D). You can see that the line on the graph is solid, meaning that it is representing ≤ or ≥, as opposed to a dotted line which would represent either > or <. This eliminates (A) and (B). Since the shaded region is above the line, that means that the values of y that satisfy the inequality are greater than the line itself, which matches (D). You can test this by picking a point in the shaded region and plugging it into the inequality to ensure the expression remains true.

4. The easiest way to solve this is through process of elimination. Start with the easiest equations to test. (C) doesn't work because it passes through the point (5, –5), but to be true the y-value must be *less than* the x-value, not equal to it. (B) doesn't work because the point (6, 19) does not make the inequality true. (D) doesn't work because the point (5, –5) does not make the inequality true. That leaves (A), which is true for all the points given in the chart.

5. The correct answer is (A). Since the shaded area is below two dotted lines, you know that the y-values that satisfy each inequality must be less than the line itself. The only option where both expressions are in the format $y < mx + b$ is (A).

6. The correct answer is (C). First, you should look for which graph shows the correct lines for $y \geq x - 2$ and $y < -2x$. Then, check to make sure that $y \geq x - 2$ is a solid line and $y < -2x$ is a dotted line. Finally, look for the shaded region in the direction of y. In the first equation, y is *greater* than or equal to, so the shading should be above the line; in the second equation, y is *less* than, so the shading should be below the line. The only option that shows all of these characteristics is (C).

7. The correct answer is (C). The circles on the ends of the line in the diagram are solid, so "or equal to" relationships at both ends of the line. You can therefore eliminate (A) and (D). Next, if you just count the tick marks, you might end up selecting (B). Note, however, that the tick marks at the ends of the graph are labeled -1 and 1. The whole range therefore falls between -1 and 1, and (C) must therefore be correct.

8. The correct answer is (C). The graph shows a solid point on 2 with a line extending to the left and ending with an arrow. That indicates that x is less than or equal to 2. None of the answer choice is in the form $x \leq 2$, but one must be equivalent to that inequality. You can eliminate (B) and (D), because they show "less than" relationships rather than "less than or equal to." Next, you can check to see which of the remaining options we can manipulate to get $x \leq 2$. Since (A) uses only integers, it will be somewhat easier to manipulate, and you can start there:

$$4 + 6x \leq 10$$
$$6x \leq 6$$
$$x \leq 1$$

(A) doesn't simplify to $x \leq 2$, which implies that (C) must be correct. To check, you can manipulate (C):

$$\frac{1}{4} + \frac{3}{16}x \leq \frac{5}{8}$$
$$\frac{4}{16} + \frac{3}{16}x \leq \frac{10}{16}$$
$$\frac{3}{16}x \leq \frac{6}{16}$$
$$3x \leq 6$$
$$x \leq 2$$

Solution Sets of Linear Inequalities
Part 18

These problems ask you to interpret a point in the solution set of a given linear inequality or system of linear inequalities.

DIRECTIONS

Select the best answer among four choices and circle the corresponding letter or record it on a separate sheet of paper.

NOTES

1. You may use a calculator, but not all problems require the use of a calculator.
2. Variables and expressions represent real numbers unless stated otherwise.
3. Figures are drawn to scale unless stated otherwise.
4. Figures lie in a plane unless stated otherwise.
5. The domain of a function f is defined as the set of all real numbers x for which $f(x)$ is also a real number, unless stated otherwise.

1

If $-4x + 11 \geq 5$, which of the following is NOT a possible value of x?

A) $-\dfrac{3}{2}$

B) $-\dfrac{3}{2}$

C) $\dfrac{3}{2}$

D) $\dfrac{5}{2}$

2

Which of the following points satisfies the system of inequalities below?

$$2x < 4 + 3y$$
$$3x > 4y - 1$$

A) $(0, 1)$

B) $(0, -1)$

C) $(1, 1)$

D) $(1, -1)$

3

How many solutions (x, y) are there for the following system of inequalities?

$$x + 2y < 3$$
$$-2x < -6 + 4y$$

A) 0

B) 1

C) 2

D) Infinitely many

4

Which of the following x-values will make the system of inequalities below have a solution set $y \geq 3$ and $y \leq 9$?

$$x + y \geq 7$$
$$2x - y \geq -1$$

A) −2

B) 0

C) 2

D) 4

5

Given the inequality $y - a > x - b$, where a and b are positive integers, which of the following must be true?

A) The point (b, a) is in the solution set.

B) The point $(-b, -a)$ is in the solution set.

C) The point $(b + 1, a)$ is in the solution set.

D) The point $(b, a + 1)$ is in the solution set.

Answers and Explanations

1. The correct answer is (D). First, you can subtract 11 from each side of the inequality to get $-4x \geq -6$. Then, divide each side by -4 to get $x \leq \frac{3}{2}$. Don't forget to reverse the direction of the inequality because you are dividing by a negative number. All the answer choices except for (D) are in this solution set. If you chose (C), you may not have noticed that the inequality has a '$\geq$', not a '$>$', so the endpoint value of $\frac{3}{2}$ is a possible value of x.

2. The correct answer is (B). Substituting in $x = 0$ and $y = -1$ will make both inequalities true. If you chose (A) or (C), you may have forgotten to substitute these points into the second equation as well as the first.

3. The correct answer is (A). You can divide the second inequality by 2 to get $-x < -3 + 2y$, and then rearrange it to get $x + 2y > 3$. However, from the first equation, you need to have $x + 2y < 3$. Since $x + 2y$ cannot be both less than and greater than 3, there are no solutions to this system.

4. The correct answer is (D). You can substitute in $x = 4$ to get the inequalities $y \geq 3$ and $y \leq 9$. (A) and (B) are incorrect because they yield no solutions for y. (C) is incorrect because it yields exactly one solution: $y = 5$.

5. The correct answer is (D). You can try plugging in each potential answer to see what would happen in the given inequality. For (A), plugging in gives you $(b) - b > (a) - a$. This simplifies to $0 > 0$, which is not true. For (B), plugging in gives you $(-a) - a > (-b) - b$. This simplifies to $a > b$, but since you don't know which of a or b is greater, this is not necessarily a true statement. For (C), you end up with $(a) - a > (b + 1) - b$. This simplifies to $0 > 1$, which is not true. Finally, for (D), you end up with $(a + 1) - a > (b) - b$. This simplifies to $1 > 0$, which is true, and therefore that point is in the solution set for the inequality.

Problem Solving and Data Analysis
Chapter 3

Chapter 3
Problem Solving and Data Analysis

Questions in the Problem Solving and Data Analysis domain test your knowledge of statistics and probability and your ability to work with sets of data. You'll need to calculate percentages, unit conversations, and averages. You'll also need to read and interpret tables and graphs, as well as perform some calculations using values selected from tables and graphs. Finally, you'll need to apply some concepts in statistics to answer questions about the properties of data sets, sometimes including hypothetical data sets that aren't presented but whose properties are described.

There are 19 specific question types in this domain:

	Problem Solving and Data Analysis				
D1	Ratios, Rates, and Units	D11	Choose an Appropriate 2-Variable Graph
D2	Compound Units	D12	Interpret 2-Variable Graphs
D3	Unit Conversion	D13	Compare Linear and Exponential Growth
D4	Percentages	D14	Estimate and Use a Line of Best Fit
D5	Choose an Appropriate 1-Variable Graph	D15	Probability
D6	Interpret 1-Variable Graphs	D16	Use Sample Data to Infer Population Data
D7	Measures of Centre and Spread	D17	Interpret Margin of Error
D8	Effect of Outliers	D18	Interpret Sample Results to a Population
D9	Compare Predicted Values to Actual Values	D19	Random Assignment
D10	Interpret Lines of Best Fit		

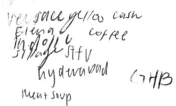

Ratios, Rates, and Units
Part 1

These problems ask you to apply proportional relationships, ratios, rates, and units in a wide variety of contexts.

DIRECTIONS

Select the best answer among four choices and circle the corresponding letter or record it on a separate sheet of paper.

NOTES

1. You may use a calculator, but not all problems require the use of a calculator.
2. Variables and expressions represent real numbers unless stated otherwise.
3. Figures are drawn to scale unless stated otherwise.
4. Figures lie in a plane unless stated otherwise.
5. The domain of a function f is defined as the set of all real numbers x for which $f(x)$ is also a real number, unless stated otherwise.

1

The densities of two metals are shown in the table below. What is the difference in weight, in grams, between a cubic meter of copper and a cubic meter of platinum? (density = mass / volume)

Metal	Density (g/cm³)
Copper	9
Platinum	21

A) 1.2×10^3

B) 1.2×10^4

C) 1.2×10^6

D) 1.2×10^7

2

Two lab assistants are preparing vials of chemicals. One assistant can prepare 4 vials per minute and the other assistant can prepare 9 vials every two minutes. If the two assistants work together, how many minutes will it take them to prepare 68 vials?

A) 4

B) 5

C) 8

D) 10

3

A 30-liter bucket is being filled with water at a rate of 2 liters per second. If the bucket loses water through a small hole at a rate of 500 milliliters per second, how long will it take, in seconds, to fill a quarter of the bucket?

A) 4

B) 5

C) 15

D) 20

4

Thea can travel at a speed of 10 meters per second, and needs to get to her office which is d meters away from her house. Let t represent the number of seconds after 8:00 AM that it is when Thea gets to work. If Thea leaves her house at 8:30 AM, which of the following is equal to t?

A) $\dfrac{d}{10}$

B) $10d$

C) $10d + 1800$

D) $\dfrac{d}{10} + 1800$

5

A trucking company records their profits each month for the years 2011 and 2012, as shown in the table below. If the ratio between the profits in December 2011 and those in December 2012 is the same as the ratio between the total profits in 2011 and those in 2012, what will the company's profits be in December 2012, in thousands of dollars?

Profit (thousands of dollars)		
Month \ Year	2011	2012
January	1000	900
February	2000	1500
March	1500	1200
April	3000	2400
May	2000	1600
June	2500	2100
July	1500	1200
August	1000	700
September	1500	1200
October	1900	1800
November	2100	1400
December	2000	?

A) 900

B) 1200

C) 1400

D) 1600

6

Given that black pens lose ink twice as fast as blue pens, and blue pens lose ink four times as fast as red pens, how many of each pen should Lucy buy so that each color runs out at the same time?

A) 8 black pens, 4 blue pens, 1 red pen

B) 8 black pens, 1 blue pen, 4 red pens

C) 1 black pen, 8 blue pens, 4 red pens

D) 1 black pen, 4 blue pens, 8 red pens

A family wants to get an enlarged photo of their dog's paw print printed. Their dog's paw measures 4 inches across, and they would like a photo that measures 3 feet across. Given that there are 12 inches in a foot, how many times larger will the picture be than the real paw?

A) 3

B) 6

C) 9

D) 12

8

Aleah reads books at a rate of 40 pages every half hour. If there are 900 pages in the book she is currently reading, what is the ratio of the number of minutes she has spent reading to the number of minutes remaining until she finishes the book, if she has been reading for t minutes already?

A) $t : 675 - t$

B) $t : 900 - t$

C) $t : 900$

D) $\dfrac{4}{3}t : (900 - t)$

If Cindy got 35 out of 40 questions correct on her first Chemistry test and 41 out of 45 questions correct on her next Chemistry test, which of the following represents the ratio of correct questions on her first test compared to the ratio of correct questions on her second test?

A) 76:85

B) 287:360

C) 315:328

D) 328:315

Answers & Explanations

1. The correct answer is (D). First, determine the difference in weight for one cubic centimeter of each metal, $21 - 9$ = 12 grams per cubic centimeter. Since $1 \text{ m} = 1 \times 10^2$ cm, one cubic meter (1 m3) is equal to $(10^2)^3 \text{ cm}^3 = 10^6$ cm^3. Since the metals have a weight difference of 12 g for each cubic centimeter, the total weight difference is $12 \frac{g}{cm^3} \times 10^6 \text{ cm}^3 = 1.2 \times 10^7$ g.

2. The correct answer is (C). The assistants' combined rate is the sum of their individual rates: $\frac{4 \text{ vials}}{1 \text{ min}} + \frac{9 \text{ vials}}{2 \text{ min}} = \frac{17 \text{ vials}}{2 \text{ min}}$. To find the number of minutes it will take the two assistants to prepare 68 vials, divide the number of vials by the rate: $68 \text{ vials} \times \frac{2 \text{ minute}}{17 \text{ vials}} = 8 \text{ minutes}$.

3. The correct answer is (B). You want to know the time it takes to fill only a quarter of the 30-liter bucket, or $\frac{30}{4} = 7.5$ L. If the bucket is being filled with water at a rate of 2 L/s and simultaneously being drained of water at a rate of 500 mL/s or 0.5 L/s, then overall it is being filled at only a rate of $2 - 0.5 = 1.5$ L/s. You can write an equation for t in seconds using this information, and then solve:

    $$7.5 \text{ L} = 1.5 \frac{L}{s} \times t$$
    $$t = \frac{7.5}{1.5} = 5 \text{ seconds}$$

    If you chose (A), you may have neglected to account for the water being drained. If you chose (C) or (D), you may have found the time needed to fill the entire bucket, either with the leak or without.

4. The correct answer is (D). The question is asking for the number of seconds it takes Thea to get to work. If her work is d meters away and she travels at 10 meters per second, then the expression for time will equal $\frac{distance}{speed}$, or $\frac{d}{10}$ seconds. However, Thea left her house 30 minutes, or 1800 seconds, after 8:00 am, so this must be added to the value of t since t measures the number of seconds that have passed since 8:00 AM.

    If you chose (A), you probably forgot to add the delay in time from when she left. If you chose (B) or (C), you mixed up the equation for time with the one for distance (speed × time).

5. The correct answer is (D). To predict what the profit in December 2012 will be, you'll need to find the average percent change from the year 2011 to 2012. This average will be equal to the average change in the first 11 months of both years, since the final month will be equal to the average and won't change it. To find this, you first need to find the monthly average profit for the first 11 months of both years. For 2011, this is (1000 + 2000 + 1500 + 3000 + 2000 + 2500 + 1500 + 1000 + 1500 + 1900 + 2100) ÷ 11 = 1818.2 thousand dollars a month. The average monthly profit for the year 2012 can be found the same way, and is 1454.5 thousand dollars. You can see that the profits decreased on average, and to find the percent decrease you take their difference divided by the original average profit:

$$\text{Average Percent Decrease} = \frac{(\text{Average Profit 2011}) - (\text{Average Profit 2012})}{\text{Average Profit 2011}} \times 100\%$$

$$= \frac{1818.2 - 1454.5}{1818.2} \times 100\%$$

$$= \frac{363.7}{1818.2} \times 100\%$$

$$\approx 20\%$$

You can predict that their profit for December 2012 will be 20% less than the profit from December 2011, or 2000 − (2000 × 0.20) = 1600 thousand dollars.

6. The correct answer is (A). This question is asking you to find the ratio of black to blue to red pens needed so that each color group will run out of ink at the same time. Black pens lose ink twice as fast as blue pens, so the ratio of black to blue is 2:1. Blue pens lose ink four times as fast as red pens, so the ratio of blue to red is $1:\frac{1}{4}$. Putting these together, you get a ratio of black to blue to red pens of $2:1:\frac{1}{4}$, or 8:4:1, meaning she should buy 8 black pens for every 4 blue pens and 1 red pen.

7. The correct answer is (C). First, notice that the measurement of the paw itself is in inches, whereas the picture's measurement is in feet. To convert the picture's measurements to inches, multiply by the conversion factor given to you in the question: $3 \text{ feet} \times \frac{12 \text{ inches}}{1 \text{ foot}} = 36$ inches. The scale factor is then 36 inches : 4 inches = 9 : 1.

8. The correct answer is (A). If Aleah reads 40 pages per half hour, you know that translates to $\frac{40 \text{ pages}}{1 \text{ half hour}} \times \frac{1 \text{ half hour}}{30 \text{ minutes}} = \frac{4}{3}$ pages per minute. From this, you can calculate that it will take her $900 \times \frac{3}{4} = 675$ minutes to finish her book. Therefore, if she has been reading for t minutes, she has $675 - t$ more minutes of reading until she is done her book, so the ratio is t: $675 - t$.

9. The correct answer is (C). The fractional ratio of Cindy's first score to her second is $\frac{35}{40}:\frac{41}{45}$. Recognize that all of the answers are in whole numbers. You can convert the fractions to whole numbers by multiplying both fractions by both denominators and then simplifying to get (45 × 35) : (40 × 41) = 1575:1640 = 315:328.

Compound Units
Part 2

These problems ask you to solve problems involving derived units.

DIRECTIONS

Select the best answer among four choices and circle the corresponding letter or record it on a separate sheet of paper.

NOTES

1. You may use a calculator, but not all problems require the use of a calculator.
2. Variables and expressions represent real numbers unless stated otherwise.
3. Figures are drawn to scale unless stated otherwise.
4. Figures lie in a plane unless stated otherwise.
5. The domain of a function f is defined as the set of all real numbers x for which $f(x)$ is also a real number, unless stated otherwise.

1

A truck drives at an average speed of 33 m/s. The driver is asked to make a delivery that is 450 km away. How many hours will it take him to make this delivery, to one decimal place?

A) 2.8

B) 3.3

C) 3.8

D) 4.3

2

Sabrina rides her bike to work every day at a speed of 12 km/h. On one particular day, she rides for 15 minutes towards her workplace before realizing that she forgot her laptop. She rides back and then proceeds to go to work. The entire trip takes her 90 minutes. How far is her workplace from her home, in kilometers?

A) 8

B) 12

C) 16

D) 20

3

Sid runs 5 miles in 40 minutes. What is Sid's average speed in miles per hour?

A) 6.5

B) 7

C) 7.5

D) 8

4

Alice buys 4 different brands of pencils. The following table shows the number of days it takes each pencil to break and the cost of each pencil. Based on Alice's data, which pencil costs the least per day of use?

Brand	Number of Days	Cost (Cents)
Lead Rocket	20	15
Little Cedar	14	20
Pensanto	28	24
Pentech	36	26

A) Lead Rocket

B) Little Cedar

C) Pensanto

D) Pentech

5

The average American English speaker speaks at a rate of about 7,800 words per hour. In 1946, Stella Pajunas set a record by typing 216 words in one minute. How many more words could she type in an hour than the average American would speak in the same amount of time?

A) 860

B) 5,160

C) 5,640

D) 7,584

Answers & Explanations

1. The correct answer is (C). To convert from meters to kilometers, you need to divide by 1000, and to convert from seconds to hours you need to divide the denominator by $60 \times 60 = 3600$, which is equivalent to multiplying the expression by 3600. This process is called dimensional analysis, and it will allow you to calculate the truck's speed to be $\frac{33 \text{ meters}}{1 \text{ second}} \times \frac{3600 \text{ seconds}}{1 \text{ hour}} \times \frac{1 \text{ kilometer}}{1000 \text{ meters}} = 118.8$ km/h. Since the trip is 450 km long, we can divide $\frac{450}{118.8} \approx 3.8$ hours

2. The correct answer is (B). Since you know that she takes $15 + 15 = 30$ minutes to retrieve her laptop from home, it takes her another $90 - 30 = 60$ minutes to get to the office. This means that it takes Sabrina 60 minutes, or 1 hour to get from her home to her office. Since she bikes at a speed of 12 km per hour, her office must be 12 km away.

3. The correct answer is (C). To find Sid's speed in miles per hour, you can write the speed in miles per minute and convert to miles per hour using a conversion factor: $\frac{5 \text{ miles}}{40 \text{ min}} \times \frac{60 \text{ min}}{1 \text{ hour}} = \frac{7.5 \text{ miles}}{\text{hour}}$.

4. The correct answer is (D). You need to determine the cost per day of each pencil by dividing the cost by the number of days. The costs per day are 0.75¢, 1.43¢, 0.86¢, and 0.72¢ respectively. Therefore, the Pentech pencils cost the least per day.

5. The correct answer is (B). To determine how many words Stella Pajunas could type in one hour, multiply her words per minute by 60 minutes in an hour: $216 \times 60 = 12,960$. To find the difference between the number of words she could type in an hour and the number of words an average speaker can say in an hour, simply subtract one from the other: $12,960 - 7,800 = 5160$.

Potatoes

Unit Conversion
Part 3

These problems ask you to solve problems involving unit conversion.

DIRECTIONS

Select the best answer among four choices and circle the corresponding letter or record it on a separate sheet of paper.

NOTES

1. You may use a calculator, but not all problems require the use of a calculator.
2. Variables and expressions represent real numbers unless stated otherwise.
3. Figures are drawn to scale unless stated otherwise.
4. Figures lie in a plane unless stated otherwise.
5. The domain of a function f is defined as the set of all real numbers x for which $f(x)$ is also a real number, unless stated otherwise.

1

Seth is driving at 36 miles per hour. How many feet does Seth travel each second? (1 mile = 5,280 feet)

A) 36
B) 52.8
C) 88
D) 105.6

2

A space shuttle in orbit around the Earth travels at a speed of 17,500 miles per hour. To land, it must be traveling at a speed of 98 meters per second. Given that there are 1.6 kilometers in a mile, what is the difference between orbital and landing speed, in kilometers per hour, to one decimal place?

A) 352.8
B) 17,402.0
C) 27,647.2
D) 28,000.0

3

If one sheep is approximately 3 feet long, how long are 3 sheep in inches (1 foot = 12 inches)?

A) 9

B) 12

C) 36

D) 108

4

A Boeing 747 travels at a speed of 248 m/s. What is this speed in kilometers per day, to the nearest 10 km/day?

A) 14,890

B) 21,430

C) 34,560

D) 89,300

5

Nicole can run at a speed of 3 meters per second. How fast can she run in kilometers per hour, to one decimal place?

A) 9.0

B) 10.8

C) 11.4

D) 12.0

Answers & Explanations

1. The correct answer is (B). You can convert miles per hour to feet per second to get: $\frac{36 \text{ miles}}{\text{hour}} \times \frac{1 \text{ hour}}{60 \text{ min}} \times \frac{1 \text{ min}}{60 \text{ sec}} \times \frac{5280 \text{ feet}}{1 \text{ mile}} = 52.8 \frac{\text{feet}}{\text{sec}}$. Don't forget to check that all of the units have cancelled out except for feet in the numerator and seconds in the denominator.

2. The correct answer is (C). The question is asking for the difference in speeds in kilometers per hour, so remember to use conversion factors to get the right units:

$$\text{Orbital} - \text{Landing} = \left(\frac{17500 \text{ miles}}{1 \text{ hour}} \times \frac{1.6 \text{ kilometers}}{1 \text{ mile}}\right) - \left(\frac{98 \text{ meters}}{1 \text{ second}} \times \frac{1 \text{ kilometer}}{1000 \text{ meters}} \times \frac{3600 \text{ seconds}}{1 \text{ hour}}\right) =$$

$$\frac{28000 \text{ kilometers}}{1 \text{ hour}} - \frac{352.8 \text{ kilometers}}{1 \text{ hour}} = 27647.2 \frac{\text{km}}{\text{h}}$$

If you got (A) or (D), you probably found one of the speeds in the right units and stopped there. If you got (B), you didn't do any unit conversions.

3. The correct answer is (D). Recall that there are 12 inches in a foot, so you can convert the length of the sheep in this way: $3 \text{ feet} \times \frac{12 \text{ inches}}{1 \text{ foot}} = 36$ inches. You want to find the length of three sheep, so multiply that number by three to get $36 \times 3 = 108$ inches.

If you got (C), you probably found the length of one sheep in inches and stopped there.

4. The correct answer is (B). To convert from meters to kilometers, you need to divide by 1000, since there are 1000 meters in a kilometer. To convert from seconds to days, you need to multiply by the number of seconds in a minute, the number of minutes in an hour, and the number of hours in a day.

$$\frac{248 \text{ meters}}{1 \text{ second}} \times \frac{1 \text{ kilometer}}{1000 \text{ meters}} \times \frac{60 \text{ seconds}}{1 \text{ minute}} \times \frac{60 \text{ minutes}}{1 \text{ hour}} \times \frac{24 \text{ hours}}{1 \text{ day}} = 21,427.2 \approx 21,430.$$

5. The correct answer is (B). To convert from meters to kilometers, you need to divide by 1000, and to convert from seconds to hours you need to divide the denominator by $60 \times 60 = 3600$, which is equivalent to multiplying the expression by 3600. This process is called dimensional analysis, and it will allow you to calculate her speed to be

$$\frac{3 \text{ meters}}{1 \text{ second}} \times \frac{3600 \text{ seconds}}{1 \text{ hour}} \times \frac{1 \text{ kilometer}}{1000 \text{ meters}} = 10.8 \text{ km/h}.$$

Percentages
Part 4

These problems ask you to solve problems using percentages, including percent increases and decreases.

DIRECTIONS

Select the best answer among four choices and circle the corresponding letter or record it on a separate sheet of paper.

NOTES

1. You may use a calculator, but not all problems require the use of a calculator.
2. Variables and expressions represent real numbers unless stated otherwise.
3. Figures are drawn to scale unless stated otherwise.
4. Figures lie in a plane unless stated otherwise.
5. The domain of a function f is defined as the set of all real numbers x for which $f(x)$ is also a real number, unless stated otherwise.

1

What is 30% of 120?

A) 24

B) 30

C) 36

D) 40

2

A scientist measures the mass of a liquid over time to determine how much of it evaporates at a certain temperature. The data for her first three measurements are shown below. If the liquid decreases by a constant percent every hour, which of the following is the best estimate for the amount of liquid remaining after 4 hours?

Time (hours)	Mass of liquid remaining (g)
0	125.0
1	100.0
2	80.0

A) 30.0

B) 51.2

C) 60.0

D) 64.0

At a department store, pants are on sale for 30% off the regular price of $40, while shirts are $30 (and are not discounted). If Jiachen buys 3 pairs of pants and a shirt, with a sales tax of 8%, how much does he spend, to the nearest cent?

A) $ 84.00

B) $ 114.00

C) $ 123.12

D) $ 162.00

In Grade 12 at a certain high school, 24% of the students take Algebra. Of those, one third take Advanced Algebra. If half of the students in the Advanced Algebra course drop it by December, what percentage of the entire grade will be taking Advanced Algebra at the start of January?

A) 1%

B) 4%

C) 6%

D) 8%

John makes 13 dollars per hour plus an initial fee of 10 dollars, and Elliot makes 16 dollars per hour with no initial fee. If they each work together for 5 hours, which of the following is true?

A) John makes approximately 5% more money than Elliot.

B) Elliot makes approximately 5% more money than John.

C) John makes approximately 7% more money than Elliot.

D) Elliot makes approximately 7% more money than John.

The following chart shows the number of high-school students in each class at 8 AM on a Monday. What percentage of all the students in class take English?

Subject Area	Number of Students
Algebra	30
English	40
Biology	30
Gym	25
Total	125

A) 20%

B) 24%

C) 32%

D) 40%

Out of a 24-hour day, Sally spends a certain percentage of her time on different activities, as shown in the chart below. How many hours did it take her to go shopping?

Daily Activities

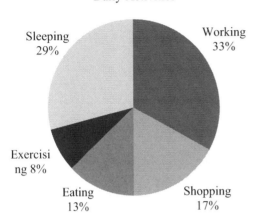

A) 3

B) 4

C) 8

D) 17

The graph below shows the number of different animals bought in a Toronto neighborhood in 2000. By 2016, the number of cats increased by 300, the number of dogs increased by 700, the number of hamsters stayed the same, and the number of birds decreased by 150. Given these new numbers, what percentage of pets bought in 2016 were hamsters, to one decimal place?

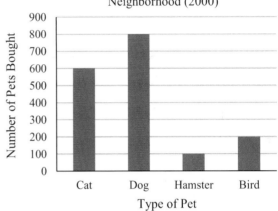

A) 3.9%

B) 4.1%

C) 5.9%

D) 6.2%

Ali goes to a Toronto Blue Jays baseball game where he records the number of hits and runs each batter has in a single game in the table below. On average, what is the chance that one of these players will score a run after getting a hit, to the nearest percent?

Name	Hits	Runs
Bautista	2	1
Donaldson	3	2
Encarnacion	1	1
Tulowitzki	3	2

A) 60%

B) 66%

C) 67%

D) 70%

A soft drink company advertises that their newest beverage has 40% less sugar than the previous version. If the previous version had 40 g of sugar per can, how many grams of sugar are in a can of the new beverage, assuming the cans are the same size?

A) 30

B) 24

C) 16

D) 0

There are 300 students in Grade 12 at a certain high school. Of those 300, 126 are taking French but not philosophy, 63 are taking philosophy but not French, and 42 are taking both French and philosophy. What percentage of the Grade 12 students are taking neither French nor philosophy?

A) 16%

B) 21%

C) 23%

D) 42%

Camille has two identical jars each filled with flour. The first is 40% full and the second is 80% full. How much more flour is in the second jar than the first jar, as a percentage of the amount of flour in the first jar?

A) 2%

B) 40%

C) 50%

D) 100%

A car dealership sells one model of car at a base price of $30,000. It also offers a premium model for 40% more than the price of the base model. If both models are on sale for 20% off their original prices, what is the difference between their sale prices?

A) $2,400

B) $9,600

C) $12,000

D) $18,000

Answers & Explanations

1. The correct answer is (C). Since 30% of a number is equal to that number multiplied by 0.30, you can calculate that 30% of 120 is equal to $0.30 \times 120 = 36$.

2. The correct answer choice is (B). Since the mass decreases by a constant percent every hour, we can use the data to determine the percent change. $\frac{100}{125} = 0.8$, so the mass decreases to 80% of its previous value each hour.

    To find the mass after 4 hours, you can multiply the mass at 2 hours by 0.8 for each additional hour: $80.0(0.8)(0.8) = 51.2$.

    If you chose (D), you may have solved for the mass after 3 hours, not after 4 hours.

3. The correct answer is (C). Pants are 30% off, meaning that they are 0.7 times their usual price of 40 dollars. To find the total cost of the clothing items, sum the price of the pants and shirts and then apply the sales tax. This is 8%, so this means the total cost is 1.08 times the amount before tax:

    $$\text{Total Cost} = \big((3 \times \$40.00 \times 0.7) + \$30.00\big) \times 1.08 = (\$84.00 + \$30.00) \times 1.08 = \$123.12$$

    If you got (A), you may have found the total cost of the pants before tax and stopped there. If you got (B), you may have found the price before the sales tax was applied. If you got (D), you may have forgotten that the pants were 30% off.

4. The correct answer is (B). To find the original percentage of students taking Advanced Algebra, multiply 24% by $\frac{1}{3}$ to get $0.24 \times 0.333 = 0.08$ or 8%. If half of the Advanced Algebra course drops the course, there will be $\frac{1}{2} \times 8\% = 4\%$ of the grade remaining in that course in January.

    If you chose (D), you probably just found the percentage of students taking Advanced Algebra originally and stopped there.

5. The correct answer is (D). If Elliot makes 16 dollars an hour, in 5 hours he makes $16 \times 5 = 80$ dollars. John makes only 13 dollars per hour, but he also gets an initial fee of 10 dollars, so he makes $(13 \times 5) + 10 = 75$ dollars. Already, you can eliminate (A) and (C), since Elliot clearly makes more money. The percent difference between the remembering to compare it to the person making less money, is therefore $\frac{|80 - 75|}{75} = \frac{5}{75} = 6.67\% \approx 7\%$.

    If you chose (B), you probably found the difference in wages in dollars instead of finding the percent difference.

6. The correct answer is (C). You need to calculate the percentage of English students out of the total number of students in class: $\frac{\text{English}}{\text{Total}} \times 100\% = \frac{40}{125} \times 100\% = 32\%$.

    If you got any of the other choices, you probably picked the wrong subject area.

7. The correct answer is (B). The chart shows the percentage of the day that Sally spends on each activity. There are 24 hours in a day, so if she spends 17% of the day shopping, that is $0.17 \times 24 = 4.08 \approx 4$ hours.

    If you got (D), you didn't convert the percentage of the day to hours. If you got (A) or (C), you accidentally took the wrong percentage of 24 hours.

8. The correct answer is (A). Notice that the graph in the question shows the number of pets bought during the year 2000, not the year 2016. However, the question gives you the information needed to calculate the final numbers in the year 2016.

    300 more cats are bought, so there are $300 + 600 = 900$ cats in 2016. The number of dogs increases by 700, for a total of $700 + 800 = 1{,}500$ dogs in 2016. The number of hamsters stays the same so there are still 100 hamsters in 2016. Finally, 150 less birds are bought, so there are $200 - 150 = 50$ birds in 2016. This means the new total number of animals is $900 + 1{,}500 + 100 + 50 = 2{,}550$. Therefore, the percentage of these that are hamsters is $\frac{100 \text{ hamsters}}{2{,}550 \text{ total}} \times 100\% = 3.9\%$.

    If you chose (D), you found the percentage of the original number of animals that were hamsters.

9. The correct answer is (C). To solve this question, you can divide the total number of runs by the total number of hits. There are 9 hits and 6 runs, and $\frac{6}{9} = 0.67$, or 67%.

    If you got (B), you most likely forgot to round up to the nearest percent.

10. The correct answer is (B). If the new can has 40% less sugar than the old can, that means it has 60% as much as the old can, so you can multiply $(40)(0.6) = 24$ to get the amount of sugar in the new can. If you got (D), you might have thought the new can had 40 g less sugar than the old can. If you got (C), you might have thought the new can had 40% as much sugar as the old can.

11. The correct answer is (C). The number of students taking neither French nor philosophy is $300 - 126 - 63 - 42 = 69$. To find the percentage of students that this represents, you can simply calculate $\frac{69}{300} = 23\%$. If you got (A), you might have found the percentage of students taking both French and philosophy.

12. The correct answer is (D). Since the jars are identical in size, the second jar has twice as much flour as the first jar, or 100% more. If you picked (B), you might have just subtracted $80 - 40$.

13. The correct answer choice is (B). Since the price of the premium model is 40% more than the price of the base model, you can find the original price of the premium model by multiplying $30,000 by 1.4 to get $42,000. Both models are on sale for 20% off, so the sale prices will be $0.8 \times \$30{,}000 = \$24{,}000$ for the base model and $0.8 \times \$42{,}000 = \$33{,}600$ for the premium model. The difference between these prices is $9,600. If you chose (C), you may have found the difference between the original prices, not the sale prices

Choose Appropriate 1-Variable Graphs
Part 5

These problems ask you to choose an appropriate graphical representation for a given data set.

DIRECTIONS

Select the best answer among four choices and circle the corresponding letter or record it on a separate sheet of paper.

NOTES

1. You may use a calculator, but not all problems require the use of a calculator.
2. Variables and expressions represent real numbers unless stated otherwise.
3. Figures are drawn to scale unless stated otherwise.
4. Figures lie in a plane unless stated otherwise.
5. The domain of a function f is defined as the set of all real numbers x for which $f(x)$ is also a real number, unless stated otherwise.

1

Which of the box plots below represents the following data?

$$\{4, 6, 6, 8, 10, 10, 11, 13, 16, 19\}$$

A)

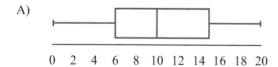

B)

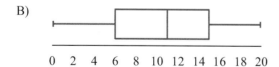

C)

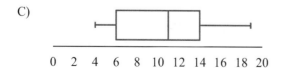

D)

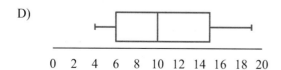

2

Which of the box plots below represents the following data?

$$\{8.1, 8.1, 8.2, 11.0, 12.1, 12.5, 13.9, 18.5, 19.0, 19.3\}$$

A)

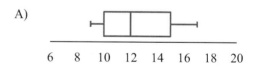

B)

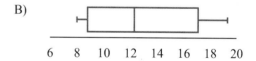

C)

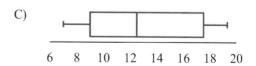

D)

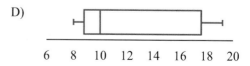

Which of the following graphs would best represent the following table of data?

Company	Profit (millions of dollars)
1	100
2	125
3	300

A)   Share of Profit Between Companies

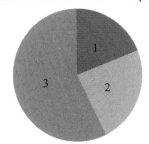

B)
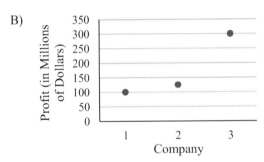

C)
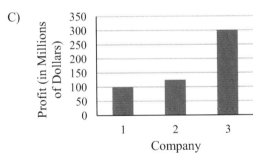

D)
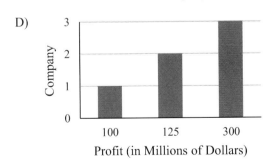

Which of the following graphs describes the data in the table below?

Profits of Company A	
Year	Profit (millions of dollars)
2000	50
2001	30
2002	35

A)
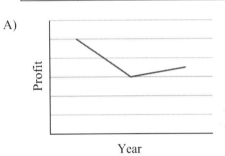

B)
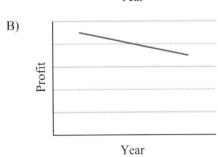

C)
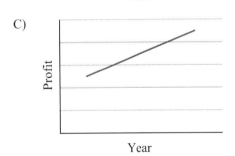

D)
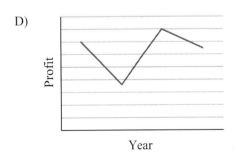

Which of the graphs below correctly represents the following frequency table?

Number	1	2	3	4	5	6	7	8	9	10
Frequency	8	9	19	11	6	11	13	7	7	16

A)
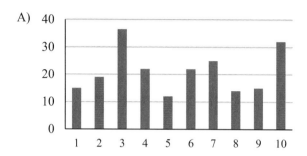

B)
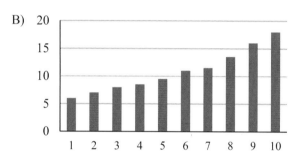

C)
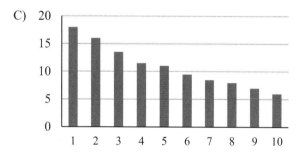

D)
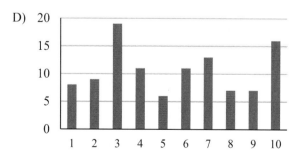

Which of the figures below is an appropriate representation of the following data?

Number	1	2	3	4	5	6	7	8	9	10
Frequency	10	1	9	6	4	1	5	3	10	9

A)
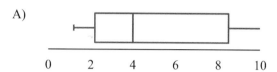

B)
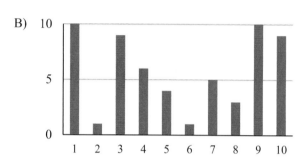

C)

D)
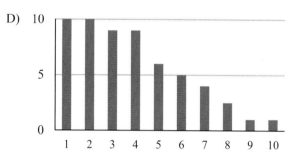

Answers & Explanations

1. The correct answer is (D). First, you can see that the data ranges from 4 to 19, limiting your options to (C) and (D). Remember that the lines of a box-plot represent the quartiles, meaning that each line divides the data into quarters. This is based on the number of data points, not their average value, so the middle line of the box represents the median, not the mean. The median of the data set is 10, which means that (D) is correct.

2. The correct answer is (B). First, you can see that the data ranges from 8.1 to 19.3, limiting your options to (B) and (D). Remember that the lines of a box-plot represent the quartiles, meaning that each line divides the data into quarters. This is based on the number of data points, not their average value, so the middle line of the box represents the median, not the mean. The median of the data set is 12.3, which means that (B) is correct.

3. The correct answer is (C). The profit depends on the company, so the companies should be along the x-axis as the independent variable, and the profit on the y-axis as the dependent variable. This eliminates answer choice (D); even though the axes are not labelled, you can see that the values along the x-axis are the profits as written in the table. The profits of each company are not part of some larger total profit, so it would not make sense to put them in a pie chart, eliminating answer choice (A). Finally, you can eliminate answer choice (B), because each company is independent from the other companies, and a scatterplot implies some kind of trend connecting their profits. (C) makes sense because you can easily compare the profits of each company.

4. The correct answer is (A). You can see from the chart that in 2000 the company's profits were high. The next year, they dropped significantly. In the final year, they had a slight uptick. Since the x-axis is measuring time from left to right, the line graph should begin at a high point, drop to a lower point, and then trend slightly upwards again. The only graph which fits this pattern is (A).

5. The correct answer is (D). Looking at the frequencies in the table, it's clear that there isn't a consistent trend upwards or downwards in either direction of numbers; rather, the frequency of each number is somewhat random. That eliminates (B) and (C), both of which show smooth trends. Next, you can match the data to one of the two remaining graphs, perhaps starting with the highest frequency number, which is 3. Be careful: though (A) and (D) may look the same at first glance, the scale of the y-axis is different in each. Graph (A) shows that number 3 has a frequency of about 38, while (D) shows that number 3 has a frequency of about 19. Answer (D) better matches the table, so it is correct.

6. The correct answer is (B). Since the table given is a frequency table, it makes sense to first check the frequency charts. Looking at (B), you can see that the height of the bar for each number matches the frequencies given in the table.
   (A) is incorrect because it has the median line drawn at 4, when the median of the data is 5. (C) is incorrect because it only ranges from 1 to 9, while the table ranges from 1 to 10. (D) is incorrect because the height of its bars do not match the frequencies in the table.

Interpret 1-Variable Graphs
Part 6

These problems ask you to interpret information from a given representation of data in context, including frequency tables, histograms, and boxplots.

DIRECTIONS

Select the best answer among four choices and circle the corresponding letter or record it on a separate sheet of paper.

NOTES

1. You may use a calculator, but not all problems require the use of a calculator.
2. Variables and expressions represent real numbers unless stated otherwise.
3. Figures are drawn to scale unless stated otherwise.
4. Figures lie in a plane unless stated otherwise.
5. The domain of a function f is defined as the set of all real numbers x for which $f(x)$ is also a real number, unless stated otherwise.

1

Bryan is a manager of a computer store, where he keeps track of the computers he sells in the table below. If x represents the number of computers he has sold with an HDD hard drive and a Doors operating system and y represents the number of computers he's sold with an SSD hard drive and a Cheetah operating system, what is the value of $x + y$?

	Hard Drive Type			
		SSD	HDD	Total
Operating System	Blueberry	0	5	u
	Cheetah	y	16	v
	Doors	25	x	z
	Total	w	108	179

A) 128

B) 133

C) 138

D) Impossible to determine.

2

The average time it takes for an amateur food-eating competitor to eat various amounts of certain foods is shown below. How long would it take to eat 10 brownies, in seconds?

	Number of Items			
	1	5	10	15
Food	Time Required to Eat (sec)			
Cupcakes	30	150	450	600
Hotdogs	60	400	900	1200
Cookies	45	300	675	900
Brownies	65	320	695	920
Pizza Slice	200	965	2090	2765

A) 320

B) 650

C) 675

D) 695

3

The following graph shows the number of gym memberships sold from January to May. How many memberships were sold in March, if 25% of the total memberships were sold in January?

Membership Sales

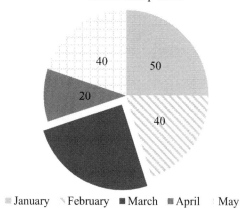

January   February   ■ March   ■ April   May

A) 40

B) 45

C) 50

D) 60

4

What is the range of the data in the bar graph below?

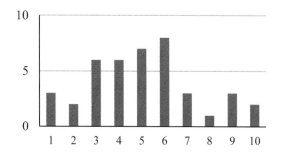

A) 1

B) 7

C) 8

D) 9

5

Which of the following statements about the graph below is NOT correct?

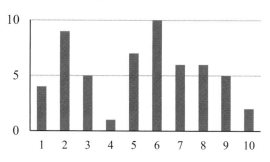

A) The range of the data is 9

B) The median of the data is 5.5

C) The mode of the data is 6

D) The minimum is 1

6

A team of researchers surveyed a random sample of 200 people in Toronto about their favorite hot drink. The results of their survey are shown below. If there are 6 million people in Toronto, how many Torontonians would most likely choose coffee as their favorite hot drink?

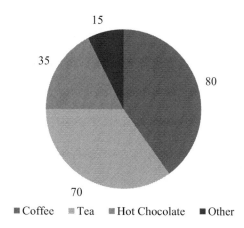

■ Coffee   ▩ Tea   ▨ Hot Chocolate   ■ Other

A) 210,000

B) 240,000

C) 2.1 million

D) 2.4 million

Answers & Explanations

1. The correct answer is (B). To find the values of x and y, it is easiest to solve for x first since all of the values in the HDD column are given. Since you know that $5 + 16 + x$ must equal 108, you can solve for $x = 87$. To solve for y, you first need to solve for w. Since the total number of computers is 179 and 108 of them have HDD hard drivers, $179 - 108 = 71$ have SSD hard drives, which is the value of w. Since you now know all the values in the SSD column, you can solve for y by subtracting 25 and 0 from 71 to get $y = 46$. The sum $x + y$ is equal to 133.

2. The correct answer is (D). To solve this question, you can simply read off the correct value from the table:

Food	Number of Items			
	1	5	10	15
Food	Time Required to Eat (sec)			
Cupcakes	30	150	450	600
Hotdogs	60	400	900	1200
Cookies	45	300	675	900
Brownies	65	320	695	920
Pizza Slice	200	965	2090	2765

3. The correct answer is (C). From the graph, you can see that there are 50 memberships sold in January. Since January sales consist of one quarter, or 25%, of all the sales, you can calculate the total number of sales by dividing 50 by 0.25 to get a total of 200 memberships. If you subtract the number of sales in other months from the total, you will get the number of sales in March, $200 - 50 - 40 - 20 - 40 = 50$.

4. The correct answer is (D). Remember, the range of a set of data refers to the actual values of every data point, not to the frequency of each number. The greatest value represented on the graph is 10, while the lowest value is 1. To find the range, simply subtract the lowest value from the greatest value: $10 - 1 = 9$.

5. The correct answer is (B). You can confirm that (A) is true by subtracting the lowest data point from the highest data point: $10 - 1 = 9$. You can confirm that (C) is true by noting that number 6 has the highest bar on the graph, which means that it has the greatest frequency, which means that it is the mode of the data. You can confirm that (D) is true by noting that the lowest number represented on the graph is 1, so it is the minimum value.

6. The correct answer is (D). Because the original survey was of a random sample, you can assume that it is representative of the population of Toronto. Therefore, the number of Torontonians who prefer coffee is equal to $\frac{80}{200} \times 6,000,000 = 2,400,000 = 2.4$ million. If you picked (B), you may have calculated the number of people who prefer tea. If you picked (A) or (C), you may have missed a decimal place.

Measures of Centre and Spread

Part 7

These problems ask you to calculate, compare, and interpret mean, median, and range, as well as compare and interpret standard deviation.

1

In a French course, a student receives the following set of grades on a series of equally weighted tests: 75%, 70%, 85%, 82%, 80%. What is their final average, to the nearest percent?

A) 78%

B) 79%

C) 80%

D) 81%

2

Each weekday, a store sells a certain number of custom TV's, as described by the table below. If a TV sells for $450, how much does the store make each day, on average?

Day	TV's Sold
Monday	100
Tuesday	150
Wednesday	200
Thursday	100
Friday	350

A) $180

B) $45,000

C) $81,000

D) $90,000

3

What is the approximate arithmetic mean of the following list of numbers, to the nearest tenth?

$$-89, 100, -24.3, \frac{3}{98}, 4.5, 8.6, -43, \frac{19}{6}$$

A) −40.0

B) −5.0

C) 1.6

D) 23.2

4

Every Tuesday in February, Alison makes some snowmen with her friends. By the beginning of March, she has made 84 snowmen. If February has 28 days, what is the average number of snowmen made per week?

A) 3

B) 12

C) 21

D) 28

5

A man has 64 cans of soup and he wants to ration them over the course of 16 days. What is the largest average number of cans he can eat per day so that he does not run out before the 16th day?

A) 2

B) 3

C) 4

D) 5

6

The average of 5 consecutive numbers is 17. What is the value of the smallest number?

A) 12

B) 13

C) 14

D) 15

7

Ethan needs to get an average of 51% to pass his course. The course comprises five equally weighted tests, and he has gotten four of them back with marks of 30%, 40%, 32%, and 78%. What grade does he need on his final test to pass?

A) 51%

B) 70%

C) 75%

D) 78%

In a 5-week span, an employee has to work an average of 35 hours each week. If the timesheet below shows how many hours she has worked in the first 4 weeks, how many hours should she work during her last week?

Week	Hours worked
1	30
2	43
3	30
4	32

A) 30

B) 35

C) 40

D) 45

Sergei rolls a die 100 times, recording his results in the table below. What is the average value shown by the die?

Die Face Value	Number of Times
1	34
2	10
3	16
4	12
5	8
6	20

A) 3.1

B) 3.2

C) 3.4

D) 3.5

What is the sum of the mean, median, and mode of the set {15, 18, 17, 10, 25, 22, 15}?

A) 48.93

B) 49.43

C) 50.93

D) 53.80

Wilson has a set of data consisting of 7 integers. If 2 numbers greater than the median and 2 less than the median are added to the set, which of the following statements must be true?

    I.   The mean has stayed the same

    II.   The median has stayed the same

    III.   The mode has stayed the same

A) I only

B) II only

C) I and II only

D) I, II and III

Answers & Explanations

1. The correct answer is (A). Since the tests are all equally weighted, you can take the average of the grades by adding all the values together and then dividing by the number of values. You get $\frac{70 + 75 + 80 + 82 + 85}{5} = \frac{392}{5} = 78\%$ as the student's final average.

   If you got (C), you found the median, not the mean.

2. The correct answer is (C). To find the store's average daily profit, first you need to find the average number of TVs sold per day: $\frac{100 + 150 + 200 + 100 + 350}{5} = 180$. Therefore, the store makes around $180 \times \$450 = 81,000$ dollars daily.

   If you picked (A), you found the average number of TVs sold and stopped there.

3. The correct answer is (B). Even though the numbers look a little unappealing, there's no other way to calculate the arithmetic mean: you have to add all the values and then divide by the number of values. You should use your calculator for this one to get $\frac{-89 + 100 - 24.3 + \frac{3}{98} + 4.5 + 8.6 - 43 + \frac{19}{6}}{8} = -5.0003 \approx -5$.

   If you got (A), you summed the numbers up and stopped there. If you got (C), you found the median. If you got (D), you only averaged the positive numbers.

4. The correct answer is (C). February has 28 days, so it has $\frac{28}{7} = 4$ weeks. If Alison made 84 snowmen in total, that means she made an average of $\frac{84 \text{ snowmen}}{4 \text{ weeks}} = 21$ snowmen per week.

   If you chose (A), you found the number of snowmen made per day.

5. The correct answer is (C). The average number of soup cans he should eat each day is equal to $\frac{64 \text{ cans}}{16 \text{ days}} = 4$ cans per day.

6. The correct answer is (D). You know that the numbers are consecutive, so the average is simply the middle number of the five. If 17 is the middle value, then $17 - 2 = 15$ is the smallest. You can check by taking the average of five consecutive numbers, starting with 15: $\frac{15 + 16 + 17 + 18 + 19}{5} = 17$.

7. The correct answer is (C). To find the grade needed, first let x represent the value of the "missing" test. You can then write out the equation for his average in the course, which you can simplify and solve for x:

$$\frac{30\% + 40\% + 32\% + 78\% + x}{5} = 51\%$$
$$180\% + x = 255\%$$
$$x = 75\%$$

If you chose (B), you probably thought the passing grade was 50%. If you chose (A), you picked the final average he needs to pass, not the grade needed on his last test.

8. The correct answer is (C). To find the hours needed for the last week, calculate the average for all five weeks, setting the average equal to 35 and x as a placeholder for the missing week:

$$\frac{30 + 43 + 30 + 32 + x}{5} = 35 \quad 135 + x = 175 \quad x = 40 \text{ hours}$$

9. The correct answer is (A). The number cube is rolled 100 times, showing each side a certain number of times (out of 100) as seen in the table. To find the average value, multiply each side by how many times it occurred (the frequency count) and then divide by the total number of rolls to get:

$$\frac{(1 \times 34) + (2 \times 10) + (3 \times 16) + (4 \times 12) + (5 \times 8) + (6 \times 20)}{100} = \frac{34 + 20 + 48 + 48 + 40 + 120}{100} = 3.1.$$

If you chose (D), you probably found the average of the number cube's faces, not the average roll value.

10. The correct answer is (B). You can determine the mean of the set by adding all the numbers together to get $15 + 18 + 17 + 10 + 25 + 22 + 15 = 122$ and dividing by the number of values in the set, 7, to get approximately 17.43. You can then calculate the median by ordering the numbers from smallest to largest to find the middle value, 17. Finally, you can determine the mode by noticing that only 15 is repeated in the set. The sum of these three values is approximately 49.43.

If you got (A), you may have only included 15 once in the list of numbers from smallest to largest, which would give you a median of 16.5.

11. The correct answer is (B). Since 2 of the numbers added are less than the median and the other 2 numbers are greater than the median, the median value will be the same since there will still be an equal number of numbers greater than and less than the median. Statement I is incorrect as you do not know how much greater than or less than the median any of the numbers are. Statement III is incorrect as you do not know if numbers have been repeated.

Effect of Outliers
Part 8

These problems ask you to describe the effect of outliers on mean and median.

1

Darryl has collected the data below about the radius of cherry trees in a park. If he now measures a tree with radius 16, which of the following statements is correct?

$$\{3, 4, 5, 5, 6, 9, 11, 11, 11, 12, 12\}$$

A) The mean and median will both increase.

B) The mean will increase and the median will remain the same.

C) The mean will remain the same and the median will increase.

D) The mean and median will both remain the same.

2

Shirley has received the grades below on quizzes in her biology class. If her teacher removes Shirley's lowest grade from the set, what will happen to her median score?

$$\{90, 95, 32, 100, 98, 85, 95\}$$

A) It will remain the same.

B) It will become less than the mean.

C) It will become equal to the mean.

D) It will change more than the mean changes.

3

$\{1, a, 3, b, 5\}$ 10b

In the ordered set above, what would happen to the mean if the value 10b were added to the set?

A) It would not change.

B) It would change by a magnitude of b.

C) It would become approximately 3 times greater.

D) It would become approximately 10 times greater.

4

$\{5, 6, 11, 29\}$

Which of the following, if added to the set above, would cause the mean of the set to change the most?

A) −10

B) 0

C) 11

D) 35

actually check!

5

$\{2, 6, 8, 28, 31\}$ 40

If the value 40 were added to the set above, which of the following would be true about the mean and median of the set?

A) Neither the mean nor the median would change.

B) The mean and the median would change equally.

C) The mean would change more than the median.

D) The median would change more than the mean.

check

6

$\{1, 4, 6, 9, 10\}$

Which pair of numbers, when added to the set above, would change neither the mean nor the median?

A) 1 and 10

B) 2 and 9

C) 3 and 9

D) 4 and 7

spicy

fruity
florals

oceanic

Allison   florals

woody   musky

Answers & Explanations

1. The correct answer is (A). Start by finding the initial median, which is 9. Then find the initial mean, which is $\frac{3+4+5+5+6+9+11+11+11+12+12}{11} \approx 8.09$. Adding 16 to the data set makes the median the average of the middle two $\frac{9+11}{2} = 10$. The mean also increases, which you know because 16 is greater than the mean of the initial data (although you can calculate the new mean as well if you want to be sure).

2. The correct answer is (A). Finding the median requires ordering the data, so start with that. The ordered set is {32, 85, 90, 95, 95, 98, 100}. Here, you can see that the median is 95. Eliminating 32 from the set makes it {85, 90, 95, 95, 98, 100}. You can see that the median is now the average of 95 and 95, which is of course 95. So, the median stays the same, and you need not even bother with determining the mean.

   If you do check the mean, you'll see that the new mean—approximately 93.83—is less than the median of 95, which eliminates (B) and (C). Since there was previously an outlier of 32, you know that the mean changed, while the median did not. So (D) is also incorrect.

3. The correct answer is (C). Since the set is ordered, you know that a must be some value from 1 to 3, and b must be some value from 3 to 5. To find the smallest possible mean for the set, assume a and b both have the smallest possible values, where $a = 1$ and $b = 3$: $\frac{1+1+3+3+5}{5} = 2.6$. To find the greatest possible mean for the set, assume a and b both have the greatest possible values, where $a = 3$ and $b = 5$: $\frac{1+3+3+5+5}{5} = 3.4$. So, the original mean for the set is somewhere between 2.6 and 3.4.

   Adding $10b$ to the first potential set means adding $10 \times 3 = 30$, while adding $10b$ to the second potential set means adding $10 \times 5 = 50$. The mean of the first set becomes $\frac{1+1+3+3+5+30}{6} \approx 7.16$, while the mean of the second set becomes $\frac{1+3+3+5+5+50}{6} \approx 11.16$. Divide each new mean by each old mean to determine how many times larger it is: $\frac{7.16}{2.6} \approx 2.75$ and $\frac{11.16}{3.4} \approx 3.28$. So, the mean of the set with $10b$ added is somewhere between 2.75 and 3.28 times greater than the original mean: in other words, it is approximately 3 times greater.

4. The correct answer is (A). First, you can find the current mean of the set: $\frac{5+6+11+29}{4} = 12.75$. The easiest way to solve this problem is to know that the value furthest from the mean will be the value that changes the mean the most if added to the set. Finding the difference between 12.75 and the four possible answers shows you that -10 is furthest from the mean, and therefore correct. Alternately, you can simply find the mean if each answer is added to the set, and see which is furthest from the original mean of 12.75, though this will take you more time. (C) is incorrect, although it may be tempting because 35 is the largest number in magnitude. However, what's important is not how far the value is from 0, but how far the value is from the mean.

5. The correct answer is (D). First, you can find the current mean and median of the set. Since the list is already ordered, it's clear that the median (the middle point of data) is 8. The mean is $\frac{2+6+8+28+31}{5} = 15$. After adding 40, the set has an even number of data points. This means that the median is equal to the average of the two middle points of data: $\frac{8+28}{2} = 18$. Additionally, the mean becomes $\frac{2+6+8+28+31+40}{6} \approx 19.16$. The difference between the two medians is $18 - 8 = 10$, while the difference between the two means is $19.16 - 15 = 4.16$. So, the median changes more.

6. The correct answer is (C). In the original set, the mean is $(1+4+6+9+10)/5 = 30/5 = 6$. The median is also 6. If 3 and 9 are added to the set, the new mean is $(1+3+4+6+9+9+10)/7 = 42/7 = 6$. Since 3 is below the original median and 9 is above the original median, the median would also stay the same.

Compare Predicted Values to Actual Values
Part 9

These problems ask you to compare data in a scatterplot to values predicted by a model that fits the data.

1

Nick is practicing for a timed math test for which he must complete 60 questions in one hour. The scatterplot below shows the number of questions Nick was able to complete in one hour on each day. The line of best fit is also shown. On the 6th day, how many more questions did Nick complete than predicted by the line of best fit?

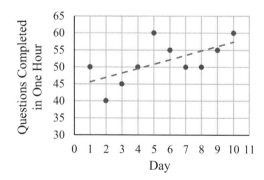

A) 10

B) 7

C) 5

D) 2

A consumer price index examines changes in the average price of a collection of products. A group of economists tracks a consumer price index and develops an algorithm to predict what the index will be for the next 4 quarters. The graph below shows their model. Which of the following data sets corresponds to the prediction of their algorithm?

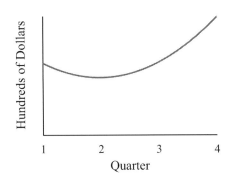

A)

x	1	2	3	4
y	1.5	3.5	4.0	3.5

B)

x	1	2	3	4
y	2.5	2.0	1.5	1.0

C)

x	1	2	3	4
y	2.5	3.0	3.5	4.0

D)

x	1	2	3	4
y	2.5	2.0	2.5	3.0

Which of the following data points is LEAST likely to be observed based on the scatterplot below?

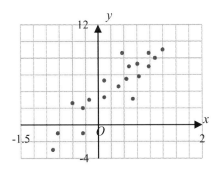

A) (0.9, 8.1)

B) (1.5, 10.4)

C) (1.8, 4.3)

D) (−0.5, 0)

Which of the following data points is MOST likely to be observed, based on the scatterplot below?

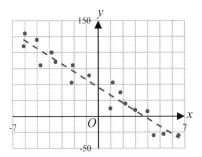

A) (5, −19)

B) (1, 16)

C) (−1, 18)

D) (−5, 75)

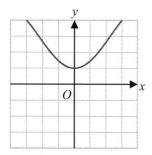

Based on the model above, which of the following points is the LEAST likely to be observed?

A) (–2, 2)

B) (0, 0)

C) (2, 3)

D) (3, 0)

1. The correct answer is (D). To solve this question, you should first identify how many questions Nick actually completed on the 6th day. From the data point for the 6th day, you can determine that Nick completed 55 questions. Now, you can use the trend line to find the number of questions it predicted Nick would be able to answer. On the 6th day, the line predicts that Nick will answer 53 questions. The difference between the actual number and the predicted number is 55 − 53 = 2.

2. The correct answer is (D). From the graph, you can see that it has a roughly quadratic shape. Now, look at the data sets to see which one corresponds best to the graph. (A) increases, then decreases. The graph is concave up, so this data set does not match. (B) decreases in a linear relationship, which does not match the graph. (C) increases in a linear relationship, which does not match the graph. (D) decreases, then increases, which matches the graph.

3. The correct answer is (C). This problem doesn't provide a line of best fit. Try sketching in your own by taking a straight edge, like your pencil or the edge of a piece of paper, and finding a place where a straight line divides the data points into two roughly equal groups. Then, sketch on your points, and see which point is furthest from your line:

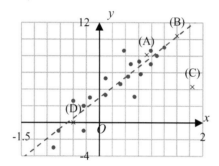

4. The correct answer is (A). First, you must notice that while the *x*-axis scales in increments of 1, the *y*-axis scales in increments of 25. From there, you can find the difference between the expected *y*-value and the actual *y*-value at each value of *x*.

For (A), the expected *y*-value minus the actual *y*-value is approximately $-15 - (-19) = 4$. For (B), the expected *y*-value minus the actual *y*-value is approximately $35 - 16 = 19$. For (C), the expected *y*-value minus the actual *y*-value is approximately $60 - 18 = 42$. For (D), the expected *y*-value minus the actual *y*-value is approximately $105 - 75 = 30$. Since (A) has the lowest difference between the expected and actual values, it is the most likely to be observed.

To double check, you can sketch out the four points to see which is closest to the model:

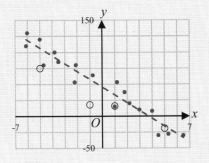

5. The correct answer is (D). The easiest way to solve this is to plot each point on the graph given:

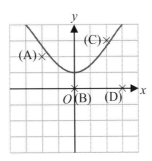

Based on the sketch above, you can see that the point that is furthest from the model is (3, 0). Since it is far from the model, it is less likely to be observed.

Interpret Lines of Best Fit
Part 10

These problems ask you to interpret the slope and intercepts of a line of best fit in context.

DIRECTIONS

Select the best answer among four choices and circle the corresponding letter or record it on a separate sheet of paper.

NOTES

1. You may use a calculator, but not all problems require the use of a calculator.
2. Variables and expressions represent real numbers unless stated otherwise.
3. Figures are drawn to scale unless stated otherwise.
4. Figures lie in a plane unless stated otherwise.
5. The domain of a function f is defined as the set of all real numbers x for which $f(x)$ is also a real number, unless stated otherwise.

1

A function is divided into four parts, as shown in the graph below. If the average slope of each region is equal to the slope of the line between the start and end points of that region, which section has the lowest average slope?

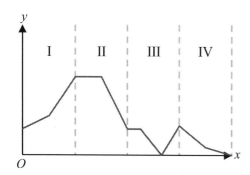

A) I

B) II

C) III

D) IV

Researchers examined the tree rings of a slow-growing desert tree. The scatterplot below shows the relationship between the number of inches of rain in a year and the width of tree rings in millimeters for that year. What can be said about the *y*-intercept?

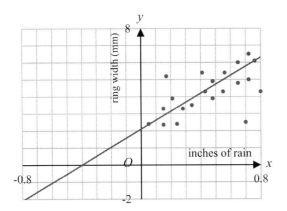

A) It should be at *y* = 0, but is higher due to variation in the data.

B) In a year with no rain, the tree ring should still be about 2 millimeters wide.

C) If there is no ring, there must have been less than 2 inches of rain that year.

D) For every inch of rain, the ring increases by 2 millimeters.

The scatterplot below shows the results of an experiment in which an air conditioner was run for 10 hours and its energy efficiency rating (EER) was measured. EER is a measure of how much cooling is produced per unit of power consumed, so a higher EER rating indicates greater efficiency. What could researchers predict about future trials using the line of best fit?

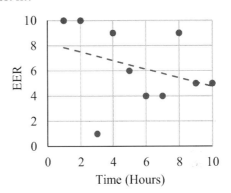

A) EER in the first two hours of future trials will likely be higher than it was in this trial.

B) After three hours, the observed EER will likely decrease to approximately 7.

C) After seven hours, the observed EER will likely decrease to approximately 4.

D) Though the EER mostly decreases over time, it is likely to increase sharply in hour 8.

The scatterplot below shows the results of a survey where participants were asked how many hours they spent each week both walking and cycling. What can be concluded from the line of best fit?

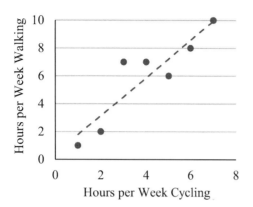

A) Someone who cycles about 10 hours per week could be expected to walk about 14 hours per week.

B) Someone who does not spend any time walking could be expected to spend 7 hours per week cycling.

C) People who spend more time cycling spend less time walking.

D) The relationship between hours spent walking and cycling is nonlinear.

The scatterplot below shows the relationship between the number of ingredients in a recipe on the x-axis and probability of success on the y-axis. What can be concluded from the line of best fit?

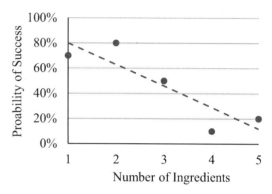

A) The probability of success increases with an increasing number of ingredients.

B) A recipe with 6 ingredients will have an estimated 0% probability of success.

C) A recipe with 1 ingredient will have an estimated 100% probability of success.

D) The probability of success decreases with a decreasing number of ingredients.

For a sample of 10 planets, the scatterplot below shows the distance from a star, in light-minutes, on the *x*-axis and surface temperature, in degrees Kelvin, on the *y*-axis. What can be concluded from the line of best fit?

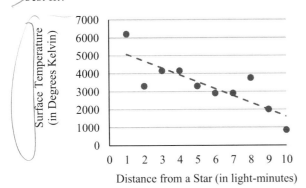

Distance from a Star (in light-minutes)

A) A planet right at the surface of the star would have a surface temperature of about 5,800 Kelvin.

B) The planet 8 light-minutes from the star is being heated by another source.

C) The relationship between surface heat and distance is exponential.

D) A planet 15 light-minutes away from the star would have a surface temperature of about 2000 degrees Kelvin.

The scatterplot below shows the population of bears in a particular section of forest between 1945 and 1995. According to the line of best fit shown, approximately how many bears were there in 1945?

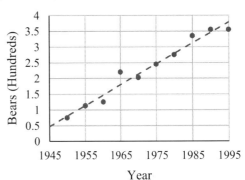

Year

A) 50

B) 70

C) 200

D) 500

Answers & Explanations

1. The correct answer is (B). Don't get caught up in the changing slopes within each section. As the question states, all you have to do is look at the starting point and the end point within each region, and determine the slope. It may help to sketch out the average slope for each question:

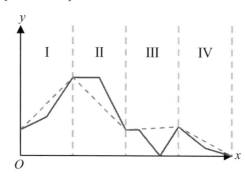

Section II has the largest negative change from its starting point to its ending point.

If you chose (C), you might have forgotten that negative slopes are smaller than any positive slope since the question does not ask for the "least steep" slope.

2. The correct answer is (B). This problem requires you to use the line of best fit to draw a conclusion about the y-intercept. The y-intercept of the line of best fit looks like it falls almost exactly at $y = 2$. Therefore, we can predict that in a year with no rain, the trend in the data suggests that a tree ring would still be 2 mm wide.

3. The correct answer is (B). This problem specifically asks about predictions the researchers could make using the line of best fit. The line of best fit is calculated using the data points, but when we use it to make predictions we shouldn't necessarily be paying attention to individual data ne of best fit. (B) is correct because the trendline at hour 3 suggests an EER of 7, even though the measured EER at hour 3 was much lower in this trial.

4. The correct answer is (A). The point (10, 14) doesn't actually appear on this graph, but we can use the formula for calculating slope from two points to determine the approximate slope of this line. We don't have gridlines to show us exact points the line of best fit crosses, but it looks like it passes very close to the points (1, 2) and (4,6), so we can use those to make our estimate: $\frac{6-2}{4-1} \approx \frac{4}{3}$. It also looks like our line wouldn't quite touch the origin, so we can estimate the formula for our line as $\frac{4x}{3}$ + (slightly less than one). If we plug in $x = 10$, then we can estimate that y is a little bit more than $13\frac{1}{3}$. That's pretty close to (10, 14), so (A) is correct.

    That said, we shouldn't necessarily start with that calculation. This problem is easier to solve by elimination. (B) is incorrect because the line of best fit actually suggests that someone who doesn't spend any time walking also wouldn't spend any time cycling. (C) is incorrect because the line of best fit actually shows a positive relationship between walking and cycling: people who do more of one also do more of the other. (D) is incorrect because the line of best fit is linear.

5. The correct answer is (B). The probability of success has declined from 80% with 1 ingredient ~15% with 5 ingredients. We can use that information to estimate the slope of the line:

$$\frac{15 - 80}{5 - 1} = -16.25$$

If we have approximately a 15% chance of success with 5 ingredients, and the line of best fit drops by about 16.25 percentage points for each ingredient added, then the line of best fit will drop below zero with the addition of another ingredient. Since probabilities always fall between 0% and 100%, that's approximately 0%.

That said, it may be quicker to solve the problem with elimination. (A) and (D) are both incorrect because it gives the wrong relationship: probability of success declines as the number of ingredients increases. (C) is incorrect because the chart shows an 80% chance of success at 1 ingredient.

6. The correct answer is (A). You can place a flat edge, like the edge of a piece of paper, against the line of best fit, and trace it back to its y-intercept:

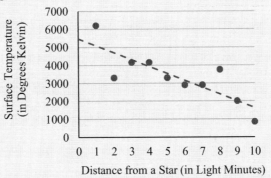

Distance from a Star (in Light Minutes)

The line of best fit has a y-intercept just below $y = 6,000$, so 5,800 is a good approximation of its value at that point. (B) is incorrect because it makes a prediction that is beyond the scope of the information presented, and (C) is incorrect because the line of best fit is linear and fits the data. (D) is incorrect because the line of best fit is already below 2000 degrees Kelvin at 10 light-minutes distance, and would drop even further if we drew it all the way out to 15 light-minutes distance.

7. The correct answer is (A). By following the line of best fit back to the left until it is above the year 1945 and reading off the value, you can see that it is at 0.5. Since the number of bears is measured in hundreds, as indicated on the y-axis, there were approximately 50 bears in 1945. If you picked (D), you might have thought the bears were measured in thousands.

Choose an Appropriate 2-Variable Graph
Part 11

These problems ask you to select a graph that represents a context, identify a value on a graph, or interpret information on the graph.

1

A scientist counts the number of bacteria in her petri dish each morning over the course of 5 days and plots her data in the graph below. Approximately how many thousands of bacteria were there at noon on the third day?

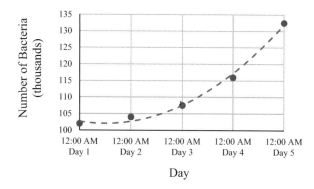

A) 104

B) 108

C) 112

D) 116

2

The number of bees owned by a pair of farmers is shown in the graph below. If the farmers need to build one artificial hive for every 300 bees, how many hives did they build in 2010?

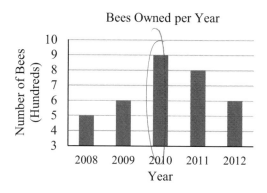

A) 2

B) 3

C) 4

D) 9

Jordan notices that the height of a kite flown in the air increases over the hour that she observes it. However, within the hour, she notices that the kite continuously bobs up and down. Which of the following graphs could represent the height of the kite over the hour, according to Jordan's observations?

A)

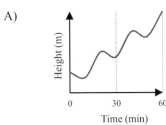

B)

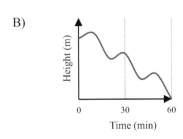

C)

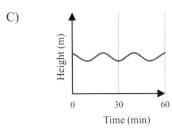

D)

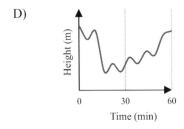

A class of 24 students each listed their favorite animal. How many students preferred birds?

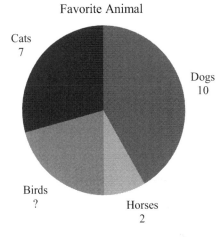

A) 2

B) 5

C) 7

D) 10

Throughout the day, an analyst receives and processes a number of emails each hour, as shown in the chart below. If she receives a total of 5,100 emails by the end of the day at 5:00PM, how many does she have left to process for tomorrow?

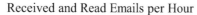

Received and Read Emails per Hour

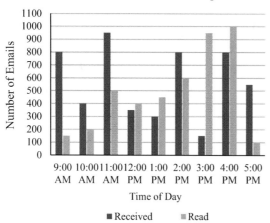

A) 0

B) 450

C) 650

D) 750

Answers & Explanations

1. The correct answer is (C). To solve this question, you simply have to read a value from the graph at the right location: noon (12:00PM) on the 3rd day means at the time halfway between 12:00AM on days 3 and 4. Observe the line of best fit and note where it intersects the x-axis at 3.5 days. You can see that it has a y-value of approximately 112 thousand bacteria.

2. The correct answer is (B). In 2010, the farmers had 900 bees, so they would have needed to build $\frac{900 \text{ bees}}{300 \frac{\text{bees}}{\text{hive}}} = 3$ hives.

    If you chose (A), you may have been looking at the wrong year on the graph. If you chose (D), you may have read the number 9 off of the graph and forgot to calculate how many hives were needed.

3. The correct answer is (A). Jordan sees that, although the height of the kite varies from minute to minute, over the course of the entire hour the height of the kite increased. Only graph (A) shows a net positive change in height from the start of the hour to the end.

4. The correct answer is (B). There are 24 students in total, and you can read from the graph that 10 prefer dogs, 7 prefer cats, and 2 prefer horses. That means that the number of students who chose birds as their favorite animal is $24 - 10 - 7 - 2 = 5$.

5. The correct answer is (D). The question is asking for the number of emails left unprocessed, which you can find by subtracting the total number processed from the total number received. You can find the total number processed by adding the amounts processed at each hour throughout the day as shown on the graph by the light-grey bars: 150 + 200 + 500 + 400 + 450 + 600 + 950 + 1,000 + 100 = 4,350. Therefore, the amount of emails leftover from the current day is equal to 5,100 − 4,350 = 750.

    If you chose (A), you accidentally added up the number of emails received as number processed. If you chose (B), you probably just subtracted the values of the last column pair (550 − 100).

Interpret 2-Variable Graphs
Part 12

These problems ask you to analyze and interpret data represented in a scatterplot or line graph or fit linear, quadratic, and exponential models to data.

1

Jordan is training for a cross country competition. She has devised a plan in which she marks out her run into three stages of three different speeds. Below is a graph of her distance traveled versus the time elapsed. Which of the following orders the regions of the graph by Jordan's speed from fastest to slowest?

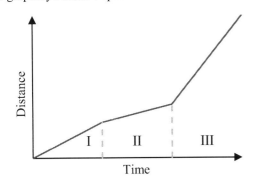

A) I, II, III

B) II, I, III

C) III, I, II

D) III, II, I

2

The revenue and costs of a company are plotted on the graph below. If profit is cost subtracted from revenue, what was the profit, in thousands of dollars, during the year 1991?

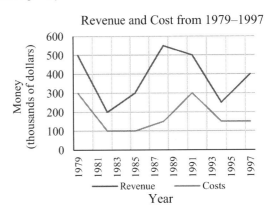

Revenue and Cost from 1979–1997

A) 200

B) 300

C) 400

D) 500

A florist sorting daisies groups them by petal length as shown in the histogram below. What is the average length of their petals, to the nearest tenth of an inch?

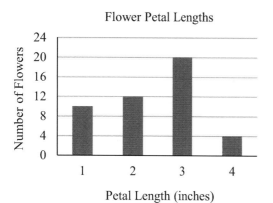

Flower Petal Lengths

A) 2.5

B) 2.4

C) 2.3

D) 2.2

The number of copies of each book a store sells is shown in the graph below. How many more copies of book A were sold than copies of book D?

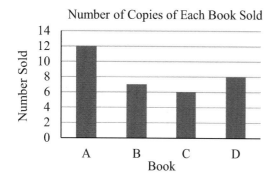

A) 4

B) 5

C) 6

D) 8

Which of the following equations could be a curve of best fit for the scatterplot below?

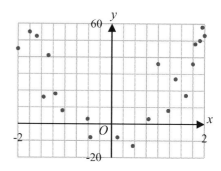

A) $y = 16x - 12$

B) $y = -16x - 12$

C) $y = 16x^2 - 12$

D) $y = -16x^2 - 12$

Answers & Explanations

1. The correct answer is (C). Speed is distance over time, which is the slope of this graph, so this question asks you to order the regions of the graph by their slopes from greatest to smallest, or from steepest to least steep. By looking at the graph, you can see that section III contains the steepest slope, followed by section I, and then by section II.

2. The correct answer is (A). The question tells you that profit = revenue – cost, so simply look for the values of revenue and cost for the year 1991 from the graph and plug them into the equation to get profit = 500 – 300 = 200 thousand dollars.

   If you chose (B) or (D), you read either revenue or cost off of the graph and stopped there.

3. The correct answer is (B). Notice that the y-axis for the number of flowers with a certain petal length increases in increments of 4, not 1 or 5. To find the average petal length, you need to find the sum of the number of flowers with each petal length, and then divide by the total number of flowers:

$$\frac{(1 \times 10) + (2 \times 12) + (3 \times 20) + (4 \times 4)}{10 + 12 + 20 + 4} = \frac{10 + 24 + 60 + 16}{46} = \frac{110}{46} = 2.4 \text{ inches}$$

   If you chose (A), you probably just found the average of the possible petal lengths, but didn't account for the different numbers of flowers with each length.

4. The correct answer is (A). From the graph, you can determine that 12 copies of book A were sold and 8 copies of book D were sold. If you subtract 8 from 12, you will get the difference in the number of books sold.

5. The correct answer is (C). This problem requires you to identify a function that models the data in the graph. The points on the scatter plot form a parabola, or a U-shaped curve, so to model it we need to use a quadratic function. (A) and (B) are both linear functions, which are never graphed as parabolas, so we can eliminate those options.

   Quadratic functions take the general form $ax^2 + bx + c$. While there are only two terms shown in the functions in our answer choices, only the coefficient a has to be a non-zero number. If there's no term equivalent to bx, that's the same as having a term in which $b = 0$:

$$y = 16x^2 + 0x - 12$$
$$y = -16x^2 + 0x - 12$$

   The direction of the parabola formed by a quadratic equation is determined by the value of a. If a is positive, the parabola opens upward—forming a U shape. If a is negative, the parabola opens downward, forming a ∩ shape. Since the data in the table look like a parabola that opens upward, the function for the line of best fit should give a positive value for a. We can therefore eliminate (D), and select (C).

Compare Linear and Exponential Growth

Part 13

These problems ask you to compare linear and exponential growth.

DIRECTIONS

Select the best answer among four choices and circle the corresponding letter or record it on a separate sheet of paper.

NOTES

1. You may use a calculator, but not all problems require the use of a calculator.
2. Variables and expressions represent real numbers unless stated otherwise.
3. Figures are drawn to scale unless stated otherwise.
4. Figures lie in a plane unless stated otherwise.
5. The domain of a function f is defined as the set of all real numbers x for which $f(x)$ is also a real number, unless stated otherwise.

1

The following table shows the increase in the population of a species of bee in a region over time. The data begins in 2010. Which of the following equations models the population of bees over time, where x is the number of years elapsed since 2010 and y is the population in tens of thousands?

Year	2010	2011	2012	2013	2014	2015
Population (tens of thousands)	0.5	1	2	4	8	16

A) $y = 0.5(2)^x$

B) $y = (2)^x$

C) $y = x^2 + 0.5$

D) $y = 2x + 0.5$

2

Every minute, a fire doubles in area. Which equation could represent this growth, where t is time in minutes and $a(t)$ is the area of the fire?

A) $a(t) = 5 + 2t$

B) $a(t) = 5(2t)$

C) $a(t) = 5(t^2)$

D) $a(t) = 5(2^t)$

The population of algae in a pond doubles every year. The population of minnows in the same pond also doubles every year, but its starting population is smaller. Which of the following graphs correctly shows the populations of algae and minnows in the pond over time?

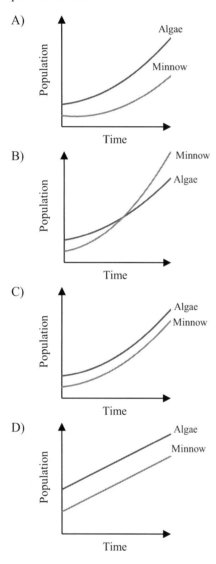

A)

B)

C)

D)

Every 18 months, computer chips become twice as powerful. During that same time, the price of a computer chip increases by $500. What can be said about the change of each quantity?

A) The chips' power is growing exponentially and their price is growing linearly.

B) The chips' power is growing linearly and their price is growing exponentially.

C) Both the chips' power and price are growing linearly.

D) Both the chips' power and price are growing exponentially.

Khalifa deposits his money in an account that earns compound interest at 5% each year, then Prasanth deposits his money in an account that gives him a bonus $150 each year. If Khalifa and Prasanth don't make any other deposits or withdrawals from their accounts, what can be said about their accounts over time?

A) Eventually, Khalifa's account will have the greater balance.

B) Eventually, Prasanth's account will have the greater balance.

C) Both accounts are growing at the same rate.

D) It is impossible to make conclusions without more information.

6

The half-life of a certain compound is five years, which means that after five years passes, half of any sample of this compound will have decayed. A scientist has 3 kilograms of this substance. Which of the following equations represents the amount of the substance remaining in kilograms, y, after x years have passed?

A) $y = 3(\frac{1}{2})^{\frac{x}{5}}$

B) $y = 3(\frac{1}{2})^{5x}$

C) $y = 3 - 5x$

D) $y = 3 - \frac{1}{2}x$

7

Julie is an editor. She gets paid a base fee of $100 for each book she edits, as well as 1 cent per word. Which of the following functions represents the amount of money Julie makes in dollars, y, for editing a book with x words in it?

A) $y = 100(0.01)^x$

B) $y = 100(1.01)^x$

C) $y = 100 + x$

D) $y = 100 + 0.01x$

8

In a colony of bacteria, the number of bacteria doubles every half hour. If there are 10 million bacteria to begin with, which of the following equations represents the number of bacteria in millions, y, in terms of the number of hours that have passed, x?

A) $y = 10(2)^x$

B) $y = 10(2)^{2x}$ — every half hour

C) $y = 10 + 2x$

D) $y = 10 + \frac{x}{2}$

Answers & Explanations

1. The correct answer is (A). First, you should recognize from the data that the population of the species doubles every year, so the equation that models the population must be exponential. This rules out (C) and (D). You can see from the data that the initial population is 0.5. Since the base equation of an exponential function is $y = a\,(r)^{bx}$ where a is the starting value, you can determine that (A) is the correct answer.

    If you chose (B), you might have forgotten than an exponential function needs to be multiplied by a starting value if the starting value is not equal to 1.

2. The correct answer is (D). Each answer choice offers a version of the function $a\,(t)$, where a = area and t = time in minutes. All of the choices indicate that the fire has an initial area of 5. If the area of the fire doubles every minute, we should multiply the area by 2 for each minute that passes. (D), $a\,(t) = 5(2^t)$ accomplishes this goal. By using the number of minutes as an exponent of the factor by which the fire grows, we can repeat the process of multiplication for each minute that passes and correctly model the exponential growth of the fire. (A) and (B) are both linear functions, so they won't correctly represent the exponential growth of the fire. (C) is an exponential function, but because it squares time that elapses rather than using time as an exponent for the actual growth factor of the fire, it won't accurately represent the fire's rate of growth.

    We can see this if we plug in a value: if the fire has been burning for 1 minute, it should double its area one time—to 10. $5(2^1) = 5(2) = 10$, so (D) correctly represents the fire's rate of growth. $5(1^2) = 5(1) = 5$, so (C) doesn't accurately represent the growth of the fire.

3. The correct answer is (A). Both populations increase at the same rate, but algae starts at a higher population than the minnows do. While the shapes of the graphs will be similar, they will not be the same. Further, since there are initially more algae than minnows, you know that the graph of the algae population is higher than the graph of the minnow population. You also know from the keyword "double" that this is exponential growth. From this information, you should be able to deduce that (A) is the only graph that correctly matches the criteria in the question.

4. The correct answer is (A). When a value increases at a constant rate, we can express the increase over time using the amount of increase as a coefficient of time. In this scenario, we could represent the increase in price as $500t$. Since there's no exponent, that function describes a straight line, and this can be described as a linear increase. When a value increase by a factor of itself over time, we need to express the amount of increase as a rate that has time as an exponent. In this scenario, we could express the rate of increase of power as 2^t. Since that function has an exponent, we need to describe it as exponential growth.

5. The correct answer is (A). Since we aren't given any information about the starting balances of the accounts, it may be tempting to select (C). If the starting account balance is very small, $150 could represent a much larger amount of money than 5% of the starting balance. Also, if Prasanth made a larger initial deposit than Khalifa, then he could maintain a higher balance for a long time. Without knowing more about their starting balances, we can't calculate the specific balance at any given point in the future, or figure out how long it will take for Khalifa's account to accrue a higher balance than Prasanth's account.

    However, compound interest is exponential: as the balance in the account increases over time, so does the rate of growth. Over a long enough period of time, the rate of growth for any exponential function will grow larger than the rate of growth for any linear function, so eventually Khalifa's account will have a higher balance than Prasanth's.

6. The correct answer is (A). Because the amount of the substance halves every five years, this relationship can be represented by an exponential function of the form $y = a\,(r)^{tx}$, where a is the initial quantity (in this case 3), r is the growth rate (in this case $\frac{1}{2}$), and t is the number of times during one unit of x (a year) that the amount of substance changes by a factor of r (in this case, $\frac{1}{5}$, since the substance takes 5 years to change by a factor of $\frac{1}{2}$).

7. The correct answer is (D). Because the amount that Julie gets paid increases by $0.01 with every word she edits, this relationship can be represented by a linear function of the form $y = mx + b$, where b is the base fee and m is the amount that she gets paid per word. If you picked (C), you might have forgotten to convert 1 cent to 0.01 dollars.

8. The correct answer is (B). Because the number of bacteria doubles every half hour, this relationship can be represented by an exponential function of the form $y = a(r)^{tx}$, where a is the initial quantity (in this case 10), r is the growth rate (in this case 2), and t is the number of times during one unit of x (an hour) that the number of bacteria changes by a factor of r (in this case 2, since the number doubles every half hour, or twice per hour).

Lines of Best Fit
Part 14

These problems ask you to estimate the line of best fit for a given scatterplot or use the line to make predictions.

DIRECTIONS

Select the best answer among four choices and circle the corresponding letter or record it on a separate sheet of paper.

NOTES

1. You may use a calculator, but not all problems require the use of a calculator.
2. Variables and expressions represent real numbers unless stated otherwise.
3. Figures are drawn to scale unless stated otherwise.
4. Figures lie in a plane unless stated otherwise.
5. The domain of a function f is defined as the set of all real numbers x for which $f(x)$ is also a real number, unless stated otherwise.

1

Which of the following curves of best fit is most appropriate for the scatter plot shown below?

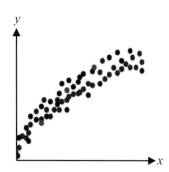

A) $y = x$

B) $y = x^2$

C) $y = 2^x$

D) $y = \sqrt{x}$

2

Which of the following could be a line of best fit for the given scatterplot?

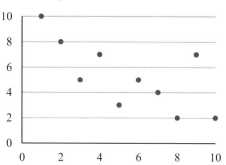

A) $y = -0.6x + 8.7$

B) $y = 0.6x + 8.7$

C) $y = -8.7x + 0.6$

D) $y = 8.7x + 0.6$

The graph below shows the curve of best fit created from a collection of data points. Which of the following scatter plots most likely represents the original data collected?

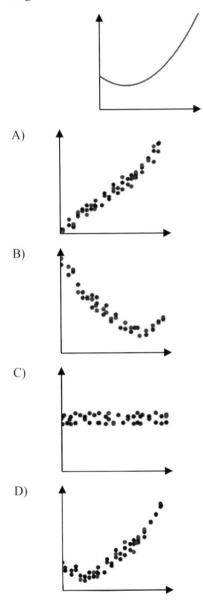

A)

B)

C)

D)

The graph below shows the average student debt in a country over the past 13 years. Based on the trend shown in this graph, which of the following predictions is most reasonable?

Average Debt per Borrower ($) in Each Year's Graduating Class

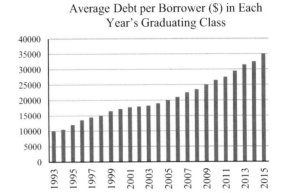

A) Average student debt will level off in the next few years.

B) Average student debt will begin to decrease in the next few years.

C) Average student debt will continue to increase in the next few years.

D) Average student debt will level off in the next few years, and then begin to rise again.

One commonly cited problem with lines of best fit is how easily a line of best fit can be altered with the addition of an outlier in the data set. The graph below shows a scatterplot as well as a line of best fit. Which of the following points, if added to the data set, would result in the steepest line of best fit?

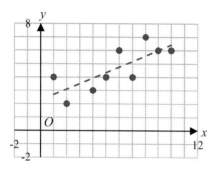

A) (11, 2)

B) (11, 4)

C) (11, 6)

D) (11, 8)

Answers & Explanations

1. The correct answer is (D). This question requires you to be familiar with the shapes of different kinds of graphs. (A) represents a linear function. (B) represents a quadratic function. (C) represents an exponential function. (D) represents a square root function. Of all the graphs shown, (D) most closely matches the shape shown in the question.

2. The correct answer is (A). This problem requires you be familiar with how the parts of a linear function shape the line that the function describes.

    In a function of the form $y = mx + b$, m is equal to the slope of the line, and b is equal to the y-intercept. The line of best fit for this data will slope downwards as it goes from left to right, so we need to select a function with a negative slope. We can therefore eliminate (B) and (D), both of which have positive slopes.

    Next, we can consider the magnitude of the slope of our lines. (B) has a slope of –0.6, so it will not be a very steep slope. The y-value at $x = 10$ will only be 6 less than its value at the y-intercept, so its coordinates at the edge of the chart will be (10, 2.7). (D) has a slope of –8.7. That's a very steep line: its y-value at $x = 1$ would be 8.7 less than its value at the y intercept, or –2.7. In other words, it will almost immediately veer off the chart completely. (B) is therefore the best formula for a line of best fit for this data.

3. The correct answer is (D). The line of best fit is a curved line that initially has a negative slope, then levels out and begins to slope upwards, increasing significantly over its original value. If you compare the shape of the graph to the scatterplots in the answer choices, (D) is the only scatterplot that matches the curve of the graph.

4. The correct answer is (C). They key phrase in this question is "based on trend shown in this graph." There may be many factors affecting student debt which are not reflected in the graph, and which could influence future levels of student debt. However, while any of the predictions could theoretically happen, (C) is best supported by the trend in the graph, which shows a steady increase in debt over time.

5. The correct answer is (D). Points (A), (B), and (C) all fall below the line of best fit, which means that they will decrease the slope of the line. Since (D) lies above the line of best fit, it will increase the slope of the line.

Probability

Part 15

These problems ask you to calculate and interpret probability and conditional probability. You may need to use the counting principle to determine a number of possible outcomes, determine average expected values for operations, or determine the probability of a certain set of outcomes given information about the probability of individual outcomes.

DIRECTIONS

Select the best answer among four choices and circle the corresponding letter or record it on a separate sheet of paper.

NOTES

1. You may use a calculator, but not all problems require the use of a calculator.
2. Variables and expressions represent real numbers unless stated otherwise.
3. Figures are drawn to scale unless stated otherwise.
4. Figures lie in a plane unless stated otherwise.
5. The domain of a function f is defined as the set of all real numbers x for which $f(x)$ is also a real number, unless stated otherwise.

1

A machine is built to attach caps to bottles. However, it sometimes malfunctions and attaches 2 or 3 caps to the same bottle instead of 1. The probabilities at which it does this are listed in the table below. What is the expected number of caps that the machine will put on a bottle?

Caps	Probability
1	0.7
2	0.2
3	0.1

A) −0.7
B) −10
C) 1.4
D) 1.7

2

A weather forecast indicates only a 20% chance of rain the following day. What is the percent chance that it doesn't rain?

A) 20%
B) 40%
C) 60%
D) 80%

3

Adrian has a trick coin that has a 75% chance of landing face up. If he tosses the coin, what are the odds it will land face-down?

A) 0

B) 1 in 4

C) 1 in 2

D) 3 in 4

4

What is the percent chance a four-sided shape, with equal sides numbered 1 to 4, will roll a 1?

A) 17%

B) 25%

C) 33%

D) 50%

5

A co-ed soccer team is made up of 4 boys and 11 girls. If a captain is selected at random, what is the percent chance the captain will be a girl?

A) 27%

B) 36%

C) 73%

D) 100%

6

George has an urn filled with toy soldiers. If he has 10 Roman legionaries, 5 Medieval knights, and 10 World War I British soldiers, what is the chance that George will randomly pick a Medieval knight?

A) 15

B) 14

C) 25

D) 12

7

In Professor Abdullah's class of 96 students, 36 of them have a Mac, 48 of them have a PC, and the rest do not use a laptop. If Professor Abdullah randomly calls upon a student in his class for an answer, what are the odds that the student does not have a computer?

A) 1 in 2

B) 1 in 4

C) 1 in 8

D) 3 in 8

8

The chance that a flower will open increases as it is exposed to more sunlight. If this flower will open 40% of the time that there is at least 5 hours of sun on any given day, and the weatherman forecasts a 60% probability of at least 6 hours of sun tomorrow, what is the probability that the flower will open tomorrow?

A) Less than 24 percent

B) Exactly 24 percent

C) At least 24 percent

D) Exactly 40 percent

9

Adonai can do between 45 and 50 push-ups without stopping. If the following table shows the probability that Adonai will do a certain number of push-ups, what is the probability that he will do at most 48 push-ups, to the nearest percent?

Push-Ups	Probability
45	0.056
46	0.169
47	0.287
48	0.241
49	0.162
50	0.085

A) 24%

B) 49%

C) 51%

D) 75%

Reyna goes to a barbeque and is equally likely to choose between sausages, burgers, and vegan patties for her main meal. If there is a 50% chance that she will drink tea, a 20% chance that she will drink coffee, and a 30% chance that she will drink water, what is the probability that she will have a burger if she chooses to drink water?

A) 10%

B) 11%

C) 30%

D) 33%

Miguel has 8 orange marbles and 7 purple marbles in a jar. He selects one marble, of unknown color, and puts it aside. What is the probability that the second marble will be the same color as the first?

A) 475

B) 715

C) 815

D) 1314

Santiago works on weekdays and brings an umbrella to work with him on Monday, Wednesday, and Friday. If it is as equally likely to rain as it is to not rain, what is the probability that Santiago will not have an umbrella and that it rains on a weekday?

A) 0.2

B) 0.3

C) 0.4

D) 0.6

All Grade 10 and Grade 11 students at Cedar Springs High School have to take either philosophy or economics, as shown in the table below. If a student cannot take both philosophy and economics in one year, what is the probability, to the nearest percent, that a randomly-selected student in Grade 11 takes philosophy?

	Grade		
	Grade 10	Grade 11	Total
Philosophy	10	12	22
Economics	16	14	30
Total	**26**	**26**	**52**

A) 38%

B) 46%

C) 55%

D) 86%

Thea has a jar containing 4 red marbles, 2 blue marbles, and 3 green marbles. She randomly draws a red marble from the jar and then puts it back. What is the probability that she will draw a red marble again on her next draw?

A) 13

B) 38

C) 49

D) 12

Yuwei made sixty cupcakes but accidentally burned twelve. Victor didn't notice and took a cupcake at random. What is the probability that Victor took a burnt cupcake?

A) 1 in 6

B) 1 in 5

C) 1 in 4

D) 5 in 6

Answers and Explanations

1. The correct answer is (C). To find a weighted average, simply multiply each number of caps by its corresponding probability (out of 1) and sum the results to get $(1 \times 0.7) + (2 \times 0.2) + (3 \times 0.1) = 1.4$ caps. It doesn't matter that this is a decimal number, because this is an expected value, an average, not how many caps actually get put on the bottle in the end.

    If you picked (B), you chose the most likely outcome but not the expected value.

2. The correct answer is (D). There is a 100% chance either rain or no rain will happen the next day. If there is a 20% chance of rain, there is a $100 - 20 = 80$ percent chance it doesn't rain.

    If you picked (A), you probably thought the question asked for the percent chance of rain.

3. The correct answer is (B). The coin toss will either result in a heads or a tails. If there is a 75% chance of heads, then there is a $100 - 75 = 25\%$ chance it will be tails, or 1 in 4 odds.
    If you chose (D), you may have thought the question asked for the odds it would be heads. If you chose (C), you probably forgot that it was a trick coin.

4. The correct answer is (B). The shape has four equal sides, so there is a 1 in 4 chance that it will land on any one of its sides, including the side marked '1.' To solve this problem, we just need to convert the fraction form of 1/4 to a percentage form. Probability questions only appear on the calculator section of the SAT, so one of the quickest ways to convert the fraction form to the percent form is to plug the fraction into your calculator, then move the decimal: $1 \div 4 = 0.25 = 25\%$. The quickest way to solve problems like this is to memorize the conversions between common fractions and percentages, so that you can recall that 1/4 = 25% without performing a calculation.

5. The correct answer is (C). Since there are 11 girls out of the $11 + 4 = 15$ total teammates, the percent chance the captain will be a girl is equal to $\frac{11}{15} \times 100\% = 73\%$.

    If you chose (A), you found the percent chance the captain will be a boy.

6. The correct answer is (A). If George has 5 Medieval knights out of $10 + 5 + 10 = 25$ toy soldiers in total, the chance that he will pick a Medieval knight is equal to $\frac{5}{25} = \frac{1}{5}$.

7. The correct answer is (C). Since there are 96 students in his class, there are $96 - 36 - 48 = 12$ students who do not use a laptop. If Professor Abdullah randomly selects a student, the chance that he or she does not have a laptop is $\frac{12}{96} = \frac{1}{8}$, meaning the odds are 1 in 8.

8. The correct answer is (C). The flower opening is conditional upon the amount of sunlight, where more increases its chances. You are given the probability of at least 6 hours of sunlight as 60% and told that there is a 40% chance that the flower will open with at least 5 hours of sunlight. Therefore, $0.6 \times 0.4 = 0.24$ or 24% chance that the flower will open with at least 5 hours of sunlight.

Since the 6 hours is greater than the 5 hours required by the flower to open at 40%, however, you can deduce that the likelihood that the flower will open if this forecast is true is greater than 40%. So, the chance that the flower will open is greater than 24 percent: 0.6×0.4 or greater = 0.24 or greater.

9. The correct answer is (D). The probability that Adonai does at least 48 push–ups is equal to the sum of the probability of him doing 45, 46, 47, and 48 push–ups, $0.056 + 0.169 + 0.287 + 0.241 = 0.753$, which is approximately equal to 75%.

If you chose (C), you may have forgotten to include the probability that Adonai does 48 push–ups, instead stopping after adding the probabilities up to 47 push–ups.

10. The correct answer is (D). It is important for this question to note that Reyna has already chosen water as her drink, so you do not need to consider the probability that she will choose water. Since she is equally likely to choose any of the 3 possible main meals, the probability that she will have a burger given that she has water is simply $\frac{1}{3}$, or 33%

If you chose (A), you probably did not notice that Reyna has already chosen water and multiplied the 30% chance she had of choosing water with the 33% chance she had of choosing a burger.

11. The correct answer is (B). There are two cases you need to consider for this question, whether the first marble Miguel picks is orange or purple. Since there is a $\frac{8}{15}$ chance that Miguel chooses an orange marble first, there is a $\frac{7}{14}$ chance that the second marble he chooses will be orange, since there is one less orange marble in the jar. You can multiply these together to find the probability that Miguel chooses 2 orange marbles, to get $\frac{8}{15} \times \frac{7}{15} = \frac{4}{15}$. Similarly, the probability of him choosing 2 purple marbles is $\frac{7}{15} \times \frac{6}{14} = \frac{3}{15}$. You can add these two together to get the probability that the second marble will be the same color as the first, $\frac{4}{15} + \frac{3}{15} = \frac{7}{15}$.

If you chose (D), you may not have used the probability of Miguel choosing the first marble, instead adding only the probability of drawing the second marble.

12. The correct answer is (A). Since Santiago works 5 days a week (weekdays) and does not bring an umbrella with him on Tuesday and Thursday, the probability that he will not have an umbrella with him is $\frac{2}{5}$, or a 40% chance. In addition, since it is as equally likely to rain as it is to not rain, there is a 50% chance that it will rain. To find the probability that both will occur, you can multiply $\frac{2}{5}$ by 50% to get 20%, meaning that there is a 20% chance that Santiago will not have an umbrella and it will rain.

If you chose (B) you most likely calculated the probability that Santiago would have an umbrella and that it would rain.

13. The correct answer is (B). Since a student cannot take both courses in the same grade, you can calculate the probability by dividing the number of Grade 11 students in philosophy (12) by the total number of Grade 11 students (26) to get 46%.

14. The correct answer is (C). First, you need to find the total number of marbles in the jar, which is $4 + 2 + 3 = 9$. Since Thea put the red marble back after drawing it, there are still 4 red marbles and 9 total marbles. It does not matter that Thea drew a red marble the first time.

If you chose (B), you may have thought that Thea did not replace the red marble she drew.

15. The correct answer is (B). We can calculate the probability of a randomly-selected cupcake being one of the burnt cupcakes by dividing the number of burnt cupcakes, 12, by the total number of cupcakes, 60. In this case, we can just set up the fraction and then simplify it. Since 12 is a factor of 60, we can simplify 12/60 to ⅕, so Victor has a ⅕ chance of taking a burnt cupcake.

amaranthine

Infer Population Data

Part 16

These problems ask you to use sample mean and sample proportion to estimate population mean and population proportion.

DIRECTIONS

Select the best answer among four choices and circle the corresponding letter or record it on a separate sheet of paper.

NOTES

1. You may use a calculator, but not all problems require the use of a calculator.
2. Variables and expressions represent real numbers unless stated otherwise.
3. Figures are drawn to scale unless stated otherwise.
4. Figures lie in a plane unless stated otherwise.
5. The domain of a function f is defined as the set of all real numbers x for which $f(x)$ is also a real number, unless stated otherwise.

1

Every weekday, a farmer reports an approximate number of berries he collects, as shown in the table below. If he always underestimates how many berries he picks, how many berries did he collect in total?

Weekday	Berries Picked
Monday	200
Tuesday	300
Wednesday	400
Thursday	200
Friday	100

A) $< 1,200$

B) $1,200$

C) $> 1,200$

D) Impossible to determine from the given information.

2

An admissions counselor examines twenty-eight randomly chosen applications and finds that eleven applicants intend to major in a science, twelve intend to major in an art, and the remaining applicants are undecided. If there are 3,500 applications, how many can be expected to be undecided?

A) 150

B) 625

C) 1,375

D) 1,500

3

A systems administrator reviews the logs for one server room and finds that the lifetime, in months, for each server is as follows:

$$\{12, 8, 8, 15, 18, 4, 13, 11, 12\}$$

What can she conclude from this data?

A) Servers in other rooms are likely to last longer.

B) A new server of this type is likely to last about 11 months.

C) Servers can generally be expected to last 15 months.

D) A new server should be switched out every 4 months.

4

A network executive is considering switching a certain show's start time from 7PM to 9PM. A poll finds that of 560 network subscribers selected at random, 220 support the switch, and the remainder oppose it. If there are 80,000 subscribers in total, how many can be expected to oppose the switch?

A) 12,077

B) 31,428

C) 48,571

D) 67,923

5

A real estate company surveyed a random sample of 1,000 residents of a certain city to find out whether they were buying or renting their home, and whether they had lived in the same residence for at least 2 years. The results of the survey are shown below. What percentage of residents of the city own their home and have lived there for at least two years?

	Same residence for < 2 years	Same residence for ≥ 2 years	Total
Owners	150	350	500
Renters	400	100	500
Total	550	450	1000

A) 15%

B) 35%

C) 45%

D) 70%

6

A fishing boat casts a net into a lake. Below is a graph showing how many of each type of fish were caught. If scientists estimate that there are 1,500 total fish in the lake, and the sample of fish that were caught is representative of the fish population of the lake, how many trout are there in the lake?

Type of Fish	Number Caught in Net
Trout	15
Bass	8
Pike	3
Perch	12
Whitefish	7

A) 250

B) 500

C) 750

D) 1000

Answers & Explanations

1. The correct answer is (C). To find the total number of berries, first add up all of the values in the "Berries Picked" column: $200 + 300 + 400 + 200 + 100 = 1{,}200$. You know that the farmer always underestimates the amount picked each day, so this means your total will be lower than the real total, and the amount collected is $> 1{,}200$.

2. The correct answer is (B). Out of 28 students, 11 plan to major in a science and 12 intend to major in an art. That leaves $28 - 11 - 12 = 5$ students who are undecided. To generalize the results of the random sample, we just divide the number of undecided students in the sample by the total sample size, and multiply that by the total population size: $(5 \div 28) \times 3{,}500 = 625$, (B).

3. The correct answer is (B). We can eliminate (A) and (D) right away because those conclusions go beyond the scope of the information provided. We aren't given any information about servers in other rooms, or about the rules for when servers should be switched out. Next, we can calculate the average lifetime of a server by adding up all of the data points and dividing the sum by the number of data points. The sum of the data points is 101, and there are 9 data points, so the servers last ~11.2 months.

4. The correct answer is (C). If 220 out of 560 network subscribers support the switch, then 340 oppose it. To generalize the results of the random sample, we just divide the number of subscribers in the sample who oppose the switch by the total sample size, and multiply that by the total population size: $(340 \div 560) \times 80{,}000 = 48571.4$, which we can round to the nearest subscriber.

5. The correct answer is (B). The number of survey respondents who fit the two desired categories is 350. The total number of survey respondents is 1,000. Therefore, the percentage of respondents who fit the two desired categories $\frac{350}{1000} = 35\%$. Because of the original survey was of a random sample, you can assume that it is representative of the whole city. Therefore, this is also the percentage of residents of the city who fit the given categories. If you chose (A), (C), or (D), you might have looked at either the wrong row or column.

6. The correct answer is (B). There were a total of $15 + 8 + 3 + 12 + 7 = 45$ fish in the net, meaning that trout accounted for $\frac{15}{45} = \frac{1}{3}$ of the fish caught. Therefore, there are $\frac{1}{3} \times 1500 = 500$ trout in the lake.

Interpret Margin of Error

Part 17

These problems ask you to interpret margin of error and understand that a larger sample size generally leads to a smaller margin of error.

1

A botanist does a preliminary study with ten plants to test a new fertilizer, where five plants are treated and five are untreated. Based on those results, he begins a full study with 200 plants, where 100 are treated and 100 are untreated. What will happen to the margin of error?

A) It will decrease because of the larger sample size.

B) It will increase because of the larger sample size.

C) It will decrease because only half the plants were treated.

D) It will increase because only half the plants were treated.

2

An emissions inspector is quantifying the carbon dioxide output of a new minivan. He calculates that the output per gallon of gasoline burned is 20.8 pounds, with a margin of error of 1.2 pounds with 95% confidence. Which of the following is a correct interpretation of this measurement?

A) 95% of cars of this model will emit 20.8 pounds of carbon dioxide per gallon of gasoline burned.

B) 5% of cars of this model will emit 1.2 pounds of carbon dioxide per gallon of gasoline burned.

C) 95% of the time, the car will emit between 20.2 and 21.4 pounds of carbon dioxide per gallon of gasoline burned.

D) 95% of the time, the car will emit between 19.6 and 22.0 pounds of carbon dioxide per gallon of gasoline burned.

A maintenance crew is checking the temperature in a large office building. They first report the average temperature of all the rooms on the first floor, and then the average temperature of all the rooms in the building. What can be said about the margin of error of these two measurements?

A) The margin of error will be larger for the building-wide measurements because of the larger sample size.

B) The margin of error will be smaller for the building-wide measurements because of the larger sample size.

C) The margin of error will not change because the measurements are from the same building.

D) The margin of error will not change because only the average temperature was reported rather than individual measurements.

Neil measures the ambient light outside his house at the same time every night for a month and finds an average value of 50 lux with a margin of error of 8 lux with 95% confidence. Based on Neil's measurements, which of the following predictions about future measurements taken at the same place and time of the night is most reasonable?

A) 95% of the time it will not be brighter than 42 lux outside of Neil's apartment.

B) 95% of the time it will not be brighter than 58 lux outside of Neil's apartment.

C) 95% of the time it will not be brighter than 46 lux outside of Neil's apartment.

D) 95% of the time it will not be brighter than 54 lux outside of Neil's apartment.

An advancement director at an opera house wants to calculate the average donation given by season ticket holders. He randomly selects 25 season-ticket holders and calculates the average donation given by those ticket holders, along with a margin of error. What would happen if he did the same for all season-ticket holders?

A) The average donation will increase.

B) The average donation will decrease.

C) The margin of error will increase.

D) The margin of error will decrease.

Answer and Explanations

1. The correct answer is (A). The margin of error for any sample of measurements will tend to decrease as the size of the set increases. To understand why, recall the Law of Large Numbers: the more times you repeat a random trial, the closer your observed average outcome will be to the theoretical average outcome.

   The margin of error is a measure of random sampling error: each time you take a measurement, random factors introduce some error. Each time you take a new sample, you repeat that random process. Thus, the greater the overall number of samples you take the closer your observed average will be to the true average.

2. The correct answer is (D). The margin of error is expressed in the same terms as the measurement that it represents, and it expresses how far away a measurement could be from its true value. Thus, a margin of error of 1.2 pounds indicates that a given measurement could be 1.2 pounds more or less than the true value. Since the emissions inspector calculated a value of 20.8 pounds, we can calculate the expected range of a measurement by adding and subtracting the margin of error to determine the upper and lower bounds of our range: $20.8 - 1.2 = 19.6$ and $20.8 + 1.2 = 22.0$, so the expected range is $19.6 - 22.0$ pounds. The confidence expresses how often a measurement will actually fall within the expected range. (D) correctly paraphrases this information.

   (A) is incorrect mainly because it ignores the margin of error. (B) is incorrect because it substitutes the margin of error for the range, instead of using the margin of error to calculate the range. (C) is incorrect because it calculates a range of 1.2 around a measure of 20.8. The full range, however, is twice the margin of error, because the range is the measurement plus or minus the margin of error.

3. The correct answer is (B). Remember that the margin of error is a measure of random sampling errors, so the more samples you take the smaller your margin of error will be. (A) incorrectly reverses this relationship. (C) is incorrect because it introduces an irrelevant idea: the maintenance crew is trying to calculate the average temperature of the building, so all of their measurements must be from the same building. The important difference between the measurements is the number of rooms having their temperature measured. (D) is incorrect because the information that the crew chooses to report doesn't determine the margin of error. To calculate averages, they must have taken individual measurements, and whether they share them with us or not doesn't change the properties of the data.

4. The correct answer is (B). We can add and subtract the margin of error from Neil's value of 50 lux to find the whole confidence interval: 42–58 lux. We should expect for measurements made under similar circumstances to fall *within* that range 95% of the time, which is the same as saying that they will NOT fall *outside* of that range 95% of the time. Each answer choice defines a range and asserts that a measurement will NOT fall into that range 95% of the time, but only (B) defines a range that doesn't overlap with the expected range of the measurement.

5. The correct answer is (D). The margin of error is a measure of random measurement error. When you increase the number of measurements, you decrease the amount of random error, and the margin of error decreases. (C) is incorrect because it reverses that relationship.

(A) and (B) are incorrect because they state that the average donation that the advancement director calculates will increase or decrease. The average he calculates probably will increase or decrease, but we can't know which: the expected average for a small random sample is the same as the expected average for a large random sample. The average that we observe in a small sample just won't be as close to the true average as the average we observe in a large sample.

Apply Sample Results to Population
Part 18

These problems ask you to understand why a result taken from random samples can be extended only to the population from which the sample was selected.

1

In the town of Lansdowne, Mohammed is collecting data for a survey on whether or not people think the number of lanes on Main Street should be reduced to allow more space for cyclists and pedestrians. How and where should he conduct his survey to most accurately determine the opinion of Lansdowne's population?

A) Post a survey online for anyone to access.

• B) Survey random people standing at a local intersection.

C) Survey people randomly as they get gas at a local gas station.

D) Survey people from randomly selected Lansdowne residents.

2

Navya takes several random soil samples from her garden on a rainy day and a sunny day, and counts the average number of worms per square meter. Based on her observations, she concludes that her city has an average of 14 worms per square meter of soil. Is this a strong conclusion?

A) Yes, because Navya chose the soil samples randomly to stay unbiased.

B) Yes, because Navya has accounted for variables in weather.

• C) No, because Navya's sample is not representative of the entire city.

D) No, because Navya has not accounted for the size of worms.

Katie is conducting a survey for her statistics course. She stands outside Pequod Coffee and surveys the people who enter their favorite coffee shop. Based on her results summarized in the table below, she concludes that 90% of people prefer Pequod Coffee over other stores. Is her conclusion justified?

Store	Number of Votes
Pequod's Coffee	85
Ahab's Grounds	3
Miles Gilberts	2
Bean There	4

A) Yes, 90% of the people surveyed liked Pequod Coffee the most.

B) No, Pequod Coffee had a special sale going on at the time.

C) No, 85% of the people surveyed liked Pequod Coffee the most.

D) No, collecting data outside Pequod Coffee leads to unreliable results.

The total population of Guam is approximately 160,000 people. The Guam Department of Public Works, or DPW, is conducting a survey to determine the models of various cars on the island. The graph below shows the data collected from a car ownership survey of 100 randomly selected employees of the DPW. Which of the following conclusions can be supported by the given information?

Car Models in Sample

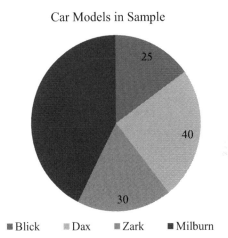

■ Blick ■ Dax ■ Zark ■ Milburn

I. DPW employees own 1.65 cars on average.
II. Residents of Guam own a total of approximately 256,000 cars.
III. A larger number of DPW employees own Zark cars than Blick cars.

A) I only

B) II only

C) I and III only

D) I, II, and III

Rahid spends the summer surveying the people at the city park in order to determine the most popular types of weather in his town of 11,000 people. He asks individuals to rank their preference for sunny, snowy, rainy, and cloudy days on a scale of 1–10. By the end of the study, he has collected over 1,000 samples. What could be most improved about Rahid's methodology?

A) He could take a greater number of samples.

B) He could ask people to rank their preferences on a scale of 1-100.

C) He could provide written surveys instead of verbal surveys to reduce bias.

D) He could take samples from more diverse locations at different times of the year.

Answers & Explanations

1. The correct answer is (D). Since the people living in the town will be most affected by a potential lane reduction of the street, Mohammed should survey people from randomly selected Lansdowne residents.

   Choice (A) is tempting but incorrect since an online survey open to everyone would mean that people from anywhere around the world would be able to vote. This does not make sense for Mohammed as not all of the respondents will actually be affected. (B) is incorrect as most people standing at a local intersection are pedestrians and likely to support enlarging sidewalks. (C) is incorrect as people filling up their vehicles are motorists and unlikely to support reducing their space.

2. The correct answer is (C). The soil in Navya's garden is likely to be unique compared to the rest of the city; it could be filled with fertilizer, specialized soil, or unique plants. So, it is not reasonable to take a sample from the garden and assume that it is representative of the entire city. This is an example of selection bias. (A) and (B) are incorrect because while choosing random samples and accounting for weather variables are both good practices, they do not counteract the fact that the samples are not representative of the whole city. (D) is incorrect because the size of worms is not necessarily as significant of a variable as the quality of the samples is.

3. The correct answer is (D). Since Katie stood outside Pequod Coffee and surveyed people entering Pequod Coffee as to what their favorite store is, you should recognize that this is an example of selection bias. This is because people who enter Pequod Coffee likely favor Pequod Coffee over other coffee stores, as they are Pequod Coffee customers going into the store to buy something. If you chose any of the other options, you did not account for this selection bias.

4. The correct answer is (A). Conclusion I makes a claim only about DPW employees. 100 employees were surveyed, and they reported owning 165 cars of various types. The survey was given to randomly selected DPW employees, so its results can be generalized to that population, and Conclusion I is supported by the information given. Conclusion II makes a claim about the residents of Guam in general. Although the survey was given to randomly selected employees of the DPW, employees of the DPW aren't necessarily representative of residents of Guam in general, so we can't generalize the results of this survey to draw conclusions about all of the residents of Guam. Conclusion II is therefore not supported by the information provided. Conclusion III makes a claim about DPW employees, but we can't be sure that it's true. The survey shows that DPW employees own more than one car each: while they own a greater number of Zark cars than Blick cars overall, it's possible that some employees own multiple Zark cars, so we can't determine which kind of car is owned by a greater number of employees. Conclusion III is therefore not supported by the information provided.

5. The correct answer is (D). People walking in the park during the summer are most likely the kinds of people who enjoy sunny summer weather. People who dislike such weather or prefer other kinds of weather are more likely to stay home, or walk in the park during other times of year. Therefore, Rahid's methods are weakened by selection bias. To improve his methodology, he could speak to people who are outside during the winter or spring; these people are more likely to prefer snowy or rainy weather. He could also choose to survey at indoor locations or online, where people remain unaffected by weather. (A) is incorrect because Rahid samples 10% of the total population, which is more than enough to draw extremely confident conclusions if selection bias is avoided. (B) is incorrect because while this may improve the precision of his results, ultimately he should still get the same level of accuracy. (C) is incorrect because written surveys are not necessarily less biased than verbal surveys.

Random Assignment
Part 19

These problems ask you to understand why random assignment provides evidence for a causal relationship.

DIRECTIONS

Select the best answer among four choices and circle the corresponding letter or record it on a separate sheet of paper.

NOTES

1. You may use a calculator, but not all problems require the use of a calculator.
2. Variables and expressions represent real numbers unless stated otherwise.
3. Figures are drawn to scale unless stated otherwise.
4. Figures lie in a plane unless stated otherwise.
5. The domain of a function f is defined as the set of all real numbers x for which $f(x)$ is also a real number, unless stated otherwise.

1

A group of scientists is testing a new hair growth cream. If the scientists want to use half of the participants as a control group and give the other half the cream, how should the scientists select the groups?

A) The control group should be the people with the most hair.

B) The control group should be the people with the least hair.

C) The control group should be made up of volunteers.

D) The control group should be chosen randomly.

2

A botanist is testing a new pesticide spray and she chooses to separate her plants into two groups for the experiment. She tests the spray on the plants that get the most sunlight, and uses the remaining plants as a control group. If the number of pests on the plants that she sprayed is reduced, what can she conclude?

A) There is a causal relationship between using the spray and reducing the number of pests because every plant that she sprayed had fewer pests.

B) There is a causal relationship between using the spray and reducing the number of pests because sunlight is more likely to attract pests to plants.

C) There is insufficient evidence for a causal relationship between using the spray and reducing the number of pests because she did not select the groups randomly.

D) There is no evidence for a causal relationship between using the spray and reducing the number of pests because the botanist only sprayed half the plants.

A pharmaceutical company testing a new drug recruits participants for a scientific study by asking for volunteers to sign up, and asking the volunteers whether they would rather be in the control group or the test group. Is this study likely to lead to meaningful results?

A) Yes, because the study is using a control group.

B) Yes, because the study allows participants to choose what group they join.

C) No, because the study is not paying the participants anything.

D) No, because the control group was not selected randomly.

A greenhouse manager wants to test whether putting his plants under red light will make them grow faster. If he randomly selects half of his tomato plants and half of his pea plants and places them under red light, is he likely to obtain meaningful results from this experiment?

A) Yes, because the plants were selected randomly.

B) Yes, because tomatoes and peas grow at the same rate.

C) No, because plants only grow faster under blue light.

D) No, because the plants were selected randomly.

Anya decides to conduct an experiment to see whether specially-designed exercise shoes can reduce pain and discomfort during everyday use. She plans to give out these shoes to a group of people, survey those people alongside people who wear their everyday shoes, and determine the levels of self-reported discomfort from each group. How should she decide who to give the athletic shoes to?

A) She should give the shoes to those who self-report the most discomfort initially.

B) She should give the shoes to those who self report the least discomfort initially.

C) She should evenly split the shoes between those who self-report the most and least initial discomfort.

D) She should randomly assign shoes with no regard to initial level of discomfort.

Answers & Explanations

1. The correct answer is (D). When placing study participants into groups, you should place them randomly to avoid having any shared variables affect the outcome of the experiment. (A), (B), and (C) are incorrect because they involve selecting groups based on shared traits: having a lot of hair, having little hair, or being volunteers. None of these selection methods are random.

2. The correct answer is (C). Because the botanist did not select the groups randomly, she cannot confidently determine the relationship between the spray and the pests. (A) is incorrect because it may be that the spray had no effect at all, while the amount of sunlight hitting the plants she chose to spray was actually the variable which reduced pests. (B) is incorrect because sunlight does not necessarily attract pests, and the selection was not random. (D) is incorrect because spraying only half the plants means that the other half acted as a control group to compare to. Having two or more groups is fine for the experiment, as long as the members of the groups are chosen randomly.

3. The correct answer is (D). When placing study participants into groups, you should place them randomly to avoid having any shared variables affect the outcome of the experiment. (A) is incorrect because using a control group does not counteract the fact that the groups were not assigned randomly. (B) is incorrect because allowing participants to choose their group is not random assignment. (C) is incorrect because paying subjects does not necessarily affect the result of the experiment.

4. The correct answer is (A). When placing experimental subjects into groups, you should place them randomly to avoid having any shared variables affect the outcome of the experiment. (B) and (C) are incorrect because it is not clear whether plants grow faster under blue light or whether peas and tomatoes grow at the same rate. (D) is incorrect because random assignment does create meaningful results.

5. The correct answer is (D). When placing study participants into groups, you should place them randomly to avoid having any shared variables affect the outcome of the experiment. (A), (B), and (C) are all incorrect because they involve grouping participants by a shared characteristic: having more pain, having less pain, or being strongly on either side of the spectrum.

Passport to Advanced Math
Chapter 4

Chapter 4
Passport to Advanced Math

Questions in the Passport to Advanced Math domain mainly test your skills with algebra that's more advanced than that in the Heart of Algebra domain. You'll need to perform various operations with rational expressions, radicals, polynomials, and quadratic. You'll also need to perform many of the same tasks Heart of Algebra requires you to carry out, but while Heart of Algebra requires you to perform those tasks with linear equations, Passport to Advanced Math will require you to perform them with nonlinear equations and functions.

There are 17 specific question types in this domain:

	Passport to Advanced Math		
P1	Rewrite Rational Expressions	P10	Interpret Nonlinear Equations
P2	Rewrite Radical Expressions	P11	Solve Nonlinear Equations for a Variable
P3	Factor Polynomials	P12	The Quadratic Formula
P4	Operations on Polynomials	P13	Create and Use Nonlinear Functions
P5	Solve Quadratics by Factoring	P14	Nonlinear Function Notation
P6	Solve Rational/Radical Equations	P15	Interpret Nonlinear Functions
P7	Solve Factored Polynomials	P16	Suitable Forms of Nonlinear Functions
P8	Absolute Value	P17	Graphs and Tables of Nonlinear Functions
P9	Solve Systems of Nonlinear Equations		

Rewrite Rational Expressions
Part 1

These problems ask you to rewrite simple rational expressions. You may need to simplify the expressions, solve for one or more variables, or express the value of some variable in terms of another.

1

If $a = \dfrac{5b}{c}$ and $b = \dfrac{5c}{d}$, what is the value of d in terms of a and c?

A) ac^2

B) $25c$

C) $\dfrac{a}{25c}$

D) $\dfrac{25}{a}$

2

$$\frac{3+y}{2x+3} = \frac{5+y}{x+3}$$

The equation above can be rewritten as which of the following?

A) $-6 = 7x + xy$

B) $-6 = 13x - xy$

C) $6 = 7x + xy$

D) $6 = 13x - xy$

$$\frac{3x^2}{6} + \frac{2x}{12} = \frac{-5}{15} + y$$

If the equation above is written in the form $ax^2 + bx + c = y$, what is the value of $a + b + c$?

A) 0

B) 1

C) 2

D) 5

$$\frac{1}{m} \times \frac{1}{n} + \frac{1}{p} =$$

A) $\dfrac{pm + pn + p^2}{mnp}$

B) $\dfrac{pn + pm + mn}{mnp}$

C) $\dfrac{p + mn}{mnp}$

D) $\dfrac{p + m + n}{mnp}$

$$\frac{x}{y} + \frac{y}{z} + \frac{z}{x} =$$

A) $\dfrac{x^2 z + y^2 x + z^2 y}{xyz}$

B) $\dfrac{xy + yz + zx}{xyz}$

C) $\dfrac{x + y + z}{xyz}$

D) $\dfrac{1}{xyz}$

Answers and Explanations

1. The correct answer is (D) To find the value of d, you can isolate d in the second equation to get $d = \frac{5c}{b}$. Since you are asked to find d in terms of a and c, you can solve the first equation for b in terms of a and c to get $b = \frac{ca}{5}$. Now you can plug this expression for b into the equation $d = \frac{5c}{b}$ to get $d = \frac{5c}{1} \times \frac{5}{ca} = \frac{25}{a}$.

2. The correct answer is (A). First you can cross multiply, then FOIL both sides, and finally combine like terms to simplify:

$$
\begin{array}{rcl}
\dfrac{3+y}{2x+3} & = & \dfrac{5+y}{x+3} \\[2mm]
(3+y)(x+3) & = & (5+y)(2x+3) \\[2mm]
3x+9+xy+3y & = & 10x+15+2xy+3y \\[2mm]
3x+9+xy & = & 10x+15+2xy \\[2mm]
3x+9 & = & 10x+15+xy \\[2mm]
9 & = & 7x+15+xy \\[2mm]
-6 & = & 7x+xy
\end{array}
$$

3. The correct answer is (B). Start by simplifying all of the fractions in the equation and separating the x terms from their coefficients:

$$
\begin{array}{rcl}
\dfrac{3x^2}{6} + \dfrac{2x}{12} & = & \dfrac{-5}{15} + y \\[2mm]
\dfrac{1x^2}{2} + \dfrac{1x}{6} & = & \dfrac{-1}{3} + y \\[2mm]
\dfrac{1}{2}x^2 + \dfrac{1}{6}x & = & -\dfrac{1}{3} + y
\end{array}
$$

Isolate y so that the equation is in standard form, and then add all the coefficients together:

$$
\begin{array}{l}
\dfrac{1}{2}x^2 + \dfrac{1}{6}x = -\dfrac{1}{3} + y \\[2mm]
\dfrac{1}{2}x^2 + \dfrac{1}{6}x + \dfrac{1}{3} = y \\[2mm]
\dfrac{1}{2} + \dfrac{1}{6} + \dfrac{1}{3} = 1
\end{array}
$$

4. The correct answer is (A). Rewrite each fraction with the same denominator, then add:

$$\left(\frac{xz}{xz} \times \frac{x}{y}\right) + \left(\frac{xy}{xy} \times \frac{y}{z}\right) + \left(\frac{yz}{yz} \times \frac{z}{x}\right) = \frac{x^2 z}{xyz} + \frac{y^2 x}{xyz} + \frac{z^2 y}{xyz} = \frac{x^2 z + y^2 x + z^2 y}{xyz}$$

5. The correct answer is (C). First, multiply the first two fractions:

$$\frac{1}{m} \times \frac{1}{n} + \frac{1}{p} = \frac{1}{mn} + \frac{1}{p}$$

Then, rewrite both fractions with common denominators and add:

$$\left(\frac{p}{p} \times \frac{1}{mn}\right) + \left(\frac{mn}{mn} \times \frac{1}{p}\right) = \frac{p}{mnp} + \frac{mn}{mnp} = \frac{p + mn}{mnp}$$

Rewrite Radical Expressions
Part 2

These problems ask you to rewrite expressions with rational exponents and radicals.

DIRECTIONS

Select the best answer among four choices and circle the corresponding letter or record it on a separate sheet of paper.

NOTES

1. You may use a calculator, but not all problems require the use of a calculator.
2. Variables and expressions represent real numbers unless stated otherwise.
3. Figures are drawn to scale unless stated otherwise.
4. Figures lie in a plane unless stated otherwise.
5. The domain of a function f is defined as the set of all real numbers x for which $f(x)$ is also a real number, unless stated otherwise.

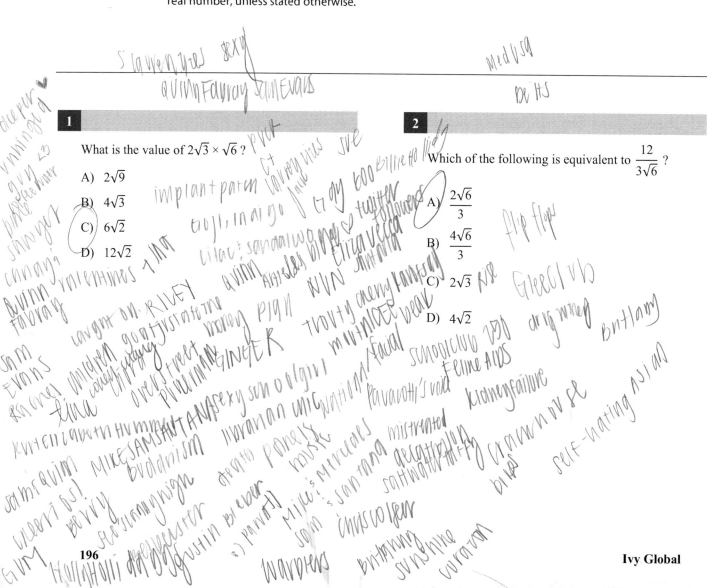

1

What is the value of $2\sqrt{3} \times \sqrt{6}$?

A) $2\sqrt{9}$

B) $4\sqrt{3}$

C) $6\sqrt{2}$

D) $12\sqrt{2}$

2

Which of the following is equivalent to $\dfrac{12}{3\sqrt{6}}$?

A) $\dfrac{2\sqrt{6}}{3}$

B) $\dfrac{4\sqrt{6}}{3}$

C) $2\sqrt{3}$

D) $4\sqrt{2}$

Ivy Global

3

What is the value of $4^{\frac{1}{3}} \times 2^{\frac{1}{3}}$?

A) $2^{\frac{2}{3}}$

B) 2

C) $2^{\frac{4}{3}}$

D) 4

4

Which of the following expressions is equivalent to $\dfrac{(10^2)(10^3)}{(10^5)^2}$?

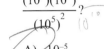

A) 10^{-5}

B) 10^{-4}

C) 10^{-1}

D) $10^{0.5}$

5

If $10^{3x+2} = \dfrac{(10^5)^{-2}(10^4)}{10^2}$, what is the value of x?

A) $\dfrac{-10}{3}$

B) $\dfrac{-5}{3}$

C) $\dfrac{1}{3}$

D) 1

6

Which of the following is equal to $27^{\frac{2}{3}}$?

A) $3^{\frac{2}{3}}$

B) $3^{\frac{4}{3}}$

C) 3^2

D) 3^3

7

If $4^x = (2^4)(16^2)$, what is the value of x?

A) 4

B) 5

C) 6

D) 7

8

Which of the following is equal to $64^{\frac{3}{2}}$?

A) 2^4

B) $2^{\frac{15}{2}}$

C) 2^8

D) 2^9

9

If $2^{x^2 + 2x - 3} = \dfrac{(2^5)(4^3)}{8^2}$, what is the value of x?

A) -1

B) 0

C) 1

D) 2

Answers and Explanations

1. The correct answer is (C). You can evaluate $2\sqrt{3} \times \sqrt{6}$ to get $2\sqrt{18}$. Then, you can factor a $\sqrt{9}$ from the radicand to get $2\sqrt{2} \times \sqrt{9} = 2\sqrt{2} \times 3 = 6\sqrt{2}$. Alternatively, you can rewrite $\sqrt{6}$ as $\sqrt{2} \times \sqrt{3}$. Multiplying this by $2\sqrt{3}$ gives you $2 \times 3 \times \sqrt{2} = 6\sqrt{2}$.

2. The correct answer is (A). To simplify this expression, first factor a 3 from the numerator and denominator to get $\frac{4}{\sqrt{6}}$. You can rationalize this expression, or remove the radical from the denominator, by multiplying the numerator

    $\frac{12\sqrt{6}}{3(6)} = \frac{2\sqrt{6}}{3}$.

3. The correct answer is (B). You can simplify this expression by rewriting $4^{\frac{1}{3}}$ with a base of 2. Since $4 = 2^2$, $4^{\frac{1}{3}} = 2^{2 \times \frac{1}{3}}$, which simplifies to $2^{\frac{2}{3}}$. Now you can evaluate the expression by adding the two powers: $2^{\frac{2}{3}} \times 2^{\frac{1}{3}} = 2^{\frac{2}{3} + \frac{1}{3}} = 2^1 = 2$.

4. The correct answer is (A). Since the numerator is the product of two exponents of base 10, you can add the powers to simplify the numerator to 10^5. In the denominator, you can multiply the two powers to simplify the denominator to 10^{10}. To divide 10^5 by 10^{10}, subtract the powers to get $10^{5-10} = 10^{-5}$.

    If you got (B), you may have multiplied the two powers in the numerator instead of adding them.

5. The correct answer is (A). You can first simplify the numerator of the right side of the equation by multiplying 5 by –2. Since the two terms share the same base you can add –10 to 4 to get 10^{-6} in the numerator. Since you are dividing two numbers with the same base, you can subtract 2 from –6, to get 10^{-8}. Since the two sides of the equation both have only one exponent of base 10, you only need to deal with the powers. You can then solve for x to get
    $x = \frac{-10}{3}$.

    $$10^{3x+2} = \frac{(10^5)^{-2}(10^4)}{10^2}$$
    $$10^{3x+2} = \frac{10^{-10+4}}{10^2}$$
    $$10^{3x+2} = 10^{-6-2}$$
    $$3x + 2 = -8$$
    $$x = -\frac{10}{3}$$

    If you got (B), you may have divided by 2 when simplifying the right side of the equation. If you got (D), you may have added 5 and –2 instead of multiplying them when simplifying the numerator.

6. The correct answer is (C). Since 27 is equal to 3^3, you can simplify the exponent $(3^3)^{\frac{2}{3}} = 3^2$ by cancelling out 3 in the exponents.

   If you got (D), you may have added the exponents 1 and 2 instead of multiplying them in the final step.

7. The correct answer is (C). To solve for x, you need to make the bases on both sides of the equation equal. All the numbers can be reduced to base 2. 4 is equal to 2^2, so $4^x = (2^2)^x = 2^{2x}$. 16 is equal to 2^4, so $16^2 = (2^4)^2 = 2^8$. Therefore, you can rewrite your equation as $2^{2x} = (2^4)(2^8)$. Since the bases are equal, you can work with the exponents alone:
   $2x = 4 + 8$. You can see that $2x = 12$, and $x = 6$.

8. The correct answer is (D). Since the answer choices all have a base of 2, you can rewrite the base in the question, 64,

   as 2^6. You can simplify the exponent $(2^6)^{\frac{3}{2}}$ by multiplying 6 by $\dfrac{3}{2}$ to get 2^9.

   If you got (B), you may have added the exponents instead of multiplying them in the final step.

9. The correct answer is (B). To solve for x, you will first need to make the bases on both sides of the equation equal.

   Since $4 = 2^2$ and $8 = 2^3$, you can change the equation to $2^{x^2 + 2x - 3} = \dfrac{(2^3)(2^2)^x}{(2^3)^2}$. You can then use exponent laws to

   simplify the right side of the equation to get $2^{x^2 + 2x - 3} = 2^{2x - 3}$. Since both sides now have base 2, you know that $x^2 + 2x - 3$ is equal to $2x - 3$. You can then solve for x to get 0.

   If you got (A) or (D), you may have added the powers in the denominator of the fraction on the right side of the equation.

Factor Polynomials
Part 3

These problems ask you to factor polynomial expressions.

1

Given that $x^3 + 4x^2 + 4x = (x + a)(x + b)(x + c)$, which one of the following is the solution for $a + b + c$?

A) 0

B) 2

C) 4

D) 6

2

Which of the following is equal to $2x^2 - x - 15$?

A) $(2x - 5)(x + 3)$

B) $(2x + 1)(x - 15)$

C) $(2x + 3)(6x - 5)$

D) $(2x + 5)(x - 3)$

3

Which of the following is equivalent to $x^2 - 5x - 14$?

A) $(x - 7)(x + 2)$

B) $(x - 7)(x - 2)$

C) $(x + 7)(x + 2)$

D) $(x + 7)(x - 2)$

4

$-12x^2 + 18x + 12 =$

A) $6(x + 1)(2x - 2)$

B) $6(-2x - 1)(x + 2)$

C) $-6(2x + 1)(x - 2)$

D) $-6(x - 1)(2x + 2)$

6

$x^3 + 3x^2 - 4x - 12 =$

A) $(x - 2)(x + 3)(x - 3)$

B) $(x - 2)(x + 2)(x - 3)$

C) $(x + 2)(x + 4)(x - 3)$

D) $(x + 2)(x + 3)(x - 3)$

5

$x^2 - 4xy - 12y^2 =$

A) $(x - 2y)(x + 6y)$

B) $(x + 2y)(x - 6y)$

C) $-(x - 2y)(x + 6y)$

D) $-(x + 2y)(x - 6y)$

Answers and Explanations

1. The correct answer is (C). You can recognize that x can be factored away from $x^3 + 4x^2 + 4x$, and you will get $x(x^2 + 4x^2 + 4)$. $x^2 + 4x^2 + 4$ can be furthered factored into a perfect square: $(x + 2)(x + 2)$ which means that a, b, and c are 0, 2 and 2. As a result, you can determine that the sum of a, b and c are $0 + 2 + 2 = 4$.

2. The correct answer is (D). The easiest way to solve this question is to FOIL each option to see which results in the correct polynomial. (A) results in $2x^2 + x - 15$, so it's incorrect. If you're observant, you may notice that this comes very close to the desired polynomial, and if you simply flip the signs of the two binomials in the answer option, you'll get the correct answer. If you don't notice this, you can continue FOILing. (B) results in $2x^2 - 14x - 15$, so it's incorrect. (C) results in $12x^2 + 8x - 15$, so it's incorrect. (D) results in $2x^2 - x - 15$, so it is correct.

3. The correct answer is (A). Given a polynomial in the form $x^2 + bx + c$, you should consider what two numbers multiply to b and add up to c. This will lead you to the two numbers that are the second terms of the binomial factors. In this case, $b = -14$ and $c = -5$. (B) is incorrect because $-7 \times -2 = 14$, not -14. (C) is incorrect because $7 \times 2 = 14$, not -14. (D) is incorrect because $7 + -2 = 5$, not -5. That leaves (A), for which $-7 \times 2 = -14$ and $-7 + 2 = -5$.

4. The correct answer is (C). First, factor out -6 from the entire expression, since 6 is the largest common factor of the three coefficients and it's easier to factor if the first term is positive. This gives you $-6(2x^2 - 3x - 2)$. From there, you can either expand the given options to determine that $(2x + 1)(x - 2)$ is the correct factorization.

5. The correct answer is (B). This is slightly different than most factoring problems because each binomial will contain two variable terms instead of a variable term and a constant. The easiest way to solve this particular question is probably to test each option by FOILing. However, you can also try setting up the two binomials yourself. Since the first term is x^2, you know that each binomial will begin with x: $(x + \_)(x + \_)$. Then, you can see that the final term is y^2 with a coefficient, so both binomials should have y terms with coefficients: $(x + \_ y)(x + \_ y)$. Finally, find what two coefficients add to -4 and multiply to -12: $(x + (-6)y)(x + (2)y) = (x + 2y)(x - 6y)$.

6. The correct answer is (B). To factor the original expression, you should group together terms that share a common factor. In this case, that factor is $(x+3)$. Remove that factor from both terms:

$$x^3 + 3x^2 - 4x - 12$$
$$(x^3 + 3x^2) - (4x + 12)$$
$$x^2(x + 3) - 4(x + 3)$$

Now, the expression consists of two terms. Remove the shared factor $(x+3)$ from both of those terms:

$$x^2(x + 3) - 4(x + 3)$$
$$(x^2 - 4)(x + 3)$$

Finally, factor the difference of squares to get the final factorization:

$$(x^2 - 4)(x + 3)$$
$$(x + 2)(x - 2)(x + 3)$$

Operations on Polynomials

Part 4

These problems ask you to add, subtract, and multiply polynomials.

1

If $(3x^2 + 4x + 1)(2x + 3) = ax^3 + bx^2 + cx + 3$, what is the value of $b - a$?

A) 2

B) 7

C) 9

D) 11

2

Which of the following is equivalent to the expression $4(4x + 1)(2x - 3)$?

A) $32x$

B) $32x^2 - 12$

C) $32x^2 - 40x - 12$

D) $32x^2 + 56x - 12$

3

Which of the following expressions is equivalent to $(4x^2 - 3y)(4x^2 + 3y)$?

A) $8x^2 + 6y$

B) $8x^2 - 6y^2$

C) $16x^2 + 9y^2$

D) $16x^4 - 9y^2$

4

Which of the following expressions is equivalent to $2x(3x - y - 5x)$?

A) $x - 2xy$

B) $-4x - 2xy$

C) $-4x^2 - 2xy$

D) $6x - 2y - 10x$

5

Which of the following expressions is equivalent to $-3x^2y(6x^7y - 11y^4)$?

A) $-18x^{14}y + 33x^2y^4$

B) $-18x^{14}y^2 - 33y^4$

C) $-18x^9y^2 + 33x^2y^5$

D) $-18x^9y - 33y^5$

6

Which of the following expressions is equal to $(3a + 7b - c) - (-5a - 2b + 8c)$?

A) $-2a + 5b - 8c$

B) $-2a + 7b - 9c$

C) $8a + 9b - 9c$

D) $8a + 5b + 7c$

7

Which of the following expressions is equal to $(x^2 - 2x + 9) + (5x^2 - 2)$?

A) $5x^2 - 2x - 18$

B) $6x^2 + x + 9$

C) $6x^2 - 4x + 7$

D) $6x^2 - 2x + 7$

8

Which one of the following is the remainder when $6x^2 - 17x + 10$ is divided by $3x - 4$?

A) -4

B) -2

C) 0

D) 2

9

If the length of a rectangle in terms of x is $3x + 6$, and its width is $7x + 9$, what is the perimeter of this rectangle?

A) $10x + 15$

B) $20x + 30$

C) $21x^2 - 15x + 54$

D) $21x^2 + 69x + 50$

Answers and Explanations

1. The correct answer is (D). You can multiply the two expressions and expand the result in the form of $ax^3 + bx^2 + cx + d$ to determine the values of a and b, which are 6 and 17 respectively. Subtract 6 from 17 to get $b - a$, which is equal to 11.

2. The correct answer is (C). First, you can expand the two binomials, $(4x + 1)(2x - 3)$, to get $8x^2 - 10x - 4$. Then, you can multiply each term by 4 to get $32x^2 - 40x - 12$.

3. The correct answer is (D). Although you can distribute the first binomial into the second, you can solve the question faster by recognizing that the expression is the expanded form of a difference of squares, which you can simplify to $(a - b)(a + b) = a^2 - b^2$. As a result, you can determine that an equivalent expression is the square of the second term subtracted from the square of the first, $16x^4 - 9y^2$.

4. The correct answer is (C). If you distribute the $2x$ to each term of the second polynomial, you will get $6x^2 - 2xy - 10x^2$. Then, you can combine like terms to simplify the expression to $-4x^2 - 2xy$.

5. The correct answer is (C). If you distribute the $-3x^2y$ to each term of the binomial, you will get the following:

$$-3x^2y(6x^7y) - (-3x^2y)(11y^4) = -18x^9y^2 + 33x^2y^5$$

6. The correct answer is (C). To simplify this expression, subtract like terms from each other:

$$3a - (-5a) = 8a, \ 7b - (-2b) = 9b, \text{ and } (-c) - 8c = -9c \text{ to get } 8a + 9b - 9c.$$

7. The correct answer is (D). If you combine like terms to add the two expressions, $x^2 + 5x^2 = 6x^2$ and $9 - 2 = 7$, you get $6x^2 - 2x + 7$.

8. The correct answer is (B). You can use remainder theorem so solve this question. Since for $3x - 4$ to equal 0, x must equal $\frac{4}{3}$, you can plug in $x = \frac{4}{3}$ into the expression $6x^2 - 17x + 10$ to get a remainder of -2.

9. The correct answer is (B). You calculate the perimeter of a shape by adding all of its sides. Since there are two of each side, the perimeter of this rectangle is equal to $2 \times (3x + 6) + 2 \times (7x + 9) = 20x + 30$.

Solve Quadratics by Factoring
Part 5

These problems ask you to solve quadratic equations in one variable by factoring or determine the conditions under which a quadratic equation has zero, one, or two real solutions.

DIRECTIONS

Select the best answer among four choices and circle the corresponding letter or record it on a separate sheet of paper.

NOTES

1. You may use a calculator, but not all problems require the use of a calculator.
2. Variables and expressions represent real numbers unless stated otherwise.
3. Figures are drawn to scale unless stated otherwise.
4. Figures lie in a plane unless stated otherwise.
5. The domain of a function f is defined as the set of all real numbers x for which $f(x)$ is also a real number, unless stated otherwise.

1

If the quadratic equation $ax^2 + bx + c = 0$ has solutions of n and $-n$, which of the following must be true?

A) $b^2 = 4ac$

B) $b = 4ac$

C) $b = 0$

D) $c = 0$

2

If the quadratic equation $ax^2 + bx + c = 0$ has no real solutions, which of the following must be true?

A) $b^2 < 4ac$

B) $b^2 > 4ac$

C) $b < 4ac$

D) $b > 4ac$

3

How many real solutions are there to the equation $x^2 + 5x + 7 = 0$?

A) 0

B) 1

C) 2

D) Infinitely many

4

In the equation $x^2 - 5x + 27 = y$, if $y = 41$, what are the possible solutions for x?

A) $-2, 7$

B) $-7, 2$

C) $2, 3$

D) $-2. 3$

5

Which of the following statements is true of the equation $f(x) = (x + 3)^2$?

A) It has no x-intercepts.

B) It has one x-intercept at -3.

C) It has one x-intercept at 3.

D) It has two x-intercepts.

6

How many positive solutions exist for x in the equation $x^2 - 1 = 0$?

A) 0

B) 1

C) 2

D) 3

7

If $(x + a)^2 = 0$ and $x = 3$, what is the value of $4a^2$?

A) -36

B) 36

C) 18

D) 9

8

If a and b are the two values of x that satisfy the equation $x^2 + 3x - 28 = 0$, what is $a + b$?

A) -3

B) 4

C) 7

D) 11

Answers and Explanations

1. The correct answer is (C). If a quadratic equation has solutions of n and $-n$, that means that the x intercepts of the parabola defined by the equation are equal distances from the origin. In other words, the parabola is reflected around the y-axis.

   The term b in a quadratic equation helps determine the position of the vertex of the parabola (the top of the arc, or bottom of the bowl, depending on which way the parabola opens). As the magnitude of b increases or decreases, so does the magnitude of the x-value of the vertex. The only time that the x-value of the vertex can be 0 is when the magnitude of b is 0. If the parabola is reflected around the y-axis, that means the vertex is at $x = 0$. Thus, it must be the case that $b = 0$.

2. The correct answer is (A). Let's look at the quadratic formula:

$$x = \frac{-b \pm \sqrt{b^2 - 4ac}}{2a}$$

   This formula requires us to find the square root of the term $b^2 - 4ac$. The term $b^2 - 4ac$ is called the *discriminant*, because it allows us to discriminate between various outcomes. If b^2 is less than $4ac$, then $b^2 - 4ac$ will be a negative number. However, squaring any real number produces a positive number, so no real number can be the square root of a negative number. Thus, there are no real solutions to the quadratic equation when $b^2 < 4ac$.

3. The correct answer is (A). Let's look at the quadratic equation, and plug in some values for a, b, and c:

$$x = \frac{-b \pm \sqrt{b^2 - 4ac}}{2a}$$

$$x = \frac{-5 \pm \sqrt{5^2 - (4)(1)(7)}}{2(1)} = \frac{-5 \pm \sqrt{25 - 28}}{2} = \frac{-5 \pm \sqrt{-3}}{2}$$

   This equation includes the term $\sqrt{-3}$. Since any real number squared is a positive number, $\sqrt{-3}$ cannot be a real number, and there are no real solutions to $x^2 + 5x + 7 = 0$.

4. The correct answer is (A). First, you can plug in 41 for y and change the equation into the more convenient form of $ax^2 + bx + c = 0$, which turns out to be $x^2 - 5x - 14 = 0$. Then, you can factor the equation to get $(x + 2)(x - 7) = 0$. As a result, you can conclude that there are two solutions for x, -2 and 7.

5. The correct answer is (B). The equation $f(x) = (x + 3)^2$ can be rewritten as $f(x) = (x + 3)(x + 3)$. Setting $f(x)$ to zero, you can determine that both factors show that x must equal -3. Therefore, there is only one x-intercept, which is at the only solution: -3. The graph is shown to the right.

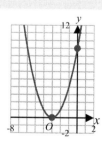

6. The correct answer is (B). $x^2 - 1$ is a difference of squares that factors into $(x - 1)(x + 1)$, which gives two solutions, $x = 1$ and -1. Since only 1 is positive, there is only one positive solution.

7. The correct answer is (B). If $x = 3$, then you can rewrite the first expression as $(a + 3)^2 = 0$. From here, you know that $a = -3$. Therefore $4a^2 = 4(-3)^2 = 4(9) = 36$.

8. The correct answer is (A). Factor the equation and you will get $(x + 7)(x - 4)$, which gives you two solutions for x: -7 and 4. As a result, $a + b = -7 + 4 = -3$.

Solve Rational/Radical Equations
Part 6

These problems ask you to solve simple rational and radical equations in one variable, including determining when a solution is extraneous.

DIRECTIONS

Select the best answer among four choices and circle the corresponding letter or record it on a separate sheet of paper.

NOTES

1. You may use a calculator, but not all problems require the use of a calculator.
2. Variables and expressions represent real numbers unless stated otherwise.
3. Figures are drawn to scale unless stated otherwise.
4. Figures lie in a plane unless stated otherwise.
5. The domain of a function f is defined as the set of all real numbers x for which $f(x)$ is also a real number, unless stated otherwise.

1

Which of the following expressions is NOT defined for $x = 4$?

A) $\dfrac{2x}{x+4}$

B) $\dfrac{2x}{x-4}$

C) $\dfrac{x+4}{2x}$

D) $\dfrac{x-4}{2x}$

2

If $t = \dfrac{r^3}{s}$, $r = -4$, and $t = 4$, what is the value of s?

A) -32

B) -16

C) 4

D) 16

3

If $f(x) = \dfrac{x-2}{x+3}$, for what value of x is $f(x)$ undefined?

A) -3

B) -2

C) 2

D) 3

4

For how many values of n is the expression $\dfrac{n-4}{n^2-3n-4}$ undefined?

A) 0

B) 1

C) 2

D) 3

5

To better understand his studying habits, Mark created a function to represent the number of hours he can work productively as a function of the number of hours he slept the previous night. His productivity function is $p(s) = \sqrt{s} + \dfrac{s}{2}$, where s represents the hours of sleep he got and p represents the number of hours he will be able to work productively the following day. If Mark slept 9 hours last night, for how many hours will he be able to work productively today?

A) 4.5

B) 7.5

C) 9

D) 10.5

6

Which of the following is NOT a valid input for the function $\dfrac{x^2-3x-28}{x-7}$?

A) -7

B) -3

C) 3

D) 7

7

For how many values of x does the function $f(x) = \dfrac{(x-3)(x+2)(x-11)}{(x-1)(x-3)(x+1)}$ NOT have an output value?

A) 1

B) 2

C) 3

D) The function has an output value for all real values of x.

Answers and Explanations

1. The correct answer is (B). Each of these expressions is undefined when the denominator is equal to 0. For the equation in (B), this occurs when $x - 4 = 0$, which you can solve to get $x = 4$

2. The correct answer is (B). To find s, manipulate the equation to solve for $s = \frac{r^3}{t}$. Then, you can substitute the given values for r and t to solve for s, $s = \frac{(-4)^3}{4} = \frac{-64}{4} = -16$.

3. The correct answer is (A). A rational function is undefined when the denominator is equal to 0. For $f(x)$, this occurs when $x + 3 = 0$, which solves to $x = -3$.

4. The correct answer is (C). An expression is undefined when the denominator is equal to 0. For this expression, that occurs when $n^2 - 3n - 4 = 0$. You can factor this expression as $(n + 1)(n - 4) = 0$ to find that $n = -1$ and 4. Therefore, the expression is undefined for two values of n.

   If you chose (B), you probably factored $n - 4$ out of the fraction, but $n = 4$ is still an undefined value for the original expression.

5. The correct answer is (B). This question may appear daunting because of its length, but once you read the question, you may see that it is a simple substitution question. The function $p(s) = \sqrt{s} + \frac{s}{2}$ gives Mark's productivity, where s is the number of hours he slept the previous night. To find Mark's productivity after 9 hours of sleep, substitute $s = 9$ into the equation and solve:

$$p(9) = \sqrt{s} + \frac{s}{2}$$
$$= \sqrt{9} + \frac{9}{2}$$
$$= 3 + 4.5$$
$$= 7.5$$

6. The correct answer is (D). A rational function is undefined at the x-value for which the denominator is equal to 0. Setting the denominator equal to 0 allows you to solve for this value. $x - 7 = 0$, so $x = 7$.

7. The correct answer is (C). A function does not have an output value, or does not exist, at any value where the denominator of the function is equal to 0. Setting the denominator equal to 0 gives three values for x: -1, 1, and 3.

   If you chose (B), you probably cancelled out $(x - 3)$ from the numerator and denominator and concluded that the function exists at $x = 3$. However, this value results in an open hole, where the function still does not exist.

Solve Factored Polynomials
Part 7

These problems ask you to solve polynomial equations in one variable that are written in factored form.

1

Which of the following is NOT a solution to the equation $x(x+3)(x-2)(x+2) = 0$?

A) -3

B) 0

C) 2

D) 3

2

What is one solution to the equation $(x-1)x^3(x-3)^2 = 0$?

A) -3

B) 0

C) -1

D) 4

If $x^3(10x + 6)(2x - 6) = 0$, x CANNOT equal

A) $-\dfrac{3}{5}$

B) 0

C) $\dfrac{5}{3}$

D) 3

Which of the following is a solution to $(x^4 + 3x + 10)(6x - 20)(x + 6) = 0$?

A) -10

B) $-\dfrac{5}{3}$

C) $\dfrac{10}{3}$

D) 6

If $\dfrac{z^2 \times z \times z^4 - 8}{4} = -2$, then z must be equal to

A) -2

B) 0

C) 4

D) Cannot be determined.

Angela
Postage stamps

Georgetown turt

Answers and Explanations

1. The correct answer is (D). The above equation is written in factored form, which means that it is composed of several terms multiplied together: x, $x + 3$, $x - 2$, and $x + 2$. When several values are multiplied together, if any one of those values is equal to zero, the entire expression will be equal to 0. For example, if $x = 2$ in the above expression, you could write:

$$2(2 + 3)(2 - 2)(2 + 2) = 2 \times 5 \times 0 \times 4 = 0$$

So, 2 is one solution to the equation, because it makes the third factor equal to 0. The other three values of x that would make one factor equal to zero are, in order, 0, -3, and -2. The only option that is not one for those four solutions is (D).

2. The correct answer is (B). The above equation is written in factored form, which means that it is composed of several terms multiplied together: $x - 1$, $x - 3$, and $\boldsymbol{x}$. When several values are multiplied together, if any one of those values is equal to 0, the entire expression will be equal to 0. The fact that some of these factors are raised to a power, like $(x - 3)^2$, does not affect the values of the solutions because 0 raised to any power is still 0. For example, if $x = 1$ in the above expression, you could write:

$$(1 - 1)1^3(1 - 3)^2 = 0 \times 1 \times 2^2 = 0$$

So, 1 is one solution to the equation, because it makes the first factor equal to 0. The other two values of x that would make one factor equal to zero are 0 and 3. However, of these three solutions, only 0 is given as an option, so (B) is correct.

3. The correct answer is (C). The above equation is written in factored form, which means that it is composed of several terms multiplied together: x, $10x + 6$, and $2x - 6$. When several values are multiplied together, if any one of those values is equal to 0, the entire expression will be equal to 0. The fact that some of these factors are raised to a power, like x^3, does not affect the values of the solutions because 0 raised to any power is still 0.

To figure out what values of x will make each factor equal to 0, you can set each of them individually as their own equation to solve for 0.

$2x - 6 = 0$	$10x + 6 = 0$	$x^3 = 0$
$2x = 6$	$10x = -6$	$x = 0$
$x = 3$	$x = -\dfrac{3}{5}$	

So, the three values of x that would make one factor equal to zero are 3, $-\dfrac{3}{5}$, and 0. The only answer option that is not one of those three values is (C).

4. The correct answer is (B). This may look like a complicated equation, but don't be discouraged. Solving it is just a matter of combining like terms and then using algebraic principles to simplify:

$$\frac{z^2 \times z \times z^4 - 8}{4} = -2$$

$$\frac{z^7 - 8}{4} = -2$$

$$z^7 - 8 = -8$$

$$z^7 = 0$$

$$z = 0$$

5. The correct answer is (C). The above equation is written in factored form, which means that it is composed of several terms multiplied together: $x + 6$, $6x - 20$, and $x^4 + 3x + 10$. When several values are multiplied together, if any one of those values is equal to 0, the entire expression will be equal to 0.

To figure out what values of x will make each factor equal to zero, you can set each of them individually as their own equation to solve for 0. Since $x^4 + 3x + 10 = 0$ is somewhat more difficult to solve, you probably want to leave it for last in case one of the easier factors gives the answer:

$$6x - 20 = 0$$

$$6x = 20$$

$$x = \frac{10}{3}$$

After solving only one of the factors for 0, you have already found the answer. Since you're just looking for one of the solutions to the equation, you don't need to worry about the others and can choose (C).

Absolute Value
Part 8 Absolve value

These problems ask you to solve <u>linear absolute value equations</u> in one variable.

DIRECTIONS

Select the best answer among four choices and circle the corresponding letter or record it on a separate sheet of paper.

NOTES

1. You may use a calculator, but not all problems require the use of a calculator.
2. Variables and expressions represent real numbers unless stated otherwise.
3. Figures are drawn to scale unless stated otherwise.
4. Figures lie in a plane unless stated otherwise.
5. The domain of a function f is defined as the set of all real numbers x for which $f(x)$ is also a real number, unless stated otherwise.

1

If $2|x-4|-10=-6$, what is the value of x?

A) $x = 12$

B) $x = 2$ or $x = -2$

C) $x = 6$ or $x = 2$

D) $x = 6$ or $x = -2$

$2|x-4| = 4$

$|x-4| = 2$

6
-2

3

If $3|x-3|+3=3$, x is equal to

A) -6

B) -3

C) 0

D) 3

2

Which of the following expressions can be <u>negative</u> <u>for some value of x?</u>

A) $|x-5|-6$

B) $|x-5|+6$

C) $|5-x|+4$

D) $|x-5|+4$

Which of the following is a solution to the equation $|2x - 6| = 4x - 2$?

A) -2

B) $\dfrac{4}{3}$

C) $\dfrac{6}{5}$

D) 7

Given $\dfrac{|x - 2|}{10} = 4$, one possible value of x is

A) -38

B) -18

C) 18

D) 38

Answers and Explanations

1. The correct answer is (C). The most reliable way to solve absolute value expressions is to treat everything inside the brackets as one big variable. That variable can be equal to either the positive or the negative version of the rest of the equation. First, isolate the absolute value brackets:

$$2|x-4|-10 = -6$$
$$2|x-4| = 4$$
$$|x-4| = 2$$

This shows that $(x-4)$ will either equal 2 or –2. You can set up two separate equations to test each option:

$$x-4 = 2 \qquad\qquad\qquad\qquad\qquad x-4 = -2$$
$$x = 6 \qquad\qquad\qquad\qquad\qquad\qquad x = 2$$

Don't forget to double check the answers you get, as absolute value expressions don't always have solutions. In this case, both solutions work, so the answer is (C).

2. The correct answer is (A). Absolute value brackets can only result in positive values or zero. Therefore, the values of (B), (C), and (D) will all be positive because they include absolute value expressions (which are positive) being added to positive integers. (A) will be negative as long as $10 \geq x \geq 0$, because 6 is being subtracted instead of added.

3. The correct answer is (D). First, isolate the absolute value brackets:

$$3|x-3|+3 = 3$$
$$3|x-3| = 0$$
$$|x-3| = 0$$

This shows that $(x-3)$ will be equal to positive or negative 0, but 0 is neither negative nor positive, you can simply solve one equation:

$$x-3 = 0$$
$$x = 3$$

Don't forget to double check the answers you get. In this case, the solution does work, so the correct answer is (D).

4. The correct answer is (B). Set up two equations to solve for x:

$$2x - 6 = 4x - 2$$
$$-4 = 2x$$
$$x = -2$$

$$2x - 6 = -(4x - 2)$$
$$6x = 8$$
$$x = \frac{4}{3}$$

Don't forget to double check the answers you get. In this case, $x = -2$ does not result in a true equation when plugged back in. However, $x = \frac{4}{3}$ does work, so the correct answer is (B).

5. The correct answer is (A). First, isolate the absolute value brackets:

$$\frac{|x - 2|}{10} = 4$$
$$|x - 2| = 40$$

This shows that $(x - 2)$ will be equal to positive or negative 40. So, you can set up two equations to solve for x:

$$x - 2 = 40$$
$$x = 42$$

$$x - 2 = -40$$
$$x = -38$$

Don't forget to double check the answers you get. In this case, both solutions work, so the correct answer is (A).

Solve Systems of Nonlinear Equations
Part 9

11 years → 7 years   (24)

These problems ask you to solve systems of linear and nonlinear equations in two variables, including relating the solutions to the graphs of the equations.

DIRECTIONS

Select the best answer among four choices and circle the corresponding letter or record it on a separate sheet of paper.

NOTES

1. You may use a calculator, but not all problems require the use of a calculator.
2. Variables and expressions represent real numbers unless stated otherwise.
3. Figures are drawn to scale unless stated otherwise.
4. Figures lie in a plane unless stated otherwise.
5. The domain of a function f is defined as the set of all real numbers x for which $f(x)$ is also a real number, unless stated otherwise.

1

If $|x - 1| = 6$, which of the following sets of ordered pairs (x, y) values satisfies the equation $x = |y - 5|$?

A) $(-5, 0)$ and $(-5, 5)$

B) $(7, -2)$ and $(7, 12)$

C) $(5, 0)$ and $(5, 5)$

D) $(7, 2)$ and $(7, -12)$

$|x - 1| = 6$
$|y - 5| = x$

2

$$y = |x - 2|, y = |x + 3|$$

What is the x-value of the solution to the system of equations given above?

A) $-\dfrac{2}{3}$

B) $-\dfrac{1}{2}$

C) $\dfrac{1}{2}$

D) $\dfrac{2}{3}$

$|x - 2| = |x + 3|$
$x - 2 = x + 3 \rightarrow$
$-x + 2 = -x - 3$

What is a solution to the system of equations composed of $y = 2x + 1$ and $y = 2x^2 + 5x + 2$?

A) $(-2, -3)$

B) $(-1, 0)$

C) $(-1, -1)$

D) $(3, 2)$

$$y = 2x^2 + 3x + 10$$
$$y = x^2 - 6x - 4$$

What is one solution to the system of equations above?

A) $(-6, 36)$

B) $(-2, 12)$

C) $(0, -6)$

D) $(4, 18)$

$$\frac{y - 8}{2} = -x$$
$$y = (x + 2)(x - 4)$$

The two equations above intersect at which of the following points?

A) $(-2, 0)$

B) $(0, 6)$

C) $(4, 0)$

D) $(8, 4)$

Answers and Explanations

1. The correct answer is (B). You can begin by solving the first equation since it's in one variable:

$$x - 1 = 6 \qquad\qquad\qquad\qquad x - 1 = -6$$
$$x = 7 \qquad\qquad\qquad\qquad\qquad x = -5$$

The second equation sets x equal to an absolute value, which implies that it must be nonnegative. That means that $x = -5$ can't satisfy that equation, so we only need to consider possible values of y given $x = 7$. Let's plug in that value:

$$y - 5 = 7 \qquad\qquad\qquad\qquad y - 5 = -7$$
$$y = 12 \qquad\qquad\qquad\qquad\qquad y = -2$$

We now have the one value of x and the two values of y that satisfy this pair of equations, which yields the two ordered pairs (7, -2) and (7, 12).

2. The correct answer is (B). Since both absolute value expressions are equal to y, you can set them equal to each other: $|x - 2| = |x + 3|$. To solve this, simply set the positive and negative versions of each side equal to each other, and test each combination:

$$x - 2 = x + 3 \qquad -(x - 2) = x + 3 \qquad x - 2 = -(x + 3) \qquad -(x - 2) = -(x + 3)$$
$$-2 = 3 \qquad\qquad 2x = -1 \qquad\qquad 2x = -1 \qquad\qquad 2 = 3$$
$$\text{No solution} \qquad\qquad x = -\frac{1}{2} \qquad\qquad x = -\frac{1}{2} \qquad\qquad \text{No solution}$$

Since each combination either has no solution or results in $x = -\frac{1}{2}$, the correct answer must be (B).

3. The correct answer is (C). Set the equations equal to one another, simplify, and then factor:

$$2x + 1 = 2x^2 + 5x + 2$$

$$0 = 2x^2 + 3x + 1$$

$$0 = (2x + 1)(x + 1)$$

$$x = -\frac{1}{2}, x = -1$$

You should notice that none of the answer options include $x = -\frac{1}{2}$, so there's no need to find its corresponding y-value. Instead, plug $x = -1$ back into the first equation to solve for y:

$$y = 2(-1) + 1$$

$$y = -1$$

So, one solution is $(-1, -1)$.

4. The correct answer is (C). To begin, rewrite both equations in their standard forms: $y = -2x + 8$ and $y = x^2 - 2x - 8$. Then, set them equal to each other and solve for x:

$$x^2 - 2x - 8 = -2x + 8$$

$$x^2 = 16$$

$$x = 4, x = -4$$

There is only one option that has either of those x-values, but to confirm that you're correct you can plug $x = 4$ back into the first equation:

$$y = -2(4) + 8$$

$$y = 0$$

5. The correct answer is (B). Set the two equations equal to one another, simplify, and then factor to solve for x:

$$2x^2 + 3x + 10 = x^2 - 6x - 4$$

$$x^2 + 9x + 14 = 0$$

$$(x + 7)(x + 2) = 0$$

$$x = -7, x = -2$$

Since only one answer option includes $x = -2$, you know the answer must be (B). To confirm, you can plug -2 back into either equation to ensure that $y = 12$.

Interpret Nonlinear Equations
Part 10

These problems ask you to interpret a solution, constant, variable, factor, or term of a nonlinear equation in one variable that represents a context.

1

The height of a ball, in meters, is given by the expression $-t^2 + 10t + 2$, where t is the time in seconds after the ball is thrown. How high is the ball off the ground, in meters, when it is thrown?

A) 0

B) 2

C) 5

D) 10

2

The number of bacteria in a petri dish, in millions, can be represented by the expression 3×2^t, where t is the number of hours that have passed since the scientists started observing the dish. What is the meaning of the number 3 in this expression?

A) The number of bacteria triples every hour.

B) The number of bacteria doubles every three hours.

C) The number of bacteria doubles three times per hour.

D) The dish had 3 million bacteria initially.

3

Susie writes down a quadratic equation to model the height of a snowball off the ground s seconds after she throws it. If she finds that the two solutions are $s = -1$ and $s = 7$, what can Susie then conclude?

A)   The snowball will hit the ground after 1 second.

B)   The snowball will hit the ground after 6 seconds.

C)   The snowball will hit the ground after 7 seconds.

D)   The snowball will hit the ground after 8 seconds.

4

A tire swing is tied to a branch, which is 10 feet off the ground. When swinging, the height of the tire, in feet, can be approximated by the equation $y = x^2 + 3$, where x is the horizontal distance that the tire is from its starting position and y is the vertical distance. Which of the following is a correct interpretation of the 3 in the equation?

A)   The tire can move up to 3 feet horizontally from its starting position.

B)   The tire can only move up to 3 feet higher than its starting position.

C)   The tire can go as high as 3 times its initial height.

D)   The tire is 3 feet off the ground when it is in its starting position.

5

Galina plants a tree at the end of spring. She models the tree's projected growth over the following 12 weeks using the equation $h = -\frac{1}{6}t^2 + 4t + 6$, where h is the height of the tree and t is the time in weeks from when she plants the tree. Which of the following can be inferred based on the coefficient of $-\frac{1}{6}t^2$?

A)   The tree will shrink in height over time.

B)   The tree will grow 6 times slower than most trees.

C)   The tree's growth rate will decline over the 12 weeks.

D)   The tree's growth rate will decrease by 3 units over 12 weeks.

Answers and Explanations

1. The correct answer is (B). At the moment the ball is thrown, no time has passed, so $t = 0$. When $t = 0$, the expression is equal to 2, so the ball is 2 meters off the ground. For quadratic equations in the standard form $y = ax^2 + bx + c$, c is the value of y when $x = 0$, in other words the y-intercept, in other words the "initial" value of y.

2. The correct answer is (D). Initially, no time has passed, so $t = 0$. When $t = 0$, the expression is equal to 3. Since the expression represents bacteria in millions, there are 3 million bacteria at the beginning of observation. In exponential equations in the standard form $y = a \times b^x$, a represents the initial value of y when $x = 0$.

3. The correct answer is (C). The solutions to a quadratic equation are the points where the equation touches the x-axis, in other words the values of x when $y = 0$, in other words the "roots." In this example, time in seconds is plotted along the x-axis, and the height of the snowball is along the y-axis. Therefore, when $y = 0$, the ball is 0 feet above the ground—meaning it has hit the ground. The two moments where the snowball hits the ground are at $x = -1$ and $x = 7$. However, since time cannot be negative, the snowball must hit the ground at $x = 7$, or 7 seconds.

4. The correct answer is (D). When the horizontal distance $x = 0$, the vertical distance $y = 3$. So, the constant "3" represents the fact that the tire is 3 feet off the ground at its starting position.

5. The correct answer is (C). Since the coefficient of the first term is negative, you know that the quadratic model will open downwards. Since the coefficient of the second term is positive, you know that the graph is shifted to the right. Since the constant is 6, you know that the graph will intersect the h-axis at $h = 6$. Using this information, you can quickly sketch a rough version of the graph:

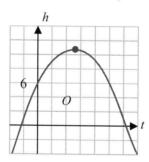

As you can see, starting from time 0, the tree grows taller, but less and less so for each unit along the t-axis. This means that the rate of growth is decreasing, until eventually the tree stops growing in height at the vertex of the parabola. Don't be confused by the fact that the height of the tree then appears to decrease: since the model is only for the next 12 weeks, the model only continues up until the vertex of the equation, which is at $t = 12$.

Solve Nonlinear Equations for a Variable
Part 11

These problems ask you to solve for the variable of interest in an equation or formula that represents a context.

DIRECTIONS

Select the best answer among four choices and circle the corresponding letter or record it on a separate sheet of paper.

NOTES

1. You may use a calculator, but not all problems require the use of a calculator.
2. Variables and expressions represent real numbers unless stated otherwise.
3. Figures are drawn to scale unless stated otherwise.
4. Figures lie in a plane unless stated otherwise.
5. The domain of a function f is defined as the set of all real numbers x for which $f(x)$ is also a real number, unless stated otherwise.

1

Given that $y = b + gx$, which of the following expressions is equal to x?

A) $\dfrac{y-b}{g}$

B) $b + gy$

C) $\dfrac{y+b}{g}$

D) $y - (b + g)$

2

Three more than quadruple a number is divided by two. If q is the new number, what was the original number, in terms of q?

A) $\dfrac{4q+3}{2}$

B) $\dfrac{q-6}{2}$

C) $\dfrac{q}{2}$

D) $\dfrac{2q-3}{4}$

The cost of Padma's trip to the store can be modeled by $0.75m + 3g + 15p = c$, where c is the total amount of money she spends, m is the number of markers she buys, g is the number of glue sticks she buys, and p is the number of poster boards she buys. If Padma wants to find the number of markers she can buy in terms of all the other variables, how can the expression be rewritten?

A) $m = \dfrac{4c}{3} - 4g - 20p$

B) $m = \dfrac{3c}{4} - \dfrac{9}{4}g - p$

C) $m = \dfrac{3c}{4} + \dfrac{9}{4}g + p$

D) $m = c - 3g - 15p$

Coulomb's Law states that the force F between two point charges can be described by the equation $F = k_e \dfrac{q_1 q_2}{r^2}$, where q_1 and q_2 are the magnitudes of the two point charges, r is the distance between their centers, and k_e is the electrostatic constant. Which of the following uses Coulomb's Law to represent the distance between two point charges in terms of magnitude, force, and the electrostatic constant?

A) $k_e = \dfrac{q_1 q_2}{Fr^2}$

B) $k_e = \dfrac{\sqrt{q_1 q_2}}{r\sqrt{F}}$

C) $r = \dfrac{k_e q_1 q_2}{F}$

D) $r = \pm\sqrt{\dfrac{k_e q_1 q_2}{F}}$

Which of the following shows the equation $x^2 + 3y^2 = 16 - y^2$ as y in terms of x?

A) $y = \pm\sqrt{4 - \dfrac{x^2}{4}}$

B) $y = \pm\sqrt{64 - 4x^2}$

C) $x = \pm\sqrt{16 - 4y^2}$

D) $x = \pm\sqrt{4 - \dfrac{y^2}{4}}$

Answers and Explanations

1. The correct answer is (A). To solve for x, simply rearrange the equation to isolate for x:

$$y = b + gx$$

$$y - b = gx$$

$$\frac{y-b}{g} = x$$

2. The correct answer is (D). Let's call the original number n. Since q is the new number, you can start by writing an equation for q based on the operations applied to n. Quadruple a number means 4 times the number, and three more than that means you add 3. This is divided by two, so:

$$\frac{4n+3}{2} = q$$

Now, rearrange and solve for n:

$$4n + 3 = 2q$$

$$4n = 2q - 3$$

$$n = \frac{2q-3}{4}$$

If you chose (A), you probably wrote out the equation for the new number and stopped there. If you chose (B), you probably misread the operations in the question as "quadruple three more than a number is divided by two," or $\frac{4 \times (n+3)}{2}$. If you chose (C), you probably forgot to add 3.

3. The correct answer is (A). The number of markers Padma buys is represented by m, so that is the variable you need to isolate. Move other terms to the opposite side of the equation, and then divide by the coefficient of m in order to get it by itself:

$$0.75m + 3g + 15p = c$$

$$0.75m = c - 3g - 15p$$

$$m = \frac{1}{0.75}c - \frac{3}{0.75}g - \frac{15}{0.75}p$$

$$m = \frac{4c}{3} - 4g - 20p$$

4. The correct answer is (D). Remember that when you multiply a fraction by any other value, the value just gets multiplied into the numerator, so $F = k_e \dfrac{q_1 q_2}{r^2}$ is equivalent to $F = \dfrac{k_e q_1 q_2}{r^2}$. The question asks you to represent the distance between two point charges, which is r. So, you need to isolate r. The easiest way to do this is to multiply both sides by r^2, divide both sides by F, and then find the square root of both sides:

$$F = k_e \frac{q_1 q_2}{r^2}$$

$$r^2 F = k_e q_1 q_2$$

$$r^2 = k_e \frac{q_1 q_2}{F}$$

$$r = \pm \sqrt{\frac{k_e q_1 q_2}{F}}$$

5. The correct answer is (A). To find the above equation "as y," you need simply to isolate y to find what it is equal to. First, combine and isolate all y terms to one side of the equation, divide by the coefficient of y, and take the square root of both sides:

$$x^2 + 3y^2 = 16 - y^2$$

$$x^2 + 4y^2 = 16$$

$$4y^2 = 16 - x^2$$

$$y^2 = 4 - \frac{x^2}{4}$$

$$y = \pm \sqrt{4 - \frac{x^2}{4}}$$

The Quadratic Formula
Part 12

These problems ask you to solve quadratic equations in one variable by using the quadratic formula or completing the square.

Select the best answer among four choices and circle the corresponding letter or record it on a separate sheet of paper.

NOTES

1. You may use a calculator, but not all problems require the use of a calculator.
2. Variables and expressions represent real numbers unless stated otherwise.
3. Figures are drawn to scale unless stated otherwise.
4. Figures lie in a plane unless stated otherwise.
5. The domain of a function f is defined as the set of all real numbers x for which $f(x)$ is also a real number, unless stated otherwise.

1

Which of the following quadratic equations has $\dfrac{-5 + \sqrt{13}}{2}$ as a solution?

A) $x^2 + 5x + 3 = 0$

B) $x^2 - 5x + 3 = 0$

C) $x^2 + 5x - 3 = 0$

D) $x^2 - 5x - 3 = 0$

2

Which of the following represents the solution set to the equation $0 = x^2 + 12x + 12$?

A) $-12 \pm \sqrt{6}$

B) $-6 \pm 2\sqrt{6}$

C) $6 \pm 2\sqrt{6}$

D) $12 \pm \sqrt{6}$

If $y = x^2 + 22x + 10$ is rewritten in the form $y = (x - h)^2 + k$, what is the value of $h - k$?

A) 28

B) 90

C) 100

D) 121

Given the equation $y = 3x^2 - 2x - 7$, if $y = 0$, what is one possible approximate value of x?

A) −2.46

B) −1.89

C) −1.23

D) 2.08

Which of the following is the solution set to the equation $2x^2 = 8 - x$?

A) $-\dfrac{1}{4} \pm \dfrac{\sqrt{65}}{4}$

B) $-1 \pm \sqrt{63}$

C) $1 \pm \sqrt{63}$

D) $\dfrac{1}{4} \pm \dfrac{\sqrt{65}}{4}$

Answers and Explanations

1. The correct answer is (A). Using the quadratic formula $x = \dfrac{-b \pm \sqrt{b^2 - 4ac}}{2a}$, you can eliminate (B) and (D) because their b term is –5, which would make the equation $\dfrac{5 + \sqrt{13}}{2}$ rather than $\dfrac{-5 + \sqrt{13}}{2}$. Since (A) and (C) differ only by their c term (3 and –3, respectively), simply calculate the discriminant ($b^2 - 4ac$) for both equations— it must equal 13 to match the given solution. For (A), $b^2 - 4ac = 25 - 4(1)(3) = 25 - 12 = 13$, so (A) is the correct answer.

2. The correct answer is (B). Use the quadratic formula to solve for x, and don't forget to simplify the radical expression:

$$x = \frac{-b \pm \sqrt{b^2 - 4ac}}{2a}$$

$$x = \frac{-12 \pm \sqrt{12^2 - 4(1)(12)}}{2(1)}$$

$$x = \frac{-12 \pm \sqrt{144 - 48}}{2}$$

$$x = -6 \pm \frac{\sqrt{96}}{2}$$

$$x = -6 \pm \frac{\sqrt{16 \times 6}}{2}$$

$$x = -6 \pm \frac{4\sqrt{6}}{2}$$

$$x = -6 \pm 2\sqrt{6}$$

3. The correct answer is (C). To transform an equation in standard form to one in vertex form, you must complete the square. To do so, determine what constant could be added to the first two terms of the polynomial to create a perfect square. In most cases, it's the square of half of the second coefficient. In other words, half of 22 is 11, so $11^2 = 121$ would be the constant needed to complete the square. Add this to both sides of the equation, rewrite your new trinomial as a perfect square, and isolate y to get the equation into vertex form:

$$y + 121 = (x^2 + 22x + 12)1 + 10$$

$$y + 121 = (x + 11)^2 + 10$$

$$y = (x + 11)^2 - 111$$

From here, you can see that $k = -111$ and $h = -11$, so– $11 - (-111) = 100$.

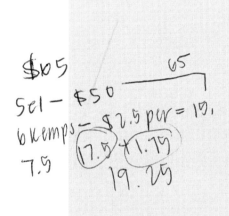

Playdon

$105
Sel – $50   65
6 kemps – $2.5 per = 10,
7.5   (7.5 + 1.75)
        19.25

this is the skin of a killer, bella

4. The correct answer is (C). Use the quadratic formula to solve for x, and then use your calculator to approximate the value:

$$x = \frac{-b \pm \sqrt{b^2 - 4ac}}{2a}$$

$$x = \frac{2 \pm \sqrt{(-2)^2 - 4(3)(-7)}}{2(3)}$$

$$x = \frac{2 \pm \sqrt{88}}{6}$$

$$x \approx 1.89 \text{ or } -1.23$$

5. The correct answer is (A). First, rewrite the equation in standard form: $2x^2 + x - 8 = 0$. Then, use the quadratic formula and simplify:

$$x = \frac{-b \pm \sqrt{b^2 - 4ac}}{2a}$$

$$x = \frac{-1 \pm \sqrt{1^2 - 4(2)(-8)}}{2(2)}$$

$$x = \frac{-1 \pm \sqrt{65}}{4}$$

$$x = -\frac{1}{4} \pm \frac{\sqrt{65}}{4}$$

Create and Use Nonlinear Functions
Part 13

These problems ask you to create and use quadratic or exponential functions to solve problems in a variety of contexts or model a relationship between quantities.

DIRECTIONS

Select the best answer among four choices and circle the corresponding letter or record it on a separate sheet of paper.

NOTES

1. You may use a calculator, but not all problems require the use of a calculator.
2. Variables and expressions represent real numbers unless stated otherwise.
3. Figures are drawn to scale unless stated otherwise.
4. Figures lie in a plane unless stated otherwise.
5. The domain of a function f is defined as the set of all real numbers x for which $f(x)$ is also a real number, unless stated otherwise.

1

Jim wants to add a frame to a square photograph. If the photograph has side lengths of x inches and the frame that surrounds the photograph is 2 inches wide, what is the area of the framed photograph in terms of x?

A) x^2

B) $x^2 + 4x + 4$

C) $x^2 + 8x - 4$

D) $x^2 + 8x + 16$

2

In a classroom, individual desks are arranged in a rectangular formation with x rows of desks and y columns of desks before a test. If 4 extra rows of desks are added and the number of columns is always double the number of rows, how many desks are there in total, in terms of x?

A) $2x^2$

B) $2x^2 + 8x$

C) $2x^2 + 12x + 16$

D) $2x^2 + 16x + 32$

A company is analyzing the cost of extracting a rare metal from a mining site. They find that the cost can be modeled as an exponential function with an initial set-up cost of $50,000. If the total cost triples for every 500 grams of metal extracted, which of the following functions represents the total cost, C, in terms of the number of kilograms of metal extracted, k?

A) $C(k) = 50{,}000(2)^{3k}$

B) $C(k) = 50{,}000(2)^{500k}$

C) $C(k) = 50{,}000(3)^{2k}$

D) $C(k) = 50{,}000(3)^{0.5k}$

When a movie theatre sells tickets for $14 each, 200 people will buy tickets to any given show. For each dollar increase in ticket price, the number of customers who will attend decreases by 7. Which of the following is an expression for revenue, if x is the number of times the ticket price is increased by one dollar?

A) $(14 + x)(200 - 7x)$

B) $(14 + x)(200 - x)$

C) $(14 - x)(200 + 7x)$

D) $2{,}800x$

The population of a town doubles every two years. If the town had an initial population of 5,000 people in 1950, which of the following functions represents the population, P, in terms of the number of years since 1950, y?

A) $P(y) = 5000(2)^{y}$

B) $P(y) = 5000(2)^{2y}$

C) $P(y) = 5000(2)^{\frac{1}{2}y}$

D) $P(y) = 5000\left(\dfrac{1}{2}\right)^{2y}$

Answers and Explanations

1.   The answer is (D). Since the frame has a width of 2 inches, the length becomes $x + 4$ as 2 inches are added on both ends of a side. You can then calculate the area by using the expression $(x + 4)(x + 4)$, which is equal to $x^2 + 8x + 16$.

2.   The correct answer is (D). When 4 extra rows are added you get a rectangular formation with $(x + 4)$ rows. Since there are always 2 times more columns than there are rows, there are $2(x + 4)$ columns. To get the number of desks, multiply rows $(x + 4)$ by columns $(2x + 8)$ to get $2x^2 + 16x + 32$.

3.   The correct answer is (C). Since the initial set-up cost is \$50,000, the cost of extracting 0 kg of metal will be \$50,000. This cost will be multiplied by a factor of 3 for every 500g or 0.5 kg of metal extracted, so you want a base of 3 for the power. The exponent must be equal to 1 for 0.5 kg of metal, which is the case when the exponent is $2k$. The function that models this correctly is (C), which shows that the cost triples for every 0.5 kg of metal extracted. If you chose (D), you probably divided the exponent by 2 instead of multiplying it by 2, which would make the cost triple for every 2.0 kg of metal instead of every 0.5 kg.

4.   The correct answer is (A). This question is asking you to write an expression for the amount of money the theatre makes. Normally the theatre makes \$14 × 200 customers = \$2,800, but you need to modify both the ticket price and the number of customers in terms of x. For each dollar increase in ticket price, $14 + x$, the number of people decreases by seven, $200 - 7x$. Therefore, the revenue of the theatre is equal to the ticket price times the number of customers: $(14 - x)(200 - 7x)$.

5.   The correct answer is (C). To answer this question, you should be familiar with the structure of exponential functions, and how they are used in word problems. An exponential function is in the form $f(x) = a\,(r)^{tx}$, where a is the starting value, r is the rate of growth, and t is the number of growth cycles that occur within one time frame, or one unit of x.

The initial population is 5000, so $a = 5000$. Since the population doubles, its rate of growth, r, is 2. The population of the town doubles every two years. This means that only $\frac{1}{2}$ of a growth cycle takes place each year. The only answer choice that correctly identifies all of these components is (C).

If you chose (B), you probably confused the phrase "every two years" with "occurring twice a year" and setting t equal to 2, not $\frac{1}{2}$.

10 ingredients

Atonement
Interstellar
Project X
Lolita
Breakfast at Tiffany's
Gone with the wind

Nonlinear Function Notation

Part 14

These problems ask you to use function notation for a quadratic, polynomial, exponential, or rational function to represent and interpret input/output pairs and points on the graph.

DIRECTIONS

Select the best answer among four choices and circle the corresponding letter or record it on a separate sheet of paper.

NOTES

1. You may use a calculator, but not all problems require the use of a calculator.
2. Variables and expressions represent real numbers unless stated otherwise.
3. Figures are drawn to scale unless stated otherwise.
4. Figures lie in a plane unless stated otherwise.
5. The domain of a function f is defined as the set of all real numbers x for which $f(x)$ is also a real number, unless stated otherwise.

1

If $h(x) = 5x^2 - 17x + 14$, what is the value of $h(4)$?

A) -14

B) -1

C) 19

D) 26

2

If the function $f(x) = 2x^3$, what is the value of $f(-2)$?

A) -16

B) -8

C) 16

D) 64

3

If $f(x) = 12x + x^2$ and $g(x) = \sqrt{x+2}$, what is the value of $f(g(7))$?

A) 117

B) 45

C) 42

D) $12\sqrt{5} + 5$

$\sqrt{7+2} = \sqrt{9} = 3$

$12(3) + 3^2$

$36 + 9 = 45$

4

If $f(x) = \sqrt{x} + 4x$ and $h(x) = 9x$, which of the following expressions is equivalent to $f(h(x))$?

A) $3\sqrt{x} + 4x$

B) $9\sqrt{x} + 4x$

C) $3\sqrt{x} + 36x$

D) $9\sqrt{x} + 36x$

$\sqrt{9x} + 4x$

$3\sqrt{x} + 4(9x)$

$36x$

5

Which of the following is not a graph of a function?

A)

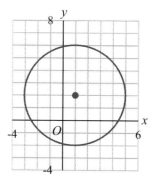

B)

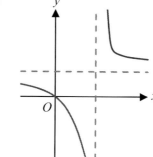

C)

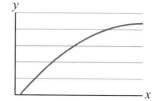

D)

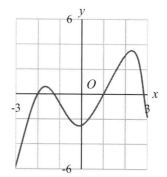

6

Which of the following is not an equation of a function?

A) $y = x^5 - 3x^3 + \dfrac{1}{2}x^2 - 19$

B) $y = 13(3^x)$

C) $(x - 12)^2 + (y + 5)^2 = 25$

D) $y = \dfrac{x^2 - 13x + 3}{x - 1}$

8

Given a function $f(x) = 3x^2 + x - 1$, what is the output when the input is 4?

A) 4

B) 48

C) 51

D) 52

7

The distance of a particle from a detector device, in meters, is given by the function $f(x) = 5x^2 - 13x + 1.3$, where x is the number of seconds elapsed. This function is used to predict the distance at any time x. What is the distance of the particle from the detector, in meters, when $x = 3$?

A) −7.7

B) 7.3

C) 8.8

D) 9.3

Answers and Explanations

1. The correct answer is (D). To solve this question, simply substitute $x = 4$ into the function and solve:

$$h(4) = 5(4)^2 - 17(4) + 14$$
$$= 5(16) - 68 + 14$$
$$= 60 - 68 + 14$$
$$= 26$$

2. The correct answer is (A). If you plug in -2 for x into the function, you get $f(-2) = 2 \times (-2)^3 = 2 \times (-8)$, which simplifies to -16.

3. The correct answer is (B). To solve this question, first find the value of $g(7) = \sqrt{7+2} = \sqrt{9} = 3$. Then, substitute this value into $f(x)$ to get $f(x) = 12(3) + 3^2 = 36 + 9 = 45$.

4. The correct answer is (C). This is a composite functions question. To solve for $f(h(x))$, substitute $h(x)$ into $f(x)$ and simplify the expression:

$$f(9x) = \sqrt{9x} + 4(9x)$$
$$= 3\sqrt{x} + 36x$$

5. The correct answer is (A). A function must have only one output value, or y-value, for every input value, or x-value in its domain. (B), (C), and (D) each have a single output for every input. (A), a circle, has input values for which there are two output values.

6. The correct answer is (C). A function must have only one output value, or y-value, for every input value, or x-value in its domain. (A) is a polynomial to the fifth power, (B) is an exponential function, and (D) is a rational function. Each of these functions have a single output for every input within its domain. (C) represents the equation of a circle, which has at least one input for which there are two output values.

7. The correct answer is (B). To find the distance of the particle from the detector at 3 seconds, substitute $x = 3$ into the function.

$$f(3) = 5(3)^2 - 13(3) + 1.3$$
$$f(3) = 5(9) - 39 + 1.3$$
$$f(3) = 45 - 39 + 1.3$$
$$f(3) = 7.3$$

8. The correct answer is (C). To solve this function, you should recognize that solving for an input value is the same as substituting that input value into the function and solving.

$$f(4) = 3(4)^2 + 4 - 1$$
$$= 3(16) + 4 - 1$$
$$= 48 + 4 - 1$$
$$= 51$$

Interpret Nonlinear Functions
Part 15

These problems ask you to interpret the meaning of an input/output pair, constant, variable, factor, or term of a quadratic or exponential function that represents a context.

1

The height, in feet, of a rocket launched in the air is given by the function $h(x) = -x^2 + 50x + 25$, where x is the number of seconds after the launch. What is the increase in the rocket's height, in feet, between 10 and 20 seconds after the launch?

A) 425

B) 200

C) 150

D) 25

2

The amount of money in Aaron's bank account can be modeled by the function $m(y) = 1{,}300 \times 1.02^y$, where y is the number of years his account has been open. What does the number 1.02 represent in this function?

A) Aaron earns 2% interest per year.

B) Aaron earns 0.02% interest per year.

C) Aaron earns 1.02% interest per year.

D) Aaron had $1.02 in his account when it opened.

If the population of trout in a pond can be modeled by the function $n(t) = 250 \times 0.9^{\frac{1}{2}t}$, where t is the number of years that trout have been in the pond, which of the following is a correct statement about the equation?

A) The number of trout in the pond halves every year.

B) The number of trout in the pond halves every 6 months.

C) The number of trout in the pond decreases by 10% every 6 months.

D) The number of trout in the pond decreases by 10% every 2 years.

Cynthia is investigating the growth of a colony of bacteria in her lab. She suspects that the colony multiplies at an exponential rate. She models its growth through the function $b(x) = 40(3)^{2x}$, where x is the number of days elapsed. What does the number 2 represent in this function?

A) The original population of the colony

B) The number of days it takes the population to triple in size

C) The number of days elapsed when the researcher determined the function

D) The number of times per day the colony grows by the growth factor of 3

A company records the number of entries to a contest. By the end of the first day, they had received 100 entries. By tracking the number of entries per day for a week, they found that the number of entries doubled every day. If the company models this information as the exponential equation $f(x) = a(r)^{bx}$, what would be the value of b?

A) 1

B) 2

C) 7

D) 100

Answers and Explanations

1. The correct answer is (B). First, find the rocket's height at 10 seconds and the rocket's height at 20 seconds. At those two points in time, $x = 10$ and $x = 20$ respectively:

$$h(x) = -(10)^2 + 50(10) + 25 \qquad\qquad h(x) = -(20)^2 + 50(20) + 25$$
$$h(x) = -100 + 500 + 25 \qquad\qquad h(x) = -400 + 1000 + 25$$
$$h(x) = 425 \qquad\qquad\qquad h(x) = 625$$

   If the height at 20 seconds is 625 feet and the height at 10 seconds is 425 feet, the increase between the two is $625 - 425 = 200$ feet.

2. The correct answer is (A). To increase a value by a percentage, you multiply that value by 1 plus the percentage you want to increase by. So, if Aaron has 2% (or $\frac{2}{100}$) interest per year, each year he can calculate his new balance by multiplying the old balance by $1 + \frac{2}{100}$, or 1.02.

3. The correct answer is (D). To decrease a value by a percentage, multiply that value by 1 minus the percentage you want to decrease by. Since the initial value is being multiplied by 0.9 every period of time, and $0.9 = 1 - 0.1$, you know that the trout decrease by 10% in each unit of time, eliminating answers (A) and (B).

   To see how often the population decreases, you can look at the exponent of 0.9. The first time the population decreases by 10%, the initial population must be multiplied by 0.9, which is equivalent to 0.9^1. For the exponent to equal 1, t would have to equal 2: $0.9^{\frac{1}{2}(2)} = 0.9^1$. So, the population decreases by 10% every 2 years.

4. The correct answer is (D). An exponential function is in the form $f(x) = a\,(r)^{tx}$, where a is the starting value, r is the rate of growth, and t is the number of growth cycles that occur within one time frame, or one unit of x. Since $t = 2$, the population of the colony must triple two times every day.

5. The correct answer is (A). An exponential function is in the form $f(x) = a\,(r)^{bx}$, where a is the starting value, r is the rate of growth, and t is the number of growth cycles that occur within one time frame, or one unit of x. Since the number of entries doubles once every day, $b = 1$.

   If you chose (B), you probably confused the rate of increase with the frequency of increase.

Suitable Forms of Nonlinear Functions
Part 16

These problems ask you to determine the most suitable form of a quadratic or exponential function to display key features of the context such as initial value, extreme values, zeroes, or doubling time.

1

In xy-coordinate space, what is the x-coordinate of the vertex of the parabola given by $y = -x^2 + 6x - 4$?

A) 3

B) -3

C) 2

D) -2

2

Leslie models the amount of money in her bank account with the function

$f(y) = (25)(1.02^y)(1.1^{2y+1})$. If y represents the number of years since Leslie opened the account, how much money, to the nearest cent, did Leslie have in the account when she opened it?

A) $25.00

B) $26.00

C) $27.50

D) $28.05

3

Given all the following equivalent quadratic equations, which form most clearly displays the least possible value of y?

A) $y = 2(x + 1)(x + 5)$

B) $y = 2x^2 + 12x + 10$

C) $y = 2(x + 3)^2 - 8$

D) $y = 2(x + 6x + 5)$

4

Zia writes a quadratic expression to represent the trajectory of her baseball as she throws it from the third floor window. Which form should she choose to most clearly convey the height of the window?

A) $h(t) = -2(8t^2 - 11t - 15)$

B) $h(t) = -16t^2 + 22t + 30$

C) $h(t) = -(16t^2 - 22t - 30)$

D) $h(t) = 2(t(11 - 8t) + 15)$

5

The profits of a large company can be modelled using a quadratic equation where y represents profits in millions of dollars. Which form best shows the points at which the company breaks even in profits, neither gaining nor losing money?

A) $y = -x^2 - 8x - 12)$

B) $y = -(x + 2)(x + 6)$

C) $y = -(x^2 + 8x + 12)$

D) $y = -(x + 4)^2 + 4$

6

Which of the following quadratic equations most clearly displays the x-value at which the graph of the equation is symmetrical?

A) $y = x^2 + 3x - 18$

B) $y = 2(x - 7)(x + 13)$

C) $y = 3(x - 2)^2 + 10$

D) $y = 3x(x - 2) + 6$

Answers and Explanations

1. The correct answer is (A). Since this question asks about the coordinates of the vertex of the parabola, it'll be helpful to get the equation into vertex form. To do this, start by factoring out -1. Then, complete the square by taking half of the second coefficient, squaring it, and adding the result to both sides of the equation (remember to account for the negative number you factored out). Finally, simplify:

$$y = -x^2 + 6x - 4$$

$$y = -(x^2 - 6x) - 4)$$

$$y + (-9) = -(x^2 - 6x + 9) - 4$$

$$y - 9 = -(x - 3)^2 - 4$$

$$y = -(x - 3)^2 + 5$$

Since vertex form is $y = a(x - h)^2 + k$ where (h, k) is the vertex, you know that the x-coordinate of the vertex is 3.

2. The correct answer is (C). This is a tricky question, because while normally the initial value in an exponential equation is the first coefficient, this equation does not adhere to the normal form. You can determine the initial amount of money in the account by plugging in $y = 0$.

$$f(t) = 25 \times 1.02^0 \times 1.1^{2(0) + 1}$$

$$f(t) = 25 \times 1 \times 1.1^1$$

$$f(t) = 25 \times 1.1 = 27.5$$

Notice that the second term still has an exponent of 1 when the account was opened. So, there was initially $27.50 in the account.

3. The correct answer is (C). The least possible value of y in an upward facing parabola is the y-value of the vertex. Since option (C) is in vertex form, it clearly shows that y-coordinate of the vertex is -8, so that is the least possible value of y.

4. The correct answer is (B). The initial height of the baseball is the height when no time has passed, or $t = 0$. In the standard form of a quadratic equation, $y = ax^2 + bx + c$, this initial height is equal to c. The only equation in this standard form is (B).

5. The correct answer is (B). The point where the company neither gains nor loses money must be where the profits are exactly 0. If the profits are represented on the y-axis, this means that the x-intercepts (in other words, the solutions) of the quadratic expression are where they break even. In factored form, the two x-intercepts are clearly visible as -2 and -6, so (B) is correct.

6. The correct answer is (C). A quadratic equation is symmetrical about the vertical line that passes through its vertex. Therefore, in knowing the x-coordinate of the vertex of a graph, you also know the line of symmetry for that quadratic graph. Since (C) is the only one of these equations in vertex form $y = a(x - h)^2 + k$, it is the only answer that clearly shows the line of symmetry—in this case, x = 2.

Graphs and Tables of Nonlinear Functions
Part 17

These problems ask you to make connections between tabular, algebraic, and graphical representations of quadratic, polynomial, exponential, or rational functions.

DIRECTIONS

Select the best answer among four choices and circle the corresponding letter or record it on a separate sheet of paper.

NOTES

1. You may use a calculator, but not all problems require the use of a calculator.
2. Variables and expressions represent real numbers unless stated otherwise.
3. Figures are drawn to scale unless stated otherwise.
4. Figures lie in a plane unless stated otherwise.
5. The domain of a function f is defined as the set of all real numbers x for which $f(x)$ is also a real number, unless stated otherwise.

1

The graphs of $f(x)$ and $g(x)$ are shown on the xy-coordinate plane to the right. Which of the following translations would transform the graph of $f(x)$ into the graph of $g(x)$?

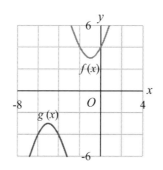

A) Reflection across the y-axis, then translation 4 units to the right

B) Reflection across the y-axis, then translation 4 units to the left

C) Reflection across the x-axis, then translation 4 units to the right

D) Reflection across the x-axis, then translation 4 units to the left

2

The functions $g(x) = x^2$ and $f(x) = x - 1$ are graphed below. For all x-values, what is the distance between the two y-values of the curves?

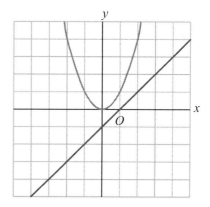

A) $x^2 - x - 1$

B) $x^2 - x + 1$

C) $x - 1 - x^2$

D) x^2

3

A quadratic function has the form $y = a(x - 1)(x - 7)$, where a is a non-zero constant. If the vertex of the parabola is located at point (c, d), what is the value of c?

A) 3

B) 4

C) 5

D) 6

4

If $c = 2$ and $b = -3$, which of the following graphs represents the equation $y = (x - b)^2 + c$?

A)

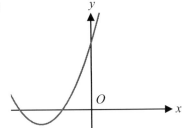

B)

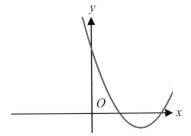

C)

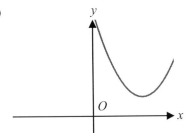

D)

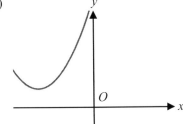

5

The graph below represents the function $q(x)$ after it was reflected about the x-axis and translated up 3 units. Which of the following graphs represents the original function $q(x)$?

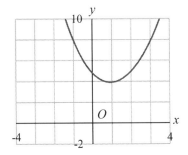

A)

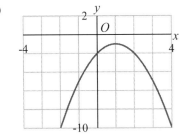

B)

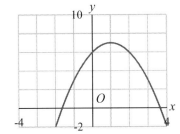

C)

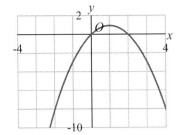

D)

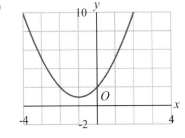

6

If the equation of the graph shown below is written in the form $y = a(x - b)(x - c)$, what is the sum of b and c?

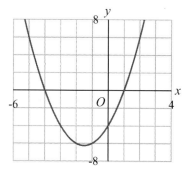

A) −4

B) −3

C) 3

D) 5

7

The graph below represents the function $g(x) = a(x - b)^2 + c$. The graph of the function $f(x) = x^2$ is also shown below. Which of the following must be true about $g(x)$?

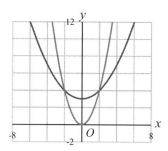

A) $a > c$

B) $a < c$

C) $a < b$

D) $b > c$

8

If the function $f(x) = (x + 4)^2 - 3$ is translated 3 units to the left, what is the equation of the new function?

A) $f(x) = (x + 4)^2 - 6$

B) $f(x) = (x + 1)^2 - 3$

C) $f(x) = (x + 7)^2 - 3$

D) $f(x) = (x + 4)^2$

1941

9

The function $h(x)$ is translated 7 units left and 4 units down, resulting in the new function

$$g(x) = \tfrac{1}{2}(x - 1)^2 + 5 \quad + 4$$

What is the equation of the original function $h(x)$?

A) $h(x) = \dfrac{1}{2}(x + 6)^2 + 5$

B) $h(x) = \dfrac{1}{2}(x - 8)^2 + 5$

C) $h(x) = \dfrac{1}{2}(x + 6)^2 + 9$

D) $h(x) = \dfrac{1}{2}(x - 8)^2 + 9$

$(-6, 9)$

10

At what x-value is the function represented by the graph below undefined?

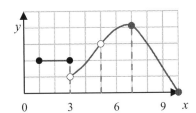

A) 0

B) 3

C) 5

D) 7

11

At which of the following values of x does the function below exist?

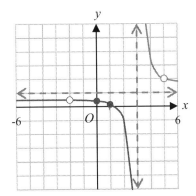

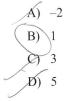

A) −2

B) 1

C) 3

D) 5

12

A parabola is concave up and has a vertex at $(3, 5)$. What is the range of the function?

g-axis

A) $y \leq 3$

B) $y \geq 3$

C) $y \leq 5$

D) $y \geq 5$

13

Which of the following equations represents the parabola shown in the xy-plane below?

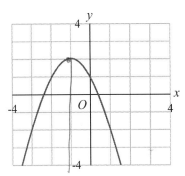

A) $y = -(x + 1)^2 + 2$

B) $y = -(x - 1)^2 + 2$

C) $y = -(x - 1)^2 - 2$

D) $y = (x + 1)^2 + 2$

Answers and Explanations

1. The correct answer is (D). In order to get from $f(x)$ to $g(x)$, the first step is to reflect $f(x)$ across the x-axis so that the parabola is now concave down. Knowing this, you can eliminate (A) and (B). Then, since $g(x)$ is to the left of $f(x)$, the parabola must be translated to the left. Of the remaining choices (C) and (D), (D) is the only choice that describes a translation to the left.

2. The correct answer is (B). From the given graph, you can see that the parabola, $g(x)$, has larger outputs for each input than the line, $f(x)$. Therefore, the positive distance between their y values is equal to $g(x) - f(x)$, or $x^2 - (x - 1) = x^2 - x + 1$.

   If you chose (A), you forgot to flip the sign on the -1. If you chose (C), you did $f(x) - g(x)$ instead.

3. The correct answer is (A). The equation of the quadratic function gives the points at which it intersects the x-axis, or the zeroes of the function: (0, 1) and (0, 7). For a quadratic function, the x-coordinate of the vertex is the midpoint between the values of the zeroes. To find this x-coordinate, use the midpoint formula: $\frac{7-1}{2} = \frac{6}{2} = 3$. Therefore, the x-coordinate of the vertex, or the value of c, is 3.

4. The correct answer is (D). If you substitute $c = 2$ and $b = -3$ into the equation, you get $y = (x + 3)^2 + 2$. The $+2$ translates the function $y = x^2$ upward 2 units. This eliminates (A) and (B). The $(x + 3)$ translates the function 3 units to the left. (D) is the only graph that correctly represents both translations.

5. The correct answer is (A). Since the answers to this question are given in graphical form, it may be easiest to solve this question using process of elimination. Visualize the reflections for choices (A), (B), (C), and (D).

   - The final graph was reflected about the x-axis, so you know that the original graph must be concave down. This eliminates (D).
   - When (B) is reflected, the resulting graph is far below the x-axis. A translation of 3 units up would not bring the graph as high up as $q(x)$.
   - When (C) is reflected, the resulting graph is below the x-axis and a translation of 3 units up will only bring the graph 2 units above the x-axis.
   - When (A) is reflected, the resulting graph is 1 unit above the x-axis and a translation of 3 units up will bring the graph 4 units above the x-axis, exactly like the final graph of $q(x)$.

6. The correct answer is (B). The values of b and c are the x-intercepts of the parabola. Looking at the graph, you can see that the parabola intercepts the x-axis at $x = -4$ and $x = 1$. The sum of these two values is -3.

7. The correct answer is (B). To solve this question, first find the values of all the constants of $g(x)$.

    - Since $g(x)$ is translated up vertically by 3 units, you know that $c = 3$.
    - Since the x-coordinate of the vertex is at 0, you know that $g(x)$ was not translated horizontally, so $b = 0$.
    - Since the parabola is flatter than the base parabola, you know that the value of a must be between 0 and 1.

    The only inequality that is true for these values is $a < c$.

    - $a > c$ is false; if this were true, $g(x)$ would be narrower than the base parabola.
    - $a < b$ is false; a must be greater than 0.
    - $b > c$ is false; $b = 0$ and $c > 0$.

8. The correct answer is (C). To solve this question, remember that a horizontal translation of a units is represented in an equation as $(x + a)$. A positive value of a moves the function to the left, so to move the equation 3 units to the left, add 3 to $(x + 4)$ to get $(x + 7)$, which is used correctly by the function in (C).

    If you chose (B), you probably translated the function to the right instead of the left or forgot that a translation to the left is represented with a positive value of a instead of a negative value.

9. The correct answer is (D). To answer this question, reverse the translations that were applied to get the new function $g(x)$. Since $g(x)$ is the result of a translation 4 units down, reverse this translation by adding 4 units to the constant "5" to get "+ 9". This eliminates (A) and (B). Since $g(x)$ is the result of a translation 7 units left, reverse this translation by subtracting 7 units from the argument to get $(x - 8)^2$. The only function $h(x)$ that correctly combines both of these reversed translations is (D). If you chose (C), you probably translated the function 7 units left, instead of right.

10. The correct answer is (C). The graph is undefined for any input value that does not have an output value, or any value of x for which the function does not exist. An open hole means that the function does not exist at that x-value. Be sure to look at the function carefully: at $x = 3$, although there is an open hole, there is a closed hole above it which means that the function does exist at $x = 3$.

11. The correct answer is (B). The function does not exist at $x = -2$ and $x = 5$ because the function has open holes at those x-values, indicating that there is no corresponding y-value. The function does not exist at $x = 3$, where there is a vertical asymptote. The function does exist at $x = 1$.

12. The correct answer is (D). Since the parabola is concave up, the range of the function will be greater than the lowest point of the parabola, or its vertex. Since the vertex is at $(3, 5)$, the minimum y-value is 5, which means that the range of the function is any y-value greater than or equal to 5, or $y \geq 5$.

13. The correct answer is (A). The vertex of the parabola shown is $(-1, 2)$. The vertex of a parabola can be found from its equation in vertex form, as a parabola with a vertex at (h, k) will have an equation of the form $y = a(x - h)^2 + k$. Plugging in -1 for h and 2 for k, you will get the equation $y = a(x + 1)^2 + 2$. Since the parabola is pointing down, you know that a must be negative, so the equation is $y = -(x + 1)^2 + 2$.

Additional Topics
Chapter 5

Chapter 5
Additional Topics

While "Additional Topics" sounds like a kind of catch-all title for a very broad domain, so you might expect it to contain a diverse array of specific topics. However, questions in this domain mostly just test your geometry and trigonometry skills. That's still quite a lot of content to cover, though: you'll need to solve problems relating to the areas and volumes of flat and solid figures, apply geometric theorems, and solve a variety of trigonometry problems involving both triangles and circles. You'll also need to perform simple calculations with complex numbers—i.e., terms including the imaginary number i.

There are 15 specific question types in this domain:

Additional Topics			
A1	Scale Factors of Figures	A9	Similar Triangle Trigonometry
A2	Area and Volume Formulae	A10	Trig Ratios of Complementary Angles
A3	Triangle Theorems and Similarity	A11	Circle Theorems and Properties
A4	Assess Conditions for Relationships or Theorems	A12	Radians and Degrees
A5	Scaling Triangles	A13	Unit Circle Trigonometry
A6	Angle and Line Theorems	A14	Equations of Circles
A7	The Pythagorean Theorem	A15	Complex Numbers
A8	Right Triangle Trigonometry		

Scale Factors of Figures
Part 1

These problems ask you to apply the idea that changing a geometric figure by a scale factor of k changes all lengths by a factor of k, changes all areas by a factor of k^2, and changes all volumes by a factor of k^3.

1

If a circle's radius is doubled, what is the effect on the circumference of the circle?

A) It stays the same.
B) It is doubled.
C) It increases by a factor of 4.
D) It increases by a factor of 8.

2

Habib moves from one apartment to another. The length and width of his new apartment are 1.5 times the length and width of his old one, respectively. His new apartment is how many times as big as his old apartment?

A) 1.5
B) 2.25
C) 3
D) 3.25

A scale model of a room is built so that its dimensions are 1/12 the dimensions of the actual room. If the actual area of the room is 8064 square inches, what is the area of the model, in inches?

A) 14

B) 56

C) 672

D) 968

Faduma is using a small box with a volume of 2 cubic feet as a model for building a large trunk. To make a proportional trunk that will have a volume of 54 cubic feet, how many times longer should the trunk's length, width, and height be?

A) 3

B) 9

C) 13

D) 27

$54 = 9 \cdot 6 = 3 \cdot 3 \cdot 3 \cdot 2$

$3x$

y

If a rectangle with sides $12x$ and $4y$ has an area of 336, what is the area of the rectangle above?

A) 16

B) 21

C) 84

D) 112

$12 \times 4y = 336$

Answers and Explanations

1. The correct answer is (B). The formula for a circle's circumference is $c = 2\pi r$, so if the radius is doubled, the new circumference will be $2\pi(2r) = 4\pi r$. You can see that this new expression is equal to $2c$, or double the circumference of the original circle.

2. The correct answer is (B). The formula for the area of a rectangle is $h \times w$, so if both the height and width increase by a factor of 1.5, the new area will be $1.5h \times 1.5w$, or $2.25hw$.

3. The correct answer is (B). The formula for the area of a rectangle is $h \times w$, so if both the height and width are multiplied by a factor of $\frac{1}{12}$, then the new area will be $\frac{1}{12}h \times \frac{1}{12}w$, or $\frac{1}{144}hw$. Since in the original room $hw = 8064$, you can plug 8064 in for hw in the new equation: $\frac{1}{144}(8064) = 56$, so (B) is correct.

4. The correct answer is (A). Since you know that the volume of a box is equal to its length, width, and height multiplied together, you can write the equation $l \times w \times h = 2$ to describe the original box. The new box has a volume of 54, and the length, width, and height are all greater by the same proportion, so you can write a similar expression using "x" as the unknown proportion: $xl \times xw \times xh = 54$. Now, by factoring out x and rewriting in terms of $l \times w \times h$, you can set these equations equal to one another:

    $$l \times w \times h = 2$$
    $$lwh = 2$$

    $$xl \times xw \times xh =$$
    $$x^3 lwh = 54$$

    $$lwh = \frac{54}{x^3}$$
    $$2 = \frac{54}{x^3}$$
    $$2x^3 = 54$$
    $$x^3 = 27$$
    $$x = 3$$

    Therefore, the proportion that each side needs to be multiplied by is 3.

5. The correct answer is (B). The formula for the area of a rectangle is $l \times w = a$, where l and w are the length and width. The rectangle given in the text has sides 12x and 4y, so its area is $12x \times 4y = 336$. The rectangle in the image's area is $3x \times y$. You might notice that the second equation seems to be the original equation divided by 4, but don't be confused: x and y are not separate terms being added together, they are the same term being multiplied together. Both formulas can be simplified: $48xy = 336$ and $3xy = a$. Now, you can see that the second equation is the first divided by 16, $\frac{336}{16} = 21$, which is the area of the rectangle in the image.

Area and Volume Formulae

Part 2

These problems as you to select the correct area or volume formula and calculate a specified value.

DIRECTIONS

Select the best answer among four choices and circle the corresponding letter or record it on a separate sheet of paper.

NOTES

1. You may use a calculator, but not all problems require the use of a calculator.
2. Variables and expressions represent real numbers unless stated otherwise.
3. Figures are drawn to scale unless stated otherwise.
4. Figures lie in a plane unless stated otherwise.
5. The domain of a function f is defined as the set of all real numbers x for which $f(x)$ is also a real number, unless stated otherwise.

1

A cylinder with a diameter of 4 inches and a height of 8 inches has a mass of 53 grams. If a second cylinder with a diameter of 8 inches is made of the same material, for which of the following heights of this second cylinder, in inches, would the two cylinders have the same mass?

(Note: density = mass / volume)

A) 2

B) 4

C) 6

D) 8

2

Peter buys wallpaper in square sheets with sides that are 2 m long and cuts them up so that he can use every piece of wallpaper he buys to cover his walls, without overlap. If he covers four walls, each 7 m wide and 3 m high, how many sheets does he need?

A) 6

B) 21

C) 28

D) 32

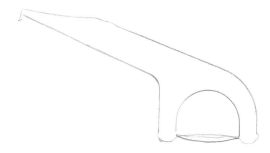

3

What is the sum of the areas of the rectangles shown in the figure below?

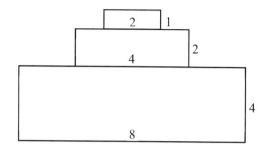

A) 21

B) 30

C) 38

D) 42

4

What is the area of the rectangle below if $x = 7$?

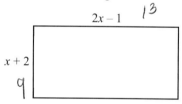

A) 54

B) 117

C) 130

D) 135

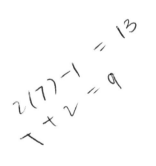

5

The figure below shows a rectangle and two squares. What is the area of the shape?

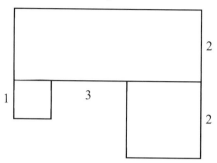

A) 13

B) 16

C) 17

D) 20

6

The figure below is made up of a square, two identical rectangles, and two identical isosceles right triangles. The hypotenuse of each triangle has a length of $\sqrt{2}$ cm, and the long side of each rectangle is twice the length of each shorter side.

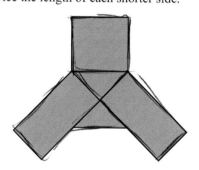

What is the area of the entire shape?

A) 7 cm^2

B) $6 + \sqrt{2}$ cm^2

C) $7 + \sqrt{2}$ cm^2

D) 8 cm^2

The figure below shows a right triangle that shares two of its sides with different rectangles. If each of the rectangles has an area of 3, what is the area of the given triangle?

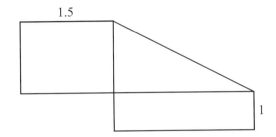

A) 0.75

B) 3

C) 5

D) 6

8

The rectangle shown below is made up of isosceles right triangles with two side lengths equal to 1.5 cm. What is the area of the rectangle?

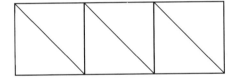

A) 4 cm^2

B) 6 cm^2

C) 6.75 cm^2

D) 8.25 cm^2

Huberto has two square cards that each have an area of 64 cm^2. He folds the first card in half along the diagonal to get a right triangle. He then attaches the second card to the hypotenuse of the triangle formed by the first card, without any overlap. What is the area of the shape Hubert creates?

A) 64 cm^2

B) 81 cm^2

C) 96 cm^2

D) 128 cm^2

10

The surface area of a cone is given by the formula $A = \pi r(r + s)$, where r is the radius and s is the slant height. A cone with the slant height of 4 cm is stacked on top of a cylinder with a height of 4 cm, as shown in the diagram below. The cone and the cylinder both have a radius of 6 cm. What is the outside surface area of the object?

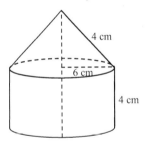

A) 64π cm^2

B) 96π cm^2

C) 108π cm^2

D) 576π cm^2

11

A swimming pool is 4 meters deep, with a length of 10 m and a width of 5 m. If the pool fills up to 3.7 m deep, how much water is in the pool, in m^3?

A) 150

B) 185

C) 190

D) 200

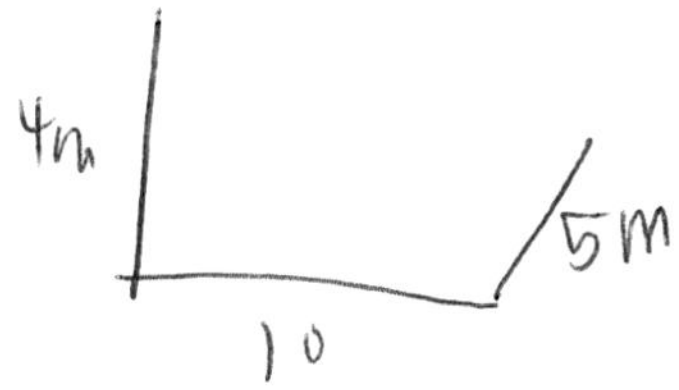

12

A farmer is laying down a 34 m long rope to enclose an area as the future pen for her hens. What is the largest area, to the nearest square meter, that she will be able to enclose?

A) 60

B) 72

C) 92

D) 108

13

If a rectangle's length is increased by 40% and its width is decreased by 40%, what is the effect on the area of the rectangle?

A) It is increased by 96%.

B) It remains unchanged.

C) It is decreased by 64%.

D) It is decreased by 16%.

Answers and Explanations

1. The correct answer is (A). First, you should recognize that since the two cylinders are made from the same material, they will have the same density. Additionally, since the cylinders have the same mass, they will have equal volumes, so the particular mass doesn't matter. The first cylinder has a radius of $\frac{4}{2} = 2$ inches and a height of 8 inches, so its volume is $2^2(8)\pi = 32\pi$ "cubic inches. The second cylinder has a radius of $\frac{8}{2} = 4$ inches and an unknown height, h, so its volume is $4^2 h\pi = 16\pi h$ cubic inches. To find h, you can set these two volumes equal to each other and solve: $32\pi = 16\pi h$, so $h = 2$ inches.

2. The correct answer is (B). Peter uses all of the wallpaper he purchased, so you only need to deal with the areas of the walls and the wallpaper to solve this question. Since the area of each wall is $7 \times 3 = 21$ m², you can determine that the total area that needs to be covered is $21 \times 4 = 84$ m² since there are four walls. Each sheet is $2 \times 2 = 4$ m², so the total number of sheets Peter will need is $84 \div 4 = 21$.

3. The correct answer is (D). The side lengths of each of the rectangles are given to you by the figure, so you need to find the area of each of the three rectangles by multiplying their side lengths and then find the sum of the three areas. The top rectangle has an area of $2 \times 1 = 2$, the middle one has an area of $4 \times 2 = 8$ and the bottom one has an area of $8 \times 4 = 32$. The total area is $32 + 8 + 2 = 42$.

4. The correct answer is (B). Since you know that x has a value of 7, you can find the length of each of the sides by plugging 7 for x into each expression. This gives you $2(7) - 1 = 13$ and $7 + 2 = 9$, so the side lengths of the rectangle are 13 and 9. Multiplying the two sides, you can get the area, which is equal to $13 \times 9 = 117$.

5. The correct answer is (C). To find the width of the rectangle, you can use the fact that all sides of a square are equal in length. Since the bottom side of the rectangle is the sum of the side lengths of the two squares and 3, you know that it is equal to $3 + 2 + 1 = 6$. As a result, you can calculate that the area of the rectangle is $6 \times 2 = 12$, which you can add to the areas of the squares, which are $1 \times 1 = 1$ and $2 \times 2 = 4$, to get $12 + 4 + 1 = 17$.

6. The correct answer is (A). It may be helpful for you to label the diagram, as shown below, before computing the area of the shape.

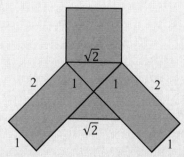

Using your knowledge of special triangles, you can determine that the length of the two shorter sides of an isosceles 45°–45°–90° right triangle is 1 if the hypotenuse has a length of $\sqrt{2}$. This means that the short sides of the rectangles have a length of 1, and the longer sides have a length of 2. Since one of the sides of the square is the hypotenuse, each side of the square must have a length of $\sqrt{2}$.

The area of each rectangle is $2 \times 1 = 2$, the area of each triangle is $(1 \times 1) \div 2 = 0.5$, and the area of the square is $(\sqrt{2})^2 = 2$. Adding the areas of two rectangles, two triangles, and the square, you get $(2 \times 2) + (0.5 \times 2) + 2 = 7$ units.

7. The correct answer is (B). Since both of the rectangles have an area of 3, you can find the unknown side lengths by dividing the area by the given lengths. Therefore, the rectangle on the left has an unknown side length of 2, and the bottom rectangle has an unknown side length of 3. This means that the two sides of the right triangle have lengths of 2 and 3. Using the formula for the area of a triangle, you will find that the area is $(2 \times 3) \div 2 = 3$.

8. The correct answer is (C). Since each of the triangles have two side lengths of 1.5 cm, you can determine that the height of the rectangle is 1.5 cm and its width is $1.5 \times 3 = 4.5$ cm. Since you have the width and height of the rectangle, you can multiply the two to get its area, $1.5 \times 4.5 = 6.75$ cm^2.

9. The correct answer is (C). The first card has an area of 64 cm^2, so folding it in half produces a triangle with an area of $64 \div 2 = 32$ cm^2. Adding this area to that of an unfolded card gives you the area of the two-card shape: $32 + 64 = 96$ cm^2.

10. The correct answer is (C). Because the cone is stacked on top of the cylinder, we only need to calculate the lateral area of both objects and the base. The lateral area of the cone is $6(4)\pi$, the lateral area of the cylinder is $2\pi(6)(4)$, and the base is $\pi(6)^2 = 36\pi$. All together, $24\pi + 48\pi + 36\pi$, the outside surface area of the object is 108π cm^2.

11. The correct answer is (B). Since you are looking for the approximate volume of the water, not the pool, you will use 3.7 m as the height instead of 4 m. You can get the volume by multiplying length, width, and height to get $3.7(10)(5) = 185$ m^3.

12. The correct answer is (C). The farmer has 34 m of rope to enclose an area. Since the shape with the largest area and the least perimeter is always a circle, it makes sense to try to arrange the rope into a circle with a circumference of 34 m. In that case, the diameter of the circle is $\frac{34}{\pi}$, "or approximately 10.8 m, and the radius is around 5.4 m, making" the area of the enclosed field approximately 92 m^2.

13. The correct answer is (D). Let x be the original length of the rectangle and let y be the original width of the rectangle, therefore the area is xy. After the change, the length is now $1.4x$ and the width is $0.6y$, which makes the area $0.84xy$. To calculate the change in percentage, use $\frac{0.84xy - xy}{xy} = -16\%$.

Triangle Theorems and Similarity
Part 3

These problems ask you to apply concepts and theorems related to congruence and similarity of triangles and the triangle sum theorem.

DIRECTIONS

Select the best answer among four choices and circle the corresponding letter or record it on a separate sheet of paper.

NOTES

1. You may use a calculator, but not all problems require the use of a calculator.
2. Variables and expressions represent real numbers unless stated otherwise.
3. Figures are drawn to scale unless stated otherwise.
4. Figures lie in a plane unless stated otherwise.
5. The domain of a function f is defined as the set of all real numbers x for which $f(x)$ is also a real number, unless stated otherwise.

1

Given the two similar triangles below, which of the following statements must be true?

A) $0 < \dfrac{b}{y} < 1$

B) $\dfrac{b}{y} < 0$

C) $\dfrac{b}{y} > 1$

D) $\dfrac{b}{y} = 1$

2

Two buildings with square bases are surveyed across an empty field. The surveyor draws a line connecting the base of the two buildings, forming two similar triangles. Given the information in the surveyor's diagram below, what is the length of the side of the smaller building that forms an edge of the triangle?

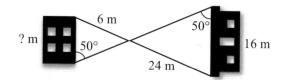

A) 3 m

B) 4 m

C) 7 m

D) 10 m

3

If a right triangle has one interior angle measure of 40 degrees, the sum of the other two angle measures must be

A) 90°

B) 130°

C) 140°

D) 180°

4

Given the two triangles below, if angle $a = 37°$, what is the measure of angle b?

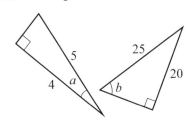

A) 37°

B) 45°

C) 53°

D) 143°

5

In the isosceles triangle below, what is a in terms of b?

A) $\dfrac{180 - b}{2}$

B) $180 - b$

C) $90 - b$

D) $2(90 - b)$

6

Olivia is designing a logo that she will later assemble using two sizes of triangular tile, as shown below.

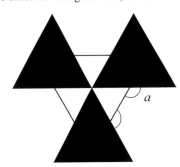

If the tiles are similar, what is the measure of angle a?

A) 30°

B) 60°

C) 90°

D) 120°

Answers and Explanations

1. The correct answer is (D). The easiest way to solve this question is through process of elimination. Because the two triangles are similar triangles, the corresponding angles are equal. Therefore, $\frac{b}{y}$ will always equal 1.

2. The correct answer is (B). To solve this question, you should recognize that the two triangles in the diagram are similar triangles:

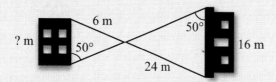

   As seen on the diagram, both triangles have angles of 50 degrees. Both triangles share the same central angle; therefore, the remaining angle must be equal as well. Now, you can set up a ratio with the known sides of the triangle and solve for the missing length.

$$\frac{16}{x} = \frac{24}{6}$$
$$x = \frac{96}{24} = 4$$

3. The correct answer is (C). The sum of the internal angles of any triangle is 180°, so if one of its angles is equal to 40°, the sum of its other angles must be 180° − 40° = 140°.

4. The correct answer is (C). The graphic indicates that these are right triangles, and we can see from the side lengths of the hypotenuses that the triangles are similar. We know that the right angle is congruent, we can infer from the similar side lengths that angle b must be congruent as well, so we can tell that these are similar triangles. The internal angles of any triangle add up to 180°, so if angle $a = 37°$, then angle b must be equal to 180° − 90° − 37° = 53°.

5. The correct answer is (A). An isosceles triangle has two equal sides. The angles opposite two equal sides must also be equal, so the angles at the bottom of the triangle shown in this diagram must be the same. Since the sum of any triangle's internal angles is equal to 180°, 180° − b can be divided equally in half to find angle a.

6. The correct answer is (D). If the large and small triangles are similar, and they all share a central angle, then each of the six angles making up that central angle is $\frac{360°}{6} = 60°$. The internal angles of a triangle add up to 180°, so the angles at the bases of each triangle must add up to 180° − 60° = 120°. Since the angle a and the angle opposite it are shown to be equal, that means the angles supplementary to them are also equal, so each angle at the base of each triangle is $\frac{120°}{2} = 60°$. If the angle supplementary to a is 60°, $a = 180° − 60° = 120°$.

Assess Conditions for Relationships or Theorems

Part 4

These problems ask you to determine which statements may be required to prove certain relationships or to satisfy a given theorem.

DIRECTIONS

Select the best answer among four choices and circle the corresponding letter or record it on a separate sheet of paper.

NOTES

1. You may use a calculator, but not all problems require the use of a calculator.
2. Variables and expressions represent real numbers unless stated otherwise.
3. Figures are drawn to scale unless stated otherwise.
4. Figures lie in a plane unless stated otherwise.
5. The domain of a function f is defined as the set of all real numbers x for which $f(x)$ is also a real number, unless stated otherwise.

1

Which of the following could be the length of x, the unknown side of the triangle?

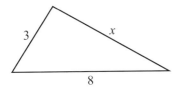

A) 4

B) 9

C) 12

D) 15

2

The two horizontal lines below are parallel. If the measure of the angle y is such that $0° < y < 90°$, which of the following CANNOT be the measure of angle x?

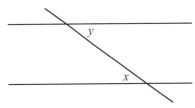

A) 3°

B) 45°

C) 89°

D) 111°

3

In the figure below, the lines *AG*, *BH* and *CI* are parallel and separated by equal distances. The lines *AC*, *DF* and *GI* are also parallel and separated by equal distances. *ABED*, *BCFE*, *DEHG* and *EFIH* are rhombuses (parallelograms with 4 equal sides) formed by these lines.

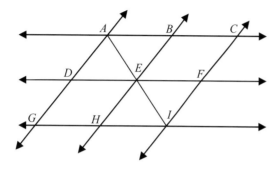

If ∠*EBA* = 80°, what is the measure of ∠*HIE*?

A) 50°

B) 60°

C) 80°

D) 100°

4

If *a* = 90°, which of the following could be true?

A) *c* = 120°

B) *b* = 90°

C) *a* + *b* = 180°

D) *a* + *c* = 120°

5

If *b* + *c* = 90°, which of the following is NOT necessarily true?

A) $a = b + c$

B) $z = \sqrt{x^2 + y^2}$

C) $\dfrac{a + b + c}{3} = 60$

D) $x + y = \sqrt{z}$

Questions 4 and 5 refer to the following information.

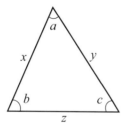

Note: The figure above is not to scale.

Fred Storage Bags: Containers

Answers and Explanations

1. The correct answer is (B). Any side length of a triangle must be greater than the difference of the other two sides, and less than their sum. Using this rule, you can determine that $5 < x < 11$. Since 4, 12 and 15 do not fit this inequality, the answer is (B).

2. The correct answer is (D). Using the properties of angles in parallel lines, you know that the measures of the angles y and x are equal. Since y is between 0° and 90°, x must also be between these two values. Answer options (A), (B) and (C) all fit within these restrictions. (D) is greater than 90° so it cannot be the measure of x.

3. The correct answer is (A). If $\angle EBA$ is 80°, $\angle EBC$ must be 100° since the two are supplementary angles. Since $ABED$ is a parallelogram, we can also infer that $\angle ADE$ is 80°, and $\angle DAB$ and $\angle DEB$ must both equal 100°. AEB and HEI are similar triangles, so $\angle AEB$ and $\angle HEI$ must be congruent angles. Since $ABED$ and $EFIH$ are similar parallelograms, $\angle DAE$ and $\angle HEI$ must also be congruent angles. That implies that the line segment AI evenly bisects $\angle HIF$, so $\angle HIE$ must be $\frac{100°}{2} = 50°$.

4. The correct answer is (D). The sum of any triangle's interior angles must equal 180°, and (D) is the only option that assigns a value to one or more of this triangle's interior angles ($c = 30°$) that makes it possible for all the angles' sum to equal 180°. (A) is incorrect because the sum of a and c would be 210°, which is greater than 180°. (B) and (C) are both incorrect because each interior angle of a triangle must have a nonzero value, and they must all add up to 180°. However, in both of these answer options, just two angles add up to 180°, leaving no possible value for the third angle.

5. The correct answer is (D). The interior angles of a triangle add up to 180°, so if $b + c = 90°$, a also equals 90°, and (A) is true. If a is a 90° angle, then z is the hypotenuse of the triangle, and the Pythagorean theorem would imply that $x^2 + y^2 = z^2$, and therefore that $z = \sqrt{x^2 + y^2}$. (B) is therefore true. Since the interior angles of a triangle add up to 180°, dividing the sum of the interior angles of a triangle by 3 will always give a result of 60°, so (C) is true.

Scaling Triangles
Part 5

These problems ask you to apply knowledge that changing a triangle by a scale factor of k changes all lengths by a factor of k, but does not change angle measures.

DIRECTIONS

Select the best answer among four choices and circle the corresponding letter or record it on a separate sheet of paper.

NOTES

1. You may use a calculator, but not all problems require the use of a calculator.
2. Variables and expressions represent real numbers unless stated otherwise.
3. Figures are drawn to scale unless stated otherwise.
4. Figures lie in a plane unless stated otherwise.
5. The domain of a function f is defined as the set of all real numbers x for which $f(x)$ is also a real number, unless stated otherwise.

Questions 1 through 3 refer to the following information.

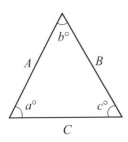

Note: The figure above is not to scale.

1

A new triangle is created with side lengths $2A$, $2B$, and $2C$. What is the sum of any two of its interior angles, in degrees?

A) 60

B) 90

C) 120

D) 180

2

A triangle has side lengths n, q, and r, as well as interior angles x, y, and z. Given the triangle above, if $\dfrac{A}{n} = \dfrac{C}{r}$, what is the measure of angle y in degrees?

A) 30

B) 45

C) 50

D) 60

A triangle has side lengths n, q, and r, as well as interior angles x, y, and z. Given the triangle above and that $n = q = r = 7A$, which of the following is true?

A) $a\left(\frac{1}{7}x\right) = 60$

B) $a = x$

C) $a = 7x$

D) $a = 14A$

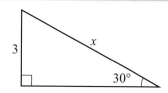

Given the triangle above and another right triangle with a hypotenuse of $4x$ and a leg of length 12, what is the measure of the angle opposite the leg of length 12?

A) 25.5°

B) 30°

C) 31°

D) 32.5°

A triangle has side lengths approximately 2.4, 3.4, and 4, with two interior angles measuring 37° and 58°. Another triangle has two sides of approximately 7.2 and 12, with two angles measuring 85° and 37°. What is the approximate measure of the third side of this triangle?

A) 8.6

B) 8.8

C) 9.0

D) 10.2

Answers and Explanations

1. The correct answer is (C). Because this is an equilateral triangle, you know that each interior angle is 60°. If all three sides are multiplied by the same value, a similar triangle will be created with the same interior angles. Therefore, any two interior angles will equal 60 + 60, which is 120°.

2. The correct answer is (D). If the ratios between two of the sides of different triangles are equal, that means that the triangles are proportional and therefore similar. In other words, both n and r can be multiplied by the same value to get A and C, respectively. So, if the triangles are similar, each individual angle must be 60°.

3. The correct answer is (B). If $n = q = r$, then the triangle is equilateral, just like the triangle with sides ABC. If they're both equilateral, all of their angles are equal to 60°, so one interior angle is equal to any other interior angle.

4. The correct answer is (B). The triangle described in the question has side lengths that are directly proportional to the triangle pictured. The drawn triangle has a hypotenuse of x and a leg of 3, and the described triangle is increased by a factor of 4 to get $4x$ and 12. Because of their proportional sides, these are similar triangles, and they will therefore have all the same interior angles. This includes the "angle opposite the leg with length 12," which is 30° in the graphic and so is 30° for the triangle described.

5. The correct answer is (D). First, you can figure out the third angle of the first triangle described: $180° - 37° - 58° = 85°$. So, the first triangle has sides 2.4, 3.4, and 4, and interior angles 37°, 58°, and 85°. The second triangle also has interior angles 85° and 37°, which means the third angle must be 58°. Since these two triangles have the same interior angles, they are similar. This means that each side of the first triangle must be proportional with each corresponding side in the second triangle. You can notice that two sides from the first triangle, 2.4 and 4, go evenly into 7.2 and 12 when multiplied by 3. So, if the sides have been increased by a factor of 3, then the third side must be $3.4 \times 3 = 10.2$.

Angle and Line Theorems

Part 6

These problems ask you to apply concepts and theorems related to lines and angles.

DIRECTIONS

Select the best answer among four choices and circle the corresponding letter or record it on a separate sheet of paper.

NOTES

1. You may use a calculator, but not all problems require the use of a calculator.
2. Variables and expressions represent real numbers unless stated otherwise.
3. Figures are drawn to scale unless stated otherwise.
4. Figures lie in a plane unless stated otherwise.
5. The domain of a function f is defined as the set of all real numbers x for which $f(x)$ is also a real number, unless stated otherwise.

1

In the figure below, the line segment $\overline{FB}$ forms the isosceles triangle FAB where it intersects the parallelogram $ACDE$. If $\angle AFB = \angle ABF = 40°$, what is the value of $\angle BCD$?

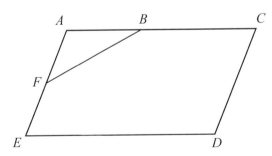

A) 40°

B) 60°

C) 80°

D) 100°

2

The triangle KHI and the isosceles triangle KIM are inscribed in the rectangle $JKLM$. Given that $\angle HIK = 20°$ and $\angle KHI = 110°$, what is the value of $\angle KIM$?

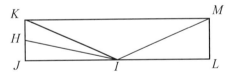

A) 40°

B) 80°

C) 100°

D) 110°

ABCD is a parallelogram where sides AB and CD are parallel, and sides BD and AC are parallel. If angle x = 135°, what is the value of angle y?

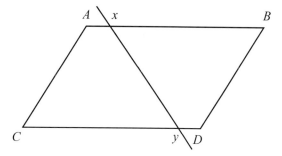

A) 35°

B) 45°

C) 135°

D) 145°

In the figure below, the lines AB, CD and EF are parallel. If angle a measures 40° and angle b measures 115°, what is the measure of angle c?

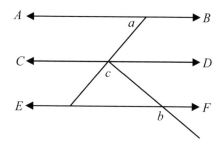

A) 25°

B) 45°

C) 55°

D) 75°

In the figure below, the lines AD and BE are parallel. If the measure of ∠ABE is 130° and the line segment $\overline{BC}$ bisects ∠ABE, what is the measure of ∠ACB?

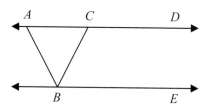

A) 25°

B) 45°

C) 65°

D) 85°

In the figure shown, the lines AG, BH and CI are parallel and are separated by equal distances. The lines AC, DF and GI are also parallel and spaced out equally. The lines AI, BH, DF and GC intersect at point E. ABED, BCFE, DEHG and EFIH are rhombuses (parallelograms with 4 equal sides) formed by these lines.

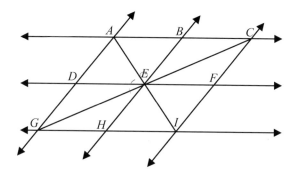

Which of the following statements is FALSE?

A) ∠DEG + ∠HIE = 180°

B) ∠DEI + ∠GIE = 180°

C) ∠CIH = 2(∠BAE)

D) ∠BEC = ∠DGE

In the parallelogram below, what is the value of angle *x*?

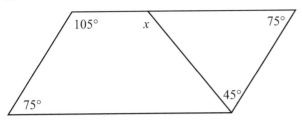

A) 45°

B) 60°

C) 105°

D) 120°

Answers and Explanations

1. The correct answer is (C). Since the sum of the angles in triangle *FAB* must be 180°, you can determine that ∠*FAB* = 180 − 2(40) = 100°. In addition, since the sum of the angles in a parallelogram is 360° and the angles facing each other, such as ∠*FAB* and ∠*EDC*, are equal, you will get the equation 360 = 2(100) + 2(∠*BCD*). You can then solve this equation to get ∠*BCD* = 80°.

   Alternatively, after finding that ∠*FAB* = 100°, you can use the fact that adjacent angles on each side of a parallelogram, such as ∠*FAB* and ∠*BCD*, are supplementary: ∠*BCD* = 180 − 100 = 80°.

2. The correct answer is (C). Since the sum of the angles in triangle *KHI* is 180°, you can determine that ∠*HKI* = 180 − ∠*KHI* − ∠*HIK* = 180 − 130 = 50°. If ∠*HKI* and ∠*IKM* are complementary angles, you know that ∠*IKM* = 90 − 50 = 40°. Finally, since KIM is an isosceles triangle, ∠*IMK* is equal to ∠*IKM*, and its internal angles must sum to 180°. You can find ∠*KIM* by subtracting the sum of the two angles (40 + 40) from 180 to get 100°.

3. The correct answer is (C). The given shape is a parallelogram, meaning that the line segments *AB* and *CD* are parallel. This means that you can use parallel angle relationships to find the value of *y* given *x*. Since *x* and *y* are alternate exterior angles, they must have the same value. The measurement of angle *y* is 135°.

4. The correct answer is (D). Since the three lines in the figure are parallel, you can use parallel angle relationships to determine the measure of *c* based on the measures of *a* and *b*. In the diagram below, if you imagine that the line with *c* and *b* next to it continued as the dashed line shown, you can see that *b* is equal to the sum of *c* and *d*. The angle *d* is the corresponding angle of *a*, therefore they are equal. Since *b* = *c* + *d*, plugg in *a* = *c* to get *b* = *a* + *c*. Plug in the given values to get 115 = 40 + *c*, which you can solve for *c* to get 75°. If you picked (A), you may have thought that *a*, *b* and *c* were supplementary angles.

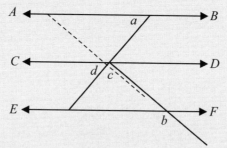

5. The correct answer is (C). If the line segment $\overline{BC}$ bisects ∠*ABE*, you know that ∠*ABE* is split into two equal angles. In this case, these angles are ∠*ABC* = ∠*CBE* = $\frac{130}{2}$ = 65°. The question asks for the value of ∠*ACB*, which is the alternate interior angle of ∠*CBE*. Therefore, you can determine that ∠*ACB* = ∠*CBE*, which is 65°.

6.   The correct answer is (A). Use process of elimination. (A) is false. Both ∠*DEG* and ∠*HIE* must be less than 90°, since they are acquired by bisecting one of the angles in a parallelogram. Therefore, their sum must be less than 180°. (B) is true since ∠*AED* and ∠*GIE* are equal because they are corresponding angles, and ∠*AED* + ∠*DEI* gives you a straight line, which has an angle of 180°. (C) is true since ∠*BAD* = ∠*CIH* because they are opposite angles in parallelogram *ACIG*, and line *AE* bisects ∠*BAD* into two equal pieces, one of which is ∠*BAE*. (D) is true since ∠*BEC* and ∠*DGE* are corresponding angles.

7.   The correct answer is (D). Since the shape is a parallelogram, you know that the sum of its internal angles must be 360°. This means that in the diagram below, the angle y is equal to $360 - (75 + 75 + 105 - 45) = 60°$. The supplementary angle of x is the alternate interior angle of y, so you can solve for x using the equation $60 + x = 180$ to get $x = 180 - 60 = 120°$.

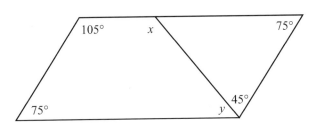

The Pythagorean Theorem
Part 7

These problems ask you to apply the Pythagorean Theorem.

DIRECTIONS

Select the best answer among four choices and circle the corresponding letter or record it on a separate sheet of paper.

NOTES

1. You may use a calculator, but not all problems require the use of a calculator.
2. Variables and expressions represent real numbers unless stated otherwise.
3. Figures are drawn to scale unless stated otherwise.
4. Figures lie in a plane unless stated otherwise.
5. The domain of a function f is defined as the set of all real numbers x for which $f(x)$ is also a real number, unless stated otherwise.

1

In the right triangle ABC, $\overline{AB}$ is 5 units long and $\overline{AC}$ is 4 units long, as shown below. If an isosceles right triangle DEF is constructed so that it has an area equal to three times that of triangle ABC, what is the length of the hypotenuse of DEF?

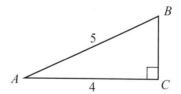

A) $6\sqrt{2}$

B) 5

C) 12

D) 15

2

What is the value of h in the trapezoid shown below?

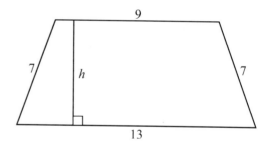

A) 2

B) $3\sqrt{5}$

C) 7

D) 9

3

Two geologists are investigating the height of a steep hill. The first geologist measures the distance along the face of the hill, while the second measures its horizontal width. They record their measurements in the figure below and try to estimate the height of the hill at its peak. Which of the following is the best estimate?

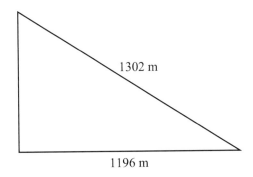

1302 m

1196 m

A) 500 m

B) 800 m

C) 920 m

D) 1200 m

4

The figure below is a right triangle. What is the value of $64 + x^2$?

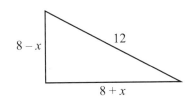

$8 - x$ 12 $8 + x$

A) 64

B) 72

C) 96

D) 144

5

In the figure below, if $\overline{BC} = 6$ and $\overline{AC}$ and $\overline{BC}$ and are parallel to the graph's axes, what is the perimeter of $\triangle ABC$?

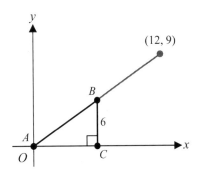

A) 14

B) 24

C) 26

D) 48

6

What is the length of the line segment, in units, contained in the first quadrant when the line $y = -\dfrac{4}{3}x + 4$ is graphed?

A) $2\sqrt{3}$

B) $2 + \sqrt{3}$

C) 5

D) 6

7

Halle is building a ramp up to her porch. If the porch is 5 feet high and the plank of wood used for the ramp is 13 feet long, what is the horizontal distance from the edge of the porch to the point where the ramp touches the ground?

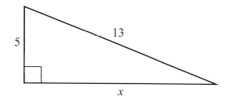

A) 12

B) $12 + \sqrt{5}$

C) 15

D) $13 + \sqrt{5}$

8

In order to protect the corners of a rectangular table, rubber triangular molds are being created to fit to the table corners. What is the length of the diagonal of each mold?

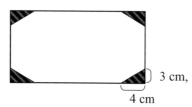

3 cm,
4 cm

A) $\sqrt{7}$ cm

B) 5 cm

C) $4 + \sqrt{3}$ cm

D) 7 cm

9

An architect wants to install triangular mirrors in the hallway of a gallery. All of the triangles are identical in shape and size. To be efficient, 6 m by 8 m rectangular mirrors were made, and then cut once along the diagonal of the rectangle. What is the length, in meters, of the diagonal that will be cut?

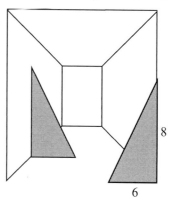

8

6

A) $6 + 2\sqrt{2}$

B) $8 + \sqrt{3}$

C) 10

D) 28

10

The two final students remaining in a game of dodgeball are standing in opposite corners of a gymnasium. What is the distance between the two students, to the nearest foot?

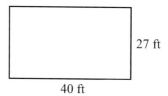

27 ft

40 ft

A) 29.5

B) 48.3

C) 51.9

D) 67.0

11

The location of two weather balloons in relation to their landing pod is mapped out below. To the nearest meter, what is the distance between the two balloons?

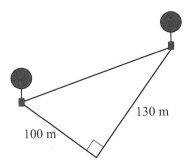

130 m

100 m

A) 100
B) 164
C) 196
D) 900

Answers and Explanations

1. The correct answer is (A). Since $\triangle ABC$ is a 3:4:5 right triangle, the missing height, $\overline{BC}$, is equal to 3. Therefore, you can find the area of $\triangle DEF$, which is three times the area of $\triangle ABC$, or $3 \times \left(\frac{1}{2} \times 4 \times 3 \right) = 18$ square units. Since $\triangle DEF$ is an isosceles right triangle, the two legs (base and height) connecting to the hypotenuse are equal:

$$\frac{1}{2} b^2 = 18$$
$$b^2 = 36$$
$$b = 6$$

    You can use the Pythagorean theorem to solve for the remaining side, the hypotenuse:

$$a^2 = b^2 + c^2$$
$$a^2 = 6^2 + 6^2$$
$$a = \sqrt{2 \times 36}$$
$$a = 6\sqrt{2}$$

    If you got (B), you probably wrote down the hypotenuse of $\triangle ABC$. If you got (D), you probably multiplied the hypotenuse of $\triangle ABC$ by three, instead of its area.

2. The correct answer is (B). The length of h must be less than 7 since h is the height of the trapezoid, which is the shortest line between the base and top, and therefore must be shorter than the sides. This allows you to eliminate (C) and (D). Then, you can picture a right triangle with the side with a length of 7 as its hypotenuse. The base of this triangle will be 2, as the base is 4 units larger than the top and half of this length extends on each side. This gives you a triangle with side lengths 7, 2, and h. Since any side of a triangle cannot be smaller than the difference between the two other sides, h must be greater than 5, eliminating (A). As a result, h is equal to 6.

3. The correct answer is (A). The two given side lengths of the triangle are 1196 m and 1302 m. While it may be tempting to directly apply the Pythagorean theorem, this is not necessary. It will be simpler if you notice that the side lengths can be approximated to 1200 m and 1300 m. As a result, the hill is a 5-12-13 special triangle with its sides multiplied by a coefficient of 100, meaning that the unknown side is $5 \times 100 = 500$ m.

4. The correct answer is (B). Given the Pythagorean Theorem, you know that $(8 - x)^2 + (8 + x)^2 = 12^2$. When you expand $(8 - x)^2 + (8 + x)^2$, you will get $2(x^2 + 64)$, which equals 144. Since the question simply asks for $64 + x^2$, you do not need to solve for x. Simply calculate $\frac{144}{2}$, which is 72, to get the answer for $64 + x^2$.

5. The correct answer is (B). You know that $\overline{BC}$ is equal to 6. Next, you need to figure out the slope of $\overline{AB}$. Since A is at (0, 0) and you know that a point on this line is (12, 9), you can find the slope:

$$\text{slope} = \frac{9-0}{12-0}$$
$$= \frac{3}{4}$$

Now, since you know the value for y, all you need to do is plug in this slope to find the value for x at point B using point-slope form:

$$y = \frac{3}{4}x + b$$
$$6 = \frac{3}{4}x + 0$$
$$\frac{6 \times 4}{3} = x = 8.$$

You know that point B is (8, 6). Because of this you know that $\overline{BC}$ = 8 With two sides of the triangle, you can use the Pythagorean theorem to find the third. Alternatively, you can recognize that 6 and 8 are two sides of the special right triangle with a ratio of 3:4:5, such that the third side must be 10. Either way, you can now determine that $\overline{AB}$ = 10. The perimeter of $\triangle ABC$ is therefore 24.

If you got (D), you found the area of the triangle. If you got (C), you used the x-value from the point (12, 8) instead of the x-value from point B.

6. The correct answer is (C). To solve this question, it might be helpful to sketch out a quick diagram.

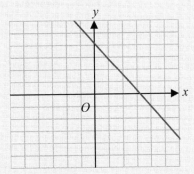

After drawing a diagram, you might realize that the x- and y-axes and the line y create a right triangle, and that the question asks you for the length of the hypotenuse of this triangle. You may have realized that this triangle is a Pythagorean triple, a 3-4-5 triangle. Since the length of the side along the x-axis is 3 units and along the y-axis is 4 units, the hypotenuse must be 5 units long.

If you didn't recognize this triangle as a Pythagorean triple, you can always solve for the missing length using the Pythagorean theorem.

7. The correct answer is (A). Recognize that this triangle is a Pythagorean triple, the triangle 5-12-13. Since two lengths, 5 and 13, are already given, you know that the missing length must be 12.

8. The correct answer is (B). You may have realized that this triangle is a Pythagorean triple, a 3-4-5 triangle. Since the length of the side along the x-axis is 3 cm and along the y-axis is 4 cm, the hypotenuse must be 5 cm long.

9. The correct answer is (C). To solve for the diagonal of the rectangle, you have two options. The first and more time-consuming option is to use the Pythagorean theorem. The second, more efficient option is to realize that the dimensions of the rectangle are 2 of the 3 lengths of a Pythagorean triple, 6-8-10. Since the sides 6 and 8 are accounted for by the dimensions of the rectangle, the length of the diagonal must be 10 m.

10. The correct answer is (B). Recognize that the smallest distance between the two students who are standing in opposite corners of a rectangular gymnasium, is the diagonal of the rectangle. You can solve for this by using the Pythagorean theorem:

$$c^2 = a^2 + b^2$$
$$c^2 = 27^2 + 40^2$$
$$c^2 = 729 + 1600$$
$$c^2 = 2329$$
$$c = \sqrt{2329} \approx 48.3$$

11. The correct answer is (B). The easiest way to solve this question is by recognizing that the triangle formed by the two weather balloons and their landing pod is a right triangle. To solve for the distance between the two balloons, you can use the Pythagorean theorem.

$$c^2 = a^2 + b^2 \quad \text{Pythagorean formula}$$
$$c^2 = 100^2 + 130^2$$
$$c^2 = 10000 + 16900 \quad \text{— expand}$$
$$c^2 = 26900 \quad \text{— simplify}$$
$$c = \sqrt{26900} \approx 164 \quad \text{— simplify}$$

plug in values

alone in wonderland

Right Triangle Trigonometry
Part 8

These problems ask you to solve problems using right triangle trigonometry, including special triangles.

DIRECTIONS

Select the best answer among four choices and circle the corresponding letter or record it on a separate sheet of paper.

NOTES

1. You may use a calculator, but not all problems require the use of a calculator.
2. Variables and expressions represent real numbers unless stated otherwise.
3. Figures are drawn to scale unless stated otherwise.
4. Figures lie in a plane unless stated otherwise.
5. The domain of a function f is defined as the set of all real numbers x for which $f(x)$ is also a real number, unless stated otherwise.

1

Which of the following is equal to $\sin \theta$?

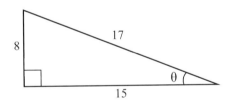

A) $\dfrac{8}{17}$

B) $\dfrac{15}{17}$

C) $\dfrac{17}{15}$

D) $\dfrac{17}{8}$

2

The cosine of an angle is $\dfrac{5}{13}$. What is the tangent of this angle?

A) $\dfrac{5}{13}$

B) $\dfrac{5}{12}$

C) $\dfrac{12}{5}$

D) $\dfrac{12}{13}$

The three points shown in the (x, y) coordinate plane below form an isosceles right triangle. What is the value of k?

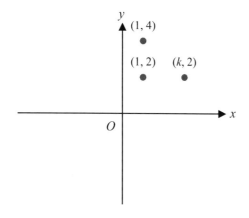

A) 1

B) 2

C) 3

D) 4

If $\sin \beta = \dfrac{7}{25}$ and $\cos \beta = \dfrac{24}{25}$, what is the value of $\tan \beta$?

A) $\dfrac{25}{7}$

B) $\dfrac{7}{24}$

C) $\dfrac{25}{24}$

D) $\dfrac{24}{7}$

A pulley system is installed next to a treehouse. Myrtle is using the system to lift a stack of books 11 feet into the treehouse. Which of the following equations represents the distance, in feet, between her and the stack of books when it is on the ground?

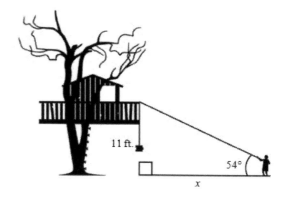

A) $x = 11\tan(54)$

B) $x = \dfrac{11}{\tan(54)}$

C) $x = \dfrac{\tan(54)}{11}$

D) $x = \dfrac{11}{\sin(54)}$

For which of the following diagrams would the trigonometric ratio $\sin(x) = \dfrac{40}{58}$ be true?

A)

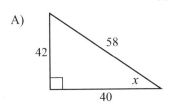

B)

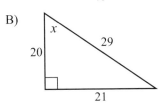

C)

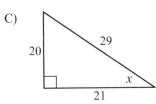

D)

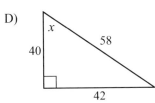

Answers and Explanations

1. The correct answer is (A). Using trigonometric ratios, you know that $\sin(\theta) = \frac{\text{opposite}}{\text{hypotenuse}}$. In the given diagram, the opposite side is 8 and the hypotenuse is 17, so this corresponds to $\sin(\theta) = \frac{8}{17}$.

2. The correct answer is (C). Since the cosine of an angle is equal to the length of the adjacent side divided by the length of the hypotenuse, this right-angled triangle has one side of length 5 (adjacent to the angle in question) and a hypotenuse of length 13. Therefore, it is a Pythagorean triple (5-12-13), so the side opposite the angle in question has length 12. Since the tangent of this angle equals opposite side divided by the adjacent side, the answer is $\frac{12}{5}$. If you chose (D), you may have found the sine of the angle.

3. The correct answer is (C). Since the triangle formed by the three points is an isosceles triangle, the distance between $(1, 4)$ and $(1, 2)$ must be equal to the distance between $(k, 2)$ and $(1, 2)$. Since $(1, 4)$ and $(1, 2)$ have the same x-coordinate, you only need to use the y-coordinates to find that the distance between them is $4 - 2 = 2$. Similarly, the y-coordinates of $(1, 2)$ and $(k, 2)$ are equal, and you know that the distance between them must be 2, you can solve for k from the equation $k - 1 = 2$ to get $k = 3$.

4. The correct answer is (B). If $\sin(\beta) = \frac{\text{opposite}}{\text{hypotenuse}}$ and $\cos(\beta) = \frac{\text{adjacent}}{\text{hypotenuse}}$," then that means that the " hypotenuse must be 25, the opposite side is 7, and the adjacent side is 24. Since $\tan(\beta) = \frac{\text{opposite}}{\text{adjacent}}$, then $\tan(\beta) = \frac{7}{24}$.

5. The correct answer is (B). First, you should set up a trigonometric ratio with the known side lengths. You cannot create the sine or cosine ratio since you don't have the length of the hypotenuse, so the only ratio you can use is tangent.

$$\tan(54) = \frac{11}{x}$$

Now, just solve for x.

$$x\tan(54) = 11$$
$$x = \frac{11}{\tan(54)}$$

6. "The correct answer is (C). In order for $\sin(x) = \frac{40}{58}$ to be true, the angle opposite x must equal 40 and the hypotenuse must equal 58. (A) is the only diagram which satisfies both of these requirements, since $\frac{20}{29} = \frac{40}{58}$.

Similar Triangle Trigonometry
Part 9

These problems ask you to use similarity to calculate values of sine, cosine, and tangent.

DIRECTIONS

Select the best answer among four choices and circle the corresponding letter or record it on a separate sheet of paper.

NOTES

1. You may use a calculator, but not all problems require the use of a calculator.
2. Variables and expressions represent real numbers unless stated otherwise.
3. Figures are drawn to scale unless stated otherwise.
4. Figures lie in a plane unless stated otherwise.
5. The domain of a function f is defined as the set of all real numbers x for which $f(x)$ is also a real number, unless stated otherwise.

1

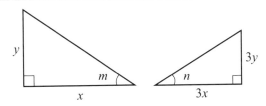

Given the two triangles above, if $\dfrac{y}{x} = \dfrac{3}{5}$, then $\tan n =$

A) $\dfrac{3}{5}$

B) $\dfrac{5}{3}$

C) $\dfrac{5}{9}$

D) $\dfrac{9}{5}$

2

Given $a = d$, $b = e$, and $c = f$, if $\sin b = 1.23$, then

$\sin e =$

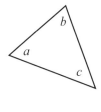
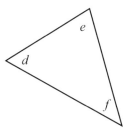

A) $\dfrac{1}{1.23}$

B) 1.23

C) -1.23

D) Cannot be determined

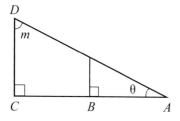

If $\sin \theta = \dfrac{3}{5}$, then $\sin m =$

A) $\dfrac{3}{5}$

B) $\dfrac{5}{3}$

C) $\dfrac{4}{5}$

D) $\dfrac{5}{4}$

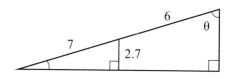

In the diagram above, $\cos \theta$ is equal to approximately

A) 0.4

B) 0.6

C) 1.4

D) 2.6

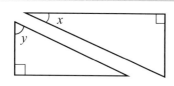

Given the two similar triangles above, if $\tan y = 4$, then $\tan x =$

A) $\dfrac{1}{4}$

B) 2

C) 4

D) Cannot be determined

Answers and Explanations

1. The correct answer is (A). First, the second triangle's legs are three times the first triangle's legs, so the two triangles must be similar. Second, if $\frac{y}{x} = \frac{3}{5}$, then y must be proportional to 3 and x must be proportional to 5. That means $3y$ is also proportional to 3 and $3x$ is also proportional to 5. Since $\tan(n) = \frac{\text{opposite}}{\text{adjacent}}$, and we know the opposite side is in proportion with 3 and the adjacent side is in proportion with 5, $\tan(n) = \frac{3}{5}$.

2. The correct answer is (B). If all three interior angles in the first triangle are equal to the corresponding angles in the second triangle, the two are similar triangles. If $\sin b = 1.23$, and e is the same angle as b, then it follows that $\sin e$ also equals 1.23.

3. The correct answer is (C). Since both line segments $\overline{EB}$ and $\overline{DC}$ are perpendicular to the base $\overline{AC}$, you know that they must also be parallel to one another. When parallel lines intersect another line such as $\overline{AC}$ or $\overline{AD}$, they create the same angle measurements at the points of intersection. This means that the larger triangle ACD has the same angles as the smaller triangle ABE, and that they are therefore similar triangles. Since $\sin(\theta) = \frac{\text{opposite}}{\text{hypotenuse}}$, you know that the opposite leg and hypotenuse are multiples of 3 and 5 respectively. If one leg is a multiple of 3 and the hypotenuse is a multiple of 5, then the other leg must be a multiple of 4, because that completes a 3-4-5 triangle (you can also determine this using the Pythagorean theorem). Finally, you know that if $\sin(m) = \frac{\text{opposite}}{\text{hypotenuse}}$, then $\sin(m) = \frac{4}{5}$.

4. The correct answer is (A). If $\tan(y) = \frac{\text{opposite}}{\text{adjacent}}$ and $\tan(y) = 4$, that means that the opposite and adjacent sides are in a 4:1 ratio $\left(\text{since 4 can be rewritten as } \frac{4}{1}\right)$. Since the two triangles are similar, they have the same angles. You can see that angle x is the complement of angle y, as they are opposite different legs in each triangle. Therefore, to find $\tan(x) = \frac{\text{opposite}}{\text{adjacent}}$, the opposite side becomes a multiple of 1 and the adjacent side becomes a multiple of 4: $\tan(x) = \frac{1}{4}$.

5. The correct answer is (A). Since the large triangle and the small one inside it are similar, angle θ and the angle marked δ on the graph to the right are identical, so $\cos\theta = \cos\delta = \frac{\text{adjacent}}{\text{hypotenuse}} = \frac{2.7}{7} = 0.385 \approx 0.4$. You don't need to do any work to figure out the side lengths of the larger triangle: because the triangles are similar, they will be in the same proportion as 2.7:7.

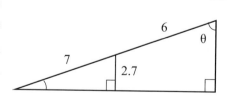

Trigonometry of Complementary Angles

Part 10

These problems ask you to solve problems using the relationship between the sine and cosine of complementary angles.

1

In the figure below, $ABCD$ is a rectangle. The sine of the angle θ is 0.4. What is the cosine of angle α?

A) 0.4

B) −0.4

C) 0.6

D) −0.6

2

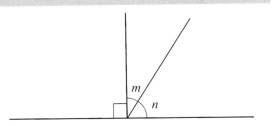

If $\sin m = 0.67$, $\cos n =$

A) 0.33

B) 0.67

C) 0.76

D) Cannot be determined

3

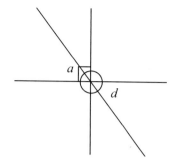

If 2sin a = 1.4, then cos d =

A) 0.3

B) 0.6

C) 0.7

D) 1.4

4

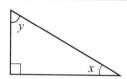

Given the figure above, sin x =

A) sin $(90 + y)$

B) sin $(90 + x)$

C) cos $(90 - x)$

D) cos $(90 - y)$

5

If the sine of one angle is equal to 0.24, then the cosine of its complementary angle

A) must be 0.24.

B) must be 0.76.

C) may be 0.24 or 0.76.

D) cannot be determined.

6

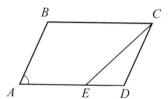

Given parallelogram $ABCD$, if the sine of angle $\angle BAD$ is $\dfrac{\sqrt{3}}{2}$ and $\overline{ED} = \overline{CD}$, then the sine of angle $\angle DCE$ is

A) $\dfrac{1}{2}$

B) $\dfrac{\sqrt{3}}{2}$

C) $\dfrac{\sqrt{2}}{2}$

D) $\sqrt{3}$

Answers and Explanations

1. The correct answer is (A). Since θ and α add up to 90°, they are complementary angles. The sine of any angle is equal to the cosine of its complementary angle. (If you don't know this, you can easily understand why by drawing a right-angled triangle with θ and α as its two acute angles!) Therefore, the cosine of α is 0.4.

2. The correct answer is (B). Since m and n add up to 90°, they are complementary. So, sin m = cos m = 0.67.

3. The correct answer is (C). Since a and d are complementary angles opposite a right angle, you know that sin a = cos d because the sine of any angle is equal to the cosine of its complement. However, since the expression says that $2 \times$ sin a = 1.4, you can simply divide both sides by 2 to find that sin a = 0.7 = cos d.

4. The correct answer is (C). A pair of complementary angles add up to 90°; in other words, if you subtract one of the angles from 90, the result will be the complementary angle. So if you have two complementary angles x and y, then $90 - x = y$ and $180 - y = x$. So, if sin x = cos y, and $y = 180 - x$, then cos(180 − x) = sin x.

5. The correct answer is (A). This is true for all acute angles. So, if the sine of one angle is 0.24, the cosine of its complement must also be 0.24.

6. The correct answer is (A). Since this is a parallelogram, sides AB and CD are parallel and intersect the base AD at the same angle. That means that both intersections create equivalent angles. So, the supplement of interior angle A is interior angle D, because they are opposite angles along the intersection of the base AD.

   You should also know from the unit circle that 60° has a sine of $\frac{\sqrt{3}}{2}$. This means that angle A is 60°, and its supplementary angle is 180 − 60 = 120. So, angle D is 120°. Since $ED = CD$, you know triangle EDC is isosceles, and angle D is the bisecting angle between the two equivalent sides. That means that the remaining two angles are each $\frac{180 - 120}{2} = 30°$. Finally, you know from the unit circle that the sin 30 is equal to $\frac{1}{2}$. So, the sin of angle DCE is $\frac{1}{2}$.

Circle Theorems and Properties

Part 11

These problems ask you to use definitions, properties, and theorems relating to circles and parts of circles to solve problems.

DIRECTIONS

Select the best answer among four choices and circle the corresponding letter or record it on a separate sheet of paper.

NOTES

1. You may use a calculator, but not all problems require the use of a calculator.
2. Variables and expressions represent real numbers unless stated otherwise.
3. Figures are drawn to scale unless stated otherwise.
4. Figures lie in a plane unless stated otherwise.
5. The domain of a function f is defined as the set of all real numbers x for which $f(x)$ is also a real number, unless stated otherwise.

1

A bullseye with a radius of 4 meters is shown below. If the radius of the central circle is 1 meter and each ring has a width of 1 meter, what is the ratio of the area of the outermost ring to that of the center circle?

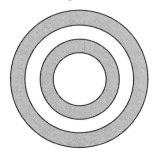

A) 4:1

B) 7:1

C) 16:π

D) 16:1

2

Given that $\overline{AB}$ and $\overline{BC}$ are $\sqrt{2}$ cm in length, and $\overline{AC}$ is the diameter of the circle shown, what is the area of the shaded region?

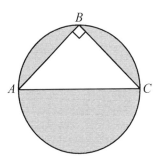

A) π cm^2

B) 1 cm^2

C) $\pi + 1$ cm^2

D) $\pi - 1$ cm^2

3

A group of mathematicians order a pizza with a radius of 12 cm and divide it up into equal slices. If one of these slices, shown below, has an area of 18π cm², what is the angle, x, of each slice?

A) 22.5°

B) 30°

C) 45°

D) 60°

4

A dolphin leaps out of the water and follows a perfect semicircle from the point where it leaves the water to where it reenters it. If these two points are 10 meters apart, what is the length of the dolphin's path through the air?

A) π meters

B) 2.5π meters

C) 5π meters

D) 10π meters

5

A and *B* are two points connected by a straight line that goes through the center of the circle, 8 units apart from each other. Given the figure below, what is the area of the circle?

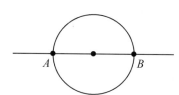

A) 4π

B) 8π

C) 16π

D) 32π

6

If the area of a circle is 16π square units, what is its circumference, in units?

A) 4π

B) 8π

C) 4

D) 8

7

In the diagram below, a circle is completely enclosed in a square. If the area of the square is 144cm², what is the area of the circle, to the nearest whole cm²?

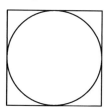

A) 100

B) 113

C) 144

D) 160

8

Given the figure below, if line segment $\overline{AC}$ passes through the center of the circle and line segment $\overline{AB}$ is 8 units long, what is the area of the circle?

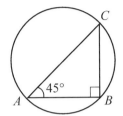

A) 8π

B) 18π

C) 32π

D) 36π

9

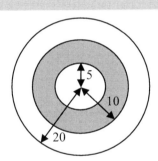

A circular dartboard has a central circle, a middle ring, and an outer ring, as shown in the diagram above. The center circle has a radius of 5 cm, the circle formed by the middle ring has a radius of 10 cm, and the dart board has a radius of 20 cm. What is the probability that a dart thrown randomly at the board will hit the middle ring?

A) 0.0625

B) 0.1875

C) 0.25

D) 0.5625

10

If O is the center of the circle below, what is the length of the highlighted arc if the indicated angle is $\frac{\pi}{3}$ radians and the radius of the circle is 3?

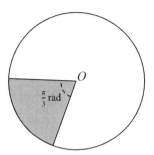

A) $\dfrac{\pi}{3}$

B) $\dfrac{\pi}{2}$

C) π

D) 2π

Answers and Explanations

1. The correct answer is (B). First you need to find the area of both the innermost ring and the entire bullseye. The area of the last ring is equal to the area of the second largest circle subtracted from the area of the whole bullseye: $(4^2 \times \pi) - (3^2 \times \pi) = 16\pi - 9\pi = 7\pi$ square meters. The area of the smallest circle is simply $1^2 \times \pi = \pi$ square meters. Therefore, the ratio of the two areas is $7\pi:\pi$, or $7:1$.

    If you chose (D), you may have found the ratio of the area of the whole bullseye to that of the smallest circle's area.

2. The correct answer is (D). The question requires you to find the area of the inner triangle, and subtract it from the area of the circle. The given triangle has two legs of equal length and a right angle, so it is an isosceles 45°-45°-90° right triangle. This is a special triangle where the hypotenuse is larger than each side by a factor of $\sqrt{2}$. This means that the hypotenuse, which is equal to the diameter of the circle, is $\sqrt{2} \times \sqrt{2} = 2$ cm long. You can find the radius of the circle by taking half of the hypotenuse, since AC is the diameter of the circle, and you'll get 1 cm. Finally, you can calculate that the area of the circle is $\pi(1)^2 = \pi$ cm^2, and the area of the triangle is $\frac{\sqrt{2} \times \sqrt{2}}{2} = 1$ cm^2. Subtracting the area of the triangle from that of the circle, you can find that the area of the shaded region is $\pi - 1$ cm^2.

3. The correct answer is (C). If the pizza has a radius of 12 cm, it has an area of $12^2\pi = 144\pi$ cm^2. Using the equation for the area of a sector, you get the following relationship: $\frac{18\pi}{144\pi} = \frac{x}{360}$. Before cross-multiplying, you can simplify the left hand side of the expression to $\frac{1}{8}$. Solving the equation after simplifying, you get $8x = 360$. As a result, the unknown angle x of each slice is 45°.

4. The correct answer is (C). From the diagram of the dolphin's path below, you can see that the diameter of this semicircle is 10 m and its radius is 5 m. The length of the dolphin's path is equal to half of the circumference of the whole circle, which is $\frac{1}{2}(10\pi) = 5\pi$ m.

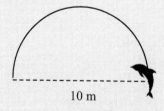

10 m

5. The correct answer is (C). As shown in the graph, line AB is the diameter of the circle. If the diameter is 8 units, the radius is half of that and is 4 units, which means that the area of the circle is 16π square units.

6. The correct answer is (B). If the area is 16π, you can use the formula for the area of the circle, πr^2, to find that the radius must be 4 units:

$$16\pi = \pi r^2$$
$$16 = r^2$$
$$r = 4$$

Since the diameter is twice that, it is 8 inches, and the circumference is 8π inches.

7. The correct answer is (B). If the area of the square is 144 cm², the length of one of the sides of the square is 12 cm, which is also the diameter of the circle. Since the radius is half the diameter, the radius is 6 cm, which means that the area, πr^2, is 36π, or approximately 113 cm².

8. The correct answer is (C). Since triangle ABC is a 45°-45°-90° triangle, its sides are in a specific ratio, as shown in the triangle below. If one leg is 8 units long, the hypotenuse would be $8\sqrt{2}$ units, which is also the diameter. The radius would therefore be $4\sqrt{2}$, making the area 32π.

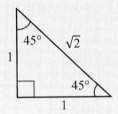

9. The correct answer is (B). The probability that the dart hits the second ring, given that it lands somewhere on the dart board, is the same as the ratio of the area of the second ring to the total area of the dart board. The total area of the dart board is 400π cm², whereas the area of the second ring is $100\pi - 25\pi = 75\pi$ cm². Therefore, the probability is $\dfrac{75\pi}{400\pi} = 0.1875$.

10. The correct answer is (C). An angle that goes around the entire circle has measure of 2π radians, so an angle of $\dfrac{\pi}{3}$ radians is $\dfrac{1}{6}$ of its size. Therefore, the length of the indicated arc is $\dfrac{1}{6}$ of the circumference of the circle. The circumference of the circle is $2\pi r = 2\pi(3) = 6\pi$, so the length of the indicated arc is π.

Radians and Degrees
Part 12

These problems ask you to solve problems using radian measure and convert between radians and degrees.

1

The arc length in the following figure is 5π. what is the diameter of the circle?

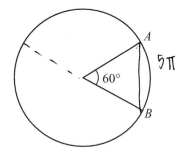

A) 10
B) 15
C) 20
D) 30

2

If a cart moves 12π inches with each rotation of its wheels, what is the area of each wheel in square inches?

A) 9π
B) 16π
C) 25π
D) 36π

3

140° is equal to which of the following radian measurements?

A) $\dfrac{7\pi}{9}$

B) $\dfrac{7\pi}{18}$

C) $\dfrac{9\pi}{18}$

D) $\dfrac{9\pi}{7}$

5

11π radians is equivalent to

A) 0°

B) 90°

C) 180°

D) 270°

4

The difference between 210° and 150° is

A) $\dfrac{\pi}{3}$ radians

B) $\dfrac{2\pi}{3}$ radians

C) $\dfrac{\pi}{6}$ radians

D) $\dfrac{\pi}{9}$ radians

Answers and Explanations

1. The correct answer is (D). The ratio of the sector angle to 360° is the same as the ratio of the arc length to the circumference of the circle. Recall that circumference is πd. You can therefore compare the two ratios:

$$\frac{\text{sector angle}}{360°} = \frac{\text{arc length}}{\text{circumference}}$$

$$\frac{60°}{360°} = \frac{5\pi}{\pi d}$$

$$\frac{1}{6} = \frac{5}{d}$$

$$d = 30$$

2. The correct answer is (D). If the cart moves 12π inches with each rotation, it means that the circumference of the wheel is 12π. As a result, you can determine that the diameter is 12 inches and the radius is 6 inches, so the area is 36π square inches.

3. The correct answer is (A). To convert from degrees to radians, simply multiply the degree measure by $\frac{\pi}{180}$: $\frac{\pi}{180} \times 140 = \frac{140\pi}{180} = \frac{7\pi}{9}$.

4. The correct answer is (A). First, you can find the difference between the two angles in degrees: $210° - 150° = 60°$. Then, you can multiply by $\frac{\pi}{180}$ to convert from degrees to radians: $\frac{\pi}{180} \times 60 = \frac{60\pi}{180} = \frac{\pi}{3}$.

5. The correct answer is (C). While it might be tempting to convert 11π into degrees, this might not actually be that helpful: $\frac{180}{\pi} \times 11\pi = \frac{1980\pi}{\pi} = 1980°$, but 1980° doesn't tell you much. Instead, you can remember from the unit circle that an entire revolution around the circle, 360°, is equal to 2π, and therefore a half a revolution is π, or 180°. Going around the circle 10 times brings you back to 0°, and adding one more π brings you half way around to 180°.

Unit Circle Trigonometry

Part 13

These problems require you to solve problems using trigonometric ratios in the unit circle.

DIRECTIONS

Select the best answer among four choices and circle the corresponding letter or record it on a separate sheet of paper.

NOTES

1. You may use a calculator, but not all problems require the use of a calculator.
2. Variables and expressions represent real numbers unless stated otherwise.
3. Figures are drawn to scale unless stated otherwise.
4. Figures lie in a plane unless stated otherwise.
5. The domain of a function f is defined as the set of all real numbers x for which $f(x)$ is also a real number, unless stated otherwise.

1

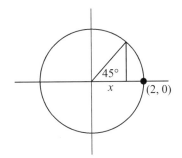

Given the diagram above, what is the length of x?

A) $\sqrt{3}$

B) $\sqrt{2}$

C) $\dfrac{\sqrt{3}}{2}$

D) $\dfrac{\sqrt{2}}{2}$

2

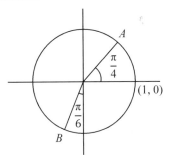

Given the circle above, what is the length of the minor arc AB?

A) $\dfrac{11\pi}{12}$

B) $\dfrac{11\pi}{24}$

C) $\dfrac{13\pi}{12}$

D) $\dfrac{13\pi}{24}$

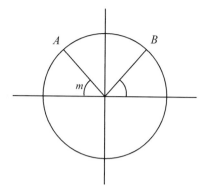

In the unit circle above, if $\cos m = \dfrac{1}{2}$, then the sine of minor arc AB is

A) $-\dfrac{1}{2}$

B) $\dfrac{1}{2}$

C) $\dfrac{\sqrt{3}}{2}$

D) $-\dfrac{\sqrt{3}}{2}$

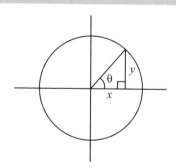

In the unit circle above, if the ratio $x{:}y$ is 4:3, what is the value of $\sin \theta$?

A) 0.2

B) 0.4

C) 0.6

D) 0.8

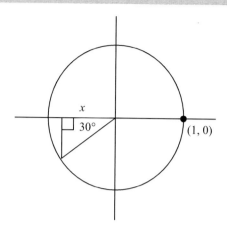

Which is the approximate length of x in the unit circle above?

A) 0.42

B) 0.50

C) 0.70

D) 0.87

Answers and Explanations

1. "The correct answer is (B). From the unit circle, you know that both the sin and cosine of 45° are equal to $\frac{\sqrt{2}}{2}$, and therefore the x and y coordinates of the point on the unit circle will be $\frac{\sqrt{2}}{2}$. So, without looking closely, you might be tempted to choose (D), since the x-coordinate is the same as the length of that leg of the triangle. However, you should notice that this is not a unit circle; the circle passes through the point (2, 0), so it has a radius of 2 instead of a radius of 1. That means that the hypotenuse will be 2 times as long, and the legs must also be 2 times as long:

$$2 \times \frac{\sqrt{2}}{2} = \sqrt{2}.$$

2. The correct answer is (A). You can find that $\frac{\pi}{4}$ is 45°, and $\frac{\pi}{6}$ is 30°. The minor arc is the shorter" "length along the circumference between the two points A and B: this includes the $\frac{\pi}{4}$ slice, the $\frac{\pi}{6}$ slice, and the entirety of the fourth quadrant, which is 90° or $\frac{\pi}{2}$. Therefore, the length of the minor arc is $\frac{\pi}{4} + \frac{\pi}{6} + \frac{\pi}{2}$. With some quick conversion to find a common denominator, you can add these all up:

$$\frac{\pi}{4} + \frac{\pi}{6} + \frac{\pi}{2} = \frac{3\pi}{12} + \frac{2\pi}{12} + \frac{6\pi}{12} = \frac{11\pi}{12}.$$

3. The correct answer is (C). Since AOB is an obtuse angle, in order to find the value of its sine, you must find the sine of its supplement. The supplement to AOB is the angle between A and the x-axis. Based on your knowledge of the unit circle, if cos $m = \frac{1}{2}$, m must be 60°. Since the diagram indicates that the angle between A and the x-axis is equal to m, it must also be 60°. The sine of 60° is $\frac{\sqrt{3}}{2}$, and you know it won't be negative because the angle is in the second quadrant.

4. The correct answer is (C). If the ratio of the two legs is 4:3, then the triangle is a 3-4-5 triangle. It appears that y is the shorter side, so since sin $(\theta) = \frac{\text{opposite}}{\text{hypotenuse}}$, sin $(\theta) = \frac{3}{5} = 0.6$.

5. The correct answer is (D). Since the given angle is 30° from the x-axis and it's in the second quadrant, you know that its cosine must be $-\frac{\sqrt{3}}{2}$. The cosine of the angle is equal to the x-coordinate, and this is a unit circle, so the length of x must be $\frac{\sqrt{3}}{2} \approx 0.87$.

Equations of Circles

Part 14

These problems ask you to solve problems related to the graphs and equations of circles in the xy-plane, including completing the square to determine properties of the circle.

DIRECTIONS

Select the best answer among four choices and circle the corresponding letter or record it on a separate sheet of paper.

NOTES

1. You may use a calculator, but not all problems require the use of a calculator.
2. Variables and expressions represent real numbers unless stated otherwise.
3. Figures are drawn to scale unless stated otherwise.
4. Figures lie in a plane unless stated otherwise.
5. The domain of a function f is defined as the set of all real numbers x for which $f(x)$ is also a real number, unless stated otherwise.

1

Alice draws a semicircle with a radius of 5 and a vertex of (3, 4) on a coordinate plane. Which of the following CANNOT be a point on the semicircle?

A) (8, 4)

B) (7, 7)

C) (–1, 1)

D) (–2, 3)

2

Which of the points shown on the xy-plane below could be the vertex of a circle with the equation $(x - 4)^2 + (y + 3)^2 = 25$?

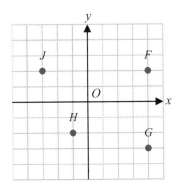

A) F

B) G

C) H

D) J

3

Which of the following points lies on the circle given by the equation $(x + 1)^2 + y^2 = 9$?

A) $(2, 0)$

B) $(0, 2)$

C) $(-2, 0)$

D) $(0, -2)$

4

What is the radius of the circle given by the equation $x^2 + y^2 = 4x - 8y - 11$?

A) 2

B) 3

C) 4

D) 5

5

What is the equation of the circle shown below?

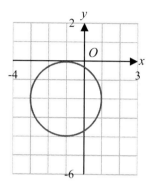

A) $(x - 1)^2 + (y - 2)^2 = 2$

B) $(x - 1)^2 + (y - 2)^2 = 4$

C) $(x + 1)^2 + (y + 2)^2 = 2$

D) $(x + 1)^2 + (y + 2)^2 = 4$

6

What is the radius of the circle represented by the equation $x^2 + y^2 + 6(y - x) = 31$?

A) 5

B) 6

C) 7

D) 8

Answers and Explanations

1. The correct answer is (D). Every point on the semicircle must be 5 units from the vertex, so you must check the distance of each point from the vertex to find one that is not equal to 5 units. Using the distance formula, (A) is $\sqrt{(8-3)^2+(4-4)^2} = 5$ units, (B) is $\sqrt{(7-3)^2+(7-4)^2} = 5$ units, and (C) is $\sqrt{(-1-3)^2+(1-4)^2} = 5$ units away from the vertex. Therefore, (A), (B) and (C) can be eliminated as they could lie on the semicircle. Applying the formula to (D), you get $\sqrt{(-2-3)^2+(3-4)^2} = \sqrt{26}$, which is greater than 5.

2. The correct answer is (B). A circle can be represented in the form $(x-h)^2 + (y-k)^2 = r^2$ where the vertex is at (h, k) and the radius is r. Using this information, you can find that the vertex of the given circle must be $(4, -3)$, a point located in Quadrant IV. The only point in the answer options located in Quadrant IV is point G.

3. The correct answer is (A). You can test each of these points individually by plugging the x and y coordinates into the given equation. Only the point given in (A) makes the equation true, which means it is the only point that lies on this circle.

4. The correct answer is (B). You can rearrange this equation until it is in the form $(x-h)^2 + (y-k)^2 = r^2$ as follows:

$$x^2 + y^2 = 4x - 8y - 11$$
$$x^2 - 4x + y^2 + 8y = -11$$
$$(x^2 - 4x + 4 - 4) + (y^2 + 8y + 16 - 16) = -11$$
$$(x^2 - 4x + 4) + (y^2 + 8y + 16) = 9$$
$$(x-2)^2 + (y+4)^2 = 3^2$$

Therefore, the circle has radius 3.

5. The correct answer is (D). The general form of a circle is $(x-h)^2 + (y-k)^2 = r^2$, where (h, k) is the center of the circle and r is its radius. From the diagram, you can see that this circle's center is $(-1, -2)$ and its radius is 2. Plugging these numbers into the general formula, you get $(x - (-1))^2 + (y - (-2))^2 = 2^2$, and simplifying, $(x + 1)^2 + (y + 2)^2 = 4$.

6. The correct answer is (C). You can begin by distributing the 6 and regrouping terms with the same variables together:

$$x^2 + y^2 + 6(y - x) = 31$$
$$x^2 + y^2 + 6y - 6x = 31$$
$$(x^2 - 6x) + (y^2 + 6y) = 31$$

Now, complete both squares:

$$(x^2 - 6x + 9) + (y^2 + 6y + 9) = 31 + 9 + 9$$
$$(x-3)^2 + (y+3)^2 = 49$$

In the standard form of a circle $(x-h)^2 + (y-k)^2 = r^2$, the constant r is the radius. Therefore, $49 = r^2$ and $7 = r$.

Complex Numbers

Part 15

These problems ask you to add, subtract, multiply, and divide complex numbers, as well as solve problems with them.

DIRECTIONS

Select the best answer among four choices and circle the corresponding letter or record it on a separate sheet of paper.

NOTES

1. You may use a calculator, but not all problems require the use of a calculator.
2. Variables and expressions represent real numbers unless stated otherwise.
3. Figures are drawn to scale unless stated otherwise.
4. Figures lie in a plane unless stated otherwise.
5. The domain of a function f is defined as the set of all real numbers x for which $f(x)$ is also a real number, unless stated otherwise.

1

If $i = \sqrt{-1}$, which values of x satisfy the equation $x^2 + 2x + 3 = 0$?

A) -3 and 1

B) -1 and 3

C) $-1 \pm \sqrt{2}i$

D) $-2 \pm \sqrt{2}i$

3

The height of a missile can be given by the inequality $h < (2 + i)(4 - 2i)$, where h is the height of the missile, in hundreds of meters. What is the lowest altitude that a plane can fly, in hundreds of meters, in order to guarantee that it will not be hit by this missile? (Note: $i = \sqrt{-1}$)

A) 4

B) 6

C) 8

D) 10

2

What is i^{8674}? Note that $i^2 = -1$.

A) $-i$

B) i

C) -1

D) 1

If $i^2 = -1$, what is the value of $(i + 5)(2i - 5)$?

A) -27

B) -23

C) $-27 + 5i$

D) $-27 - 5i$

If $i^2 = -1$, which of the following is equivalent to $\dfrac{i^2 + 2i - 3}{4i - 8}$?

A) $\dfrac{3}{8}$

B) $\dfrac{1}{2}$

C) $\dfrac{3}{2}$

D) $\dfrac{(i - 3)(i + 1)}{4(i - 2)}$

If $i = \sqrt{-1}$, which of the following is equivalent to $\dfrac{i}{2i - 3}$?

A) $\dfrac{2 - 3i}{5}$

B) $\dfrac{2 + 3i}{5}$

C) $\dfrac{2 - 3i}{13}$

D) $\dfrac{2 + 3i}{13}$

If $i^2 = -1$, what is the value of $(2i + 1)(i - 3)$?

A) $-5(i - 1)$

B) $-5(i + 1)$

C) $-2i - 3$

D) $2i - 3$

In the complex number plane, the x-axis is represented by all real numbers, and the y-axis is represented by all imaginary numbers, i. What complex number is represented by the point in the complex plane below?

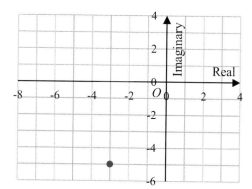

A) $3 - 5i$

B) $3 + 5i$

C) $-3 - 5i$

D) $-3i - 5$

In the imaginary number system, $i = \sqrt{-1}$. If $0 = (x - 2i)(2x - i) + 2$, which of the following is a real solution for x?

A) -2

B) $-\dfrac{2}{5}$

C) 0

D) $\dfrac{2}{5}$

If $i = \sqrt{-1}$, which expression is equal to $3i^4x^2 + 2i^2x^2 + 4i^4 - 5$?

A) $3x^2i - x^2 + 4i - 5$

B) $(x + 1)(x - 1)$

C) $(x + 1)(x + 1)$

D) $x^2 + 1$

Answers and Explanations

1. The correct answer is (C). If you apply the quadratic formula, you get " $x = \frac{-2 \pm \sqrt{2^2 - 4(1)(3)}}{2(1)} = \frac{-2 \pm \sqrt{-8}}{2}$. Since $\sqrt{-1}$ is equal to i, you can substitute i for $\sqrt{-1}$ "in the equation to get $x = \frac{-2 \pm \sqrt{8}i}{2}$, "which you can further simplify to $x = -1 \pm \sqrt{2}i$. If you got (A), you may have factored the original equation as $(x + 3)(x - 1) = 0$, which is incorrect. If you got (D), you may have forgotten to divide the -2 term in the fraction's numerator by the denominator 2.

2. The correct answer is (C). Although this question may seem quite daunting at first, it becomes much simpler if you realize that there is a sequence involving the exponents of i: $i^1 = i$, $i^2 = -1$, $i^3 = -i$, $i^4 = 1$ This pattern continues to repeat in the same order for all positive powers of i. Since both 2 divided by 4 and 8674 divided by 4 give a remainder of 2, you can conclude that i^{8674} is equal to i^2, or -1.

3. The correct answer is (D). Since the missile is always at a height less than $(2 + i)(4 - 2i)$, you can find the lowest height the plane may fly to avoid being hit by the missile by multiplying the two binomials. Using FOIL, you get $8 + 4i - 4i - 2i^2$, which you can simplify to $6 - 2(-1) = 10$. If you got (B), you may have evaluated the product of the last two parts of the binomial, $-2i^2$, as -2 instead of $+2$. If you got (C), you may not have evaluated the product of the last two parts of the binomial, $i(-2i)$.

4. The correct answer is (C). If you expand $(i + 5)(2i - 5)$ using FOIL, you are left with $2i^2 + 5i - 25$. Since the question tells you that $i^2 = -1$, you can plug -1 in for i^2 to get $-2 - 5i - 25 = -27 + 5i$.

   If you got (B), you may have subtracted $2i^2$ from -25 instead of adding it and neglected to multiply the two single-order imaginary terms. If you got (D), you may have reversed the subtraction of the two single-order imaginary terms.

5. The correct answer is (B). For questions with complex numbers, remember that the square of i^2 is equal to -1. If you evaluate the numerator, you can determine that it is equal to $-1 - 3 + 2i$, which can be simplified to $2(i - 2)$. Similarly, you can factor out the 4 in the denominator to get $4(i - 2)$. Since $i - 2$ is in both the numerator and denominator, you can cancel it out to get $\frac{2(i - 2)}{4(i - 2)} = \frac{1}{2}$.

   If you chose (D), you did not factor the quadratic in the numerator correctly.

6. The correct answer is (C). In order to simplify the fraction, you need to remove the complex number from the denominator. Since you know that $i = \sqrt{-1}$, by squaring i you get $i^2 = -1$. In order to get i^2 in the denominator, you can multiply both the denominator and numerator of the fraction by the expression $2i + 3$, which makes the denominator a difference of squares: $\frac{i(2i + 3)}{(2i - 3)(2i + 3)} = \frac{2i^2 + 3i}{4i^2 - 9}$.

Plug in -1 for i^2 to get $\dfrac{-2+3i}{-13}$. To make the denominator positive, you can multiply both the denominator and numerator by -1 to get $\dfrac{2-3i}{13}$.

If you got (A), you may have subtracted 9 from positive 4 instead of negative 4 in the last step in the denominator.

7. The correct answer is (B). If you expand the two binomials using FOIL, you get $2i^2 - 5i - 3$. If you plug in -1 for i^2, you will get $-2 - 5i - 3$, which can be simplified to $-5(i + 1)$.

If you got (A), you may have forgotten the negative sign in front of the -5 when simplifying.

8. The correct answer is (C). The question explains how you need to interpret the xy-graph of the complex number plane. You can find the real part of the complex number by looking at the x-coordinate of the point. This is equal to -3. You can then find the imaginary part of the complex number by looking at the y-coordinate. This is equal to -5. Putting both of these together, you can determine that the complex number is equal to $-3 - 5i$. If you got (A), you found the point in the standard (x, y) coordinate plane.

9. The correct answer is (C). First, multiply and simplify the factored part of the expression:
$$(x - 2i)(2x - i)$$
$$= 2x^2 - ix - 4ix + 2i^2$$
$$= 2x^2 - 5ix - 2$$

Next, add this to the rest of the right side of the equation and factor:
$$2x^2 - 5ix - 2 + 2$$
$$= 2x^2 - 5ix$$
$$= x(2x - 5i)$$

Since this is equal to 0, you know that x is either 0 or $\dfrac{5i}{2}$. The question asks for a real number, so the answer is 0.

If you got (D), you forgot that the 5 multiplied i in the numerator.

10. The correct answer is (B). First, evaluate the terms with i. You know that $i = \sqrt{-1}$, so $i^2 = -1$. Therefore, since $i^4 = i^2 \times i^2$, $i^4 = (-1)(-1)$, or 1. Plugging these two values into the expression, you get the following:
$$3i^4x^2 + 2i^2x^2 + 4i^4 - 5$$
$$= 3(1)x^2 + 2(-1)x^2 + 4(1) - 5$$
$$= x^2 - 1$$

You know that this expression is just a difference of squares, so it can be factored as $(x + 1)(x - 1)$.

If you got (C), you didn't evaluate the difference of squares correctly.